T0164509

"I don't know anyone who can match the high definition clarity of John Loftus when it comes to navigating the labyrinthine world of Christian evangelical apologetics for the general public. This is a relentless and incisive critique of the pseudo-scholarship that passes for genuine intellectual inquiry under the name of Christian apologetics."

—Dr. Hector Avalos, Professor of Religious Studies at Iowa State University and author of *The End of Biblical Studies* (2007), *Slavery, Abolitionism, and the Ethics of Biblical Scholarship* (2011), and *The Bad Jesus: The Ethics of New Testament Ethics* (2015)

"Loftus is one of the few atheists who actually understands religion. This book displays the knowledge of a Christian theologian as well as rationality of an atheist. Both sides can learn a lot from it."

—Dr. David Eller, author of *Natural Atheism* (2004), *Atheism Advanced: Further Thoughts of a Freethinker* (2008), and *Introducing Anthropology of Religion: Culture to the Ultimate* (2014)

"Once again, Loftus raises the bar in the enduring conversation between atheists and Christian apologists with *How to Defend the Christian Faith*. This book will sharpen and hone the argument for either side, and woe to the unread debater going against someone who has absorbed this book's relentless reasoning. I highly recommend this book for anyone who debates religion—on either side."

—David Silverman, President of American Atheists, Inc.

"For years I have despaired about the sorry state of Christian apologetics, and even sorrier state of Christian apologists. If there be Christian truth, it lies beyond the reach of rational inquiry, and perhaps that is OK. In *How to Defend the Christian Faith*, John Loftus lays waste to a colosseum full of bad arguments, including my own tentative efforts at the problem of evil. (Loftus says I am "ignorant" but less ignorant than Ken Ham, which was a relief.) Believers should read Loftus' engaging assault on their intellectual champions. They will be dismayed at how often they agree. I know I was."

—Karl Giberson, Scholar-in-Residence in Science & Religion at Stonehill College, and author of *Saving the Original Sinner: How Christians Have Used the Bible's First Man to Oppress, Inspire, and Make Sense of the World* (2015)

"The world has just become a richer place. Who can calculate the added value to our planet when bright, young aspiring apologists decide to redirect their talents and energies to evidence-based careers? Many of them—the ones who sincerely care about truth—will certainly do that after reading the wise counsel in John Loftus' caring and sobering book. *How to Defend the Christian Faith* is a welcome mutual aid for Apologists Anonymous."

—Dan Barker, author of *Life Driven Purpose: How an Atheist Finds Meaning* (2015), and Co-President of the Freedom From Religion Foundation

"I will watch any movie with Denzel Washington in it and I will buy any book written by John Loftus. The former—well, he's just one hell of an actor, and the latter, because he is one hell of a thinker and writer. His mastery of the material shows a depth that most writers simply could never accomplish. This book adds to the body of work being done so eloquently and convincingly by this 'second wave' generation of New Atheists. But even better, it raises the bar on how good scholarship should be done. Kudos to Loftus for another amazing text that will stand the test of time. My advice to readers? Buy it! Read it! Tell others about it, especially those who need it the most—evangelicals and believers who need a dose of objective reality and science-based reasoning."

—Sharon Nichols, retired Associate Professor of Geography, College of DuPage, Glen Ellyn, IL, and former President of the Illinois Geographical Society

"Loftus once again exposes the intellectual and moral bankruptcy of Christian apologetics. As the title promises, Loftus offers practical advice to the believer in his or her quest to defend the indefensible. The book's greatest strength is its accurate exposition of the apologist's challenges. Loftus documents the moral weaknesses of God's biblical commandments, the absurdity of a God who cannot do a better job revealing Himself, and the intellectual dishonesty that religious adherence requires. With wit and insight, Loftus offers the believer the tricks necessary to remain in the faith and to persuade others to do likewise. Self-delusion and deception are necessary attributes and Loftus humorously explains how it is done from someone who has been there. This is a great book for the believer who is ready to take an honest look at the moral and intellectual cost of his or her faith."

—Carolyn Hyppolite, MA, author of *Still Small Voices: The Testimony of a Born Again Atheist* (2014)

HOW TO *DEFEND*
THE CHRISTIAN FAITH

Advice from an Atheist

JOHN W. LOFTUS

Foreword by Peter Boghossian

Pitchstone Publishing
Durham, North Carolina

Pitchstone Publishing
Durham, North Carolina
www.pitchstonepublishing.com

10 9 8 7 6 5 4 3 2 1

Library of Congress Cataloging-in-Publication Data

Loftus, John W.
  How to defend the Christian faith : advice from an atheist / John W. Loftus ;
foreword by Peter Boghossian.
     pages cm
  Includes bibliographical references.
  ISBN 978-1-63431-056-7 (pbk. : alk. paper)
  1. Christianity—Controversial literature. 2. Apologetics—Methodology. I. Title.
  BL2775.3.L63 2015
  230—dc23
                                2015015166

Dedication

I dedicate this book to several scholarly friends who have greatly influenced my thinking.

On the darker side I am most grateful to Christian apologists James D. Stauss (1929–2014) and William Lane Craig.

On the brighter side I am most grateful to four atheist intellectual giants, Hector Avalos, Peter Boghossian, Jerry Coyne, and David Eller.

David Eller's luminous works contain important perspectives you won't find from anyone else in today's world. We are all in his debt. You aren't a fully informed person if you're not reading them.

Peter Boghossian's brilliant book, *A Manual for Creating Atheists*, is a significant game changer coming from a one-of-a-kind intellectual strategist. He's raising up a grassroots atheist movement to help believers realize they're pretending to know what they don't know when they claim to know with 100 percent certainty their faith is true.

Jerry Coyne, in his published works and daily writing on his website (https://whyevolutionistrue.wordpress.com/), is doling out one beating after another to religious and faith-based reasoning. No other scientist of his stature is writing so much, so knowledgeably, and so passionately. His influence is being felt around the world.

Hector Avalos is expertly leading a second wave of atheist biblical scholars following the first wave of new atheists. His writings are multidisciplinary in scope (covering biblical, scientific, ethical, and political issues), cross-cultural in nature (in both English and Spanish), and utilize a variety of venues (scholarly books, journals, blog posts, and newspapers). He is a one-man demolition machine when it comes to debunking Christianity and its influence in today's world.

Contents

Foreword

. . . be ready always to give an answer to every man
that asketh you a reason of the hope that is in you . . .
—1 Peter 3:15

If you're a Christian, and you read only one book about how to defend your faith, this is that book. It is the one book on apologetics whose guidance, advice, and recommendations will lead you to what is true.

In order to discern truth from falsity, you need a resisting opponent. In the martial arts, for example, if you want to figure out which techniques work and which do not, you will need to try them on someone who does not want them to work—in other words, someone who wants to win the fight. Resisting opponents act as correcting mechanisms, that is, as a way to keep your ideas about reality in check. Getting to the truth requires checking your beliefs mercilessly against reality.

How to Defend the Christian Faith is the ultimate resisting opponent for the Christian apologist. It is the titleholder in the Ultimate Apologist Championship. Take it down, and you will be the new belt holder. You will know that your ideas about reality actually correspond to reality and you will have arrived at truth.

Like John Loftus, I am a professional atheist. And like many Christians, I want to know what's true. I do my best to have an open mind and sincerely consider ideas that do not comport with my understanding of reality, even entertaining those ideas that make me feel uncomfortable. If Christians have some truth I don't know, I want to know what that is so that I can know it too.

Every year I speak about faith, God, and religion to thousands of people around the world. At every one of my events, Christian apologists attempt to

9

publically defend their Christian faith during the open question-and-answer sessions. After only a few minutes of back-and-forth questions their arguments always unravel—yet their conviction remains.

One lesson I've learned from these years of public engagements with Christian apologists is that the arguments they offer for their faith are not the reason they have faith. Arguments for God or for specific propositions within their religious tradition have nothing to do with why they believe. I know this because when I ask apologists, "If you were shown, to your satisfaction, that the argument you presented was untrue, would you still believe?" virtually every apologist, when pressed, replies, "Yes." (And those who do not respond affirmatively claim it is impossible that their arguments could be untrue.) For Christian defenders of the faith, I have found that convictions masquerade as reasons, arguments do not anchor beliefs, and the public defense of faith-based assertions is among the most noble of virtues. If you're a Christian reading this you may be different in this respect. You may be willing to follow the truth, no matter where it leads—which is, as Loftus argues, the only way to defend Christianity.

Thus for the Christian apologist reason and argument are charades. So too are the vociferous protestations that the core propositions in their faith tradition (the virgin birth, Christ's crucifixion, the resurrection, etc.) are true. Truth is a casualty of faith. Dishonesty, insincerity, and self-deception germinate the moment one becomes an apologist. When one becomes convinced they have the truth they stop seeking the truth. As Bertrand Russell wrote, the will to find out is bartered for the wish to believe.

Enter John W. Loftus' *How to Defend the Christian Faith*: A pointedly honest, forthright, and sincere way to approach a defense of Christianity. And Loftus, one of the world's leading atheists, is uniquely qualified for this task. He was groomed by the who's who of the top echelon of Christian apologists: William Lane Craig, James D. Strauss, Paul Feinberg, Stuart Hackett, Kenneth Kantzer (known as the dean of evangelicalism), Marc F. Greisbach (past President of the American Catholic Philosophical Association), and Ron Feenstra (Director of Doctoral Studies at Calvin Theological Seminary). *How to Defend the Christian Faith* is a desperately needed lifebuoy that can prevent both would-be and seasoned apologists from drowning in a sea of dangerous nonsense.

How to Defend the Christian Faith explains exactly how this can be accomplished. Such an ambitious task has never been undertaken from the perspective of someone who lacks belief, yet it is vital because so few Christian apologists actually know how to defend their faith to the informed doubter.

And because none of Christianity's claims can be rationally derived based on the available evidence, persuasive defenders of the faith are necessary to ensure Christianity's survival. This is because the truths of Christianity cannot be "reasoned to"—they cannot be derived absent messengers. Without apologists and proselytizers, Christianity would not survive a single generation. With *How to Defend the Christian Faith*, and because Christianity is on the decline in the West, Christians are paradoxically placed in the uncomfortable yet fortunate position of turning to an atheist to shackle them to the value of truth.

Yet Loftus does not whitewash the difficulty for potential apologists. *How to Defend the Christian Faith* is not a feel-good, self-congratulatory book that deceives believers into thinking they can easily persuade others—or themselves—that the hope they have is aligned with reality. Rather, it's a call to honest self-reflection for lifelong seekers of truth, while providing methods and a roadmap for exactly how to proceed. In a crystal-clear, plainspoken style, he levels with apologists. As a former apologist, he's done all the work. Loftus knows exactly what's needed to defend Christianity, and he articulates arguments apologists must answer to achieve their ultimate goal: eternal salvation through Jesus Christ.

From apologetical methods, to mechanisms for evaluating and adjudicating claims in the Christian faith tradition, to exploring what an unshakeable commitment to truth looks like, *How to Defend the Christian Faith* takes readers on the ultimate journey into Christianity. Even beyond becoming knowledgeable about how to defend core tenets of the Christian faith, reading and engaging with this book offers a unique opportunity to be honest and to know exactly what it means to argue for Christianity. (And much of what Loftus has to offer, especially as it relates to reason and rationality, is of value not just to Christians but also to atheists and anyone genuinely curious about finding out what's true.)

How to Defend the Christian Faith is the Omega of literally thousands of years of intellectual history devoted to the defense of Christianity. It is the ultimate corrective mechanism for the Christian faith, and the definitive guide to Christian apologetics and for Christian apologists. You will never have to read another book about how to defend your faith—and, after reading this book, you may never want to.

Peter Boghossian
Portland, Oregon

Introduction

In what is known as the *Great Commission* (Matthew 28:19–20), Jesus presumably challenged the earliest disciples to proselytize (or evangelize) and disciple (or tutor) others. They had just graduated from classes taught by the master disciple-maker himself and were charged with discipling others just as Jesus had discipled them. Following their example all Christians are to be "witnesses" on behalf of the Christian faith (Acts 1:8). They should also always be prepared to defend their Christian faith (1 Peter 3:15). This witnessing, proselytizing, discipling, tutoring, training, teaching, and defending are required of every single Christian to some degree. So this book is for every Christian who wants to be better at these tasks.

There are, however, special classes of professional people who devote their careers to these tasks. Someone who defends the Christian faith professionally is known as an apologist. They are also variously described as evangelists, proselytizers, missionaries, ministers, preachers, disciplers, pastors, or teachers. Christians who aren't one of these professionals must financially support, encourage, and pray for these professional workers (Matthew 9:35–38).

The word "apologetics" comes from the Greek word *apologia*. It referred to what defendants would do in a courtroom in response to any accusations made against them. They would try to provide a defense (an *apologia*) against the charges. The accused would try to literally "speak away" (*apo*—away, *logia*—speech) the accusation(s). So apologetics is the act of providing a defense of one's particular faith. The better one does this the better of an apologist he or she is known to be.

The triple aims of Christian apologetics are to (1) provide a positive case for concluding Christianity is true above all other religious and/or nonreligious contenders; (2) defend the reasonableness of Christianity against any objections brought against it; and (3) persuade non-Christians to accept the Christian faith. The first aim is called *positive apologetics*. The second aim is called *negative apologetics*. The third aim I'll call *persuasion apologetics*.

This book is written by an atheist, a nonbeliever, to Christians who feel called by their God to defend their faith from the arguments of atheists like me. As someone who had formerly been trained to defend the Christian faith by some of the best recognized apologists in our generation—and who now argues against it—what I'll say should be helpful. My goal is to show Christians how to defend their faith—that is, to do apologetics—correctly, if it can be done at all. It's also intended for atheists who want to argue Christians out of their faith, since the arguments contained within should be useful for this purpose.

Given the state of apologetics this book is sorely needed. Even Christian apologist Dr. Randal Rauser admits he has "a lot of reasons to be dissatisfied with the current state of Christian apologetics." The biggest problem is

> the way apologetics is often taught. Rather than be trained as thinkers, many apologists seem keen to learn by rote a bunch of factoids and arguments peppered with impressive quotes from select sources. This is a desperately boring and unimaginative approach, and it suggests that the common stereotype of the apologist as merely trained to present a sales-pitch is not undeserved.
>
> We need independent, creative thinkers who are equipped to think about the world in novel ways and explore the grounds for—and against—their beliefs from a fresh, and honest perspective free of spin and informed by their own unique experiences, interest, and context.
>
> There are dozens more arguments waiting to be discovered, and innumerable creative ways one could present them, contextualized to the particular time and place in which one finds oneself. . . . And as apologists begin exploring new ways to defend their beliefs, apologetics will benefit in the long run.[1]

Reading this book will be a good thing no matter what the result. Perhaps in some cases it may help potential defenders of Christianity accomplish what Rauser wishes apologetics programs would do. Maybe some aspiring apologist will figure out how to do apologetics better from reading it, since no one has done it well so far, in my opinion. If it helps in this way that's a good thing, right? Then would-be apologists will be better at their task by reading it. Of course, I'm writing the book because the case for Christianity is so bad I can offer honest advice for doing apologetics better, and it still won't be good enough.

Perhaps in some other cases this book might even convince potential apologists that defending Christianity is defending the indefensible. So they may be convinced to stop pursuing a career in apologetics when it dawns on them the challenge is much too great. If it helps in this way that too is a good thing, right? They might as well know this in advance of pursuing such a profession. Then they could pursue other interests and find some other productive work to do in life. Perhaps in still a few other cases aspiring apologists might even abandon their faith from reading this book. If it helps in this way that too is a good thing, right? I would welcome this result of course, since I myself abandoned my faith based on conclusions I made. Truth is its own reward. Since, as I'll argue later, we should be honest life-long seekers of the truth, then arriving at truth is a good thing no matter what the result.

The title to this book is intentionally provocative. Atheists will criticize it because there simply isn't a way to help Christians do what it proposes, defend the indefensible. Any atheist proposing to write such a book must not be a true atheist. He's either an unconvinced atheist, or worse, a secret believer. Perhaps he's motivated by money? Well I assure my readers that if anyone is motivated by money, it isn't me. And I equally assure them I have not changed my mind. I am still an intellectually committed atheist. Sufficient evidence is lacking to accept Christianity as the truth. Trying to enter into a relationship with a supernatural Being who does not exist is like trying to have a relationship with an invisible imaginary friend. Anyone who has read my other works can see why I think this way. And I stand by those works.

Christians will also criticize the title of this book because I cannot be sincere in writing it. Surely I'm no more interested in helping Christians learn how to defend their faith than a vegan who writes a cookbook for meat eaters with beef, chicken, pork, and fish recipes. The truth is that I really am going to offer some sincere honest advice to would-be Christian apologists, especially in Part 1. I'll also be offering a lot of snarky tongue-in-cheek advice, especially in Parts 2 and 3. I'll offer some positive advice for what budding apologists should do, as well as negative advice—lots of it—for what they should not do. If apologists truly seek to challenge nonbelievers to accept Christianity, they will be helped by listening to me, an atheist who was trained by the best to be a Christian apologist.

In chapter one I challenge readers with the most important question of all when it comes to defending the Christian faith. It's the obvious elephant in the room that very few Christians even notice. *Why is it necessary to defend the Christian faith at all?* I mean, really, if people want to pursue a goal they should know why they are doing so. I argue there shouldn't be any reason to defend Christianity. I challenge readers interested in pursuing that goal to ponder this question. Answer that question before proceeding any further. I argue that God, if he exists, should do all the work himself—without needing any apologists—thereby attaining much better results than apologists could ever possibly get.

In Part 1 of the book, I will offer some positive advice to aspiring defenders of the faith. It is honest and helpful advice. It is also essential advice. I wish I had been given this guidance when I first sought to defend the faith that I was raised to believe. It's counsel that all apologists should take very seriously. No matter what else you like or dislike about the book, this part is worth the price of admission.

In chapter two, I want potential apologists to know precisely how challenging the task of apologetics will turn out to be. It doesn't dawn on us when we begin pursuing a goal how hard it can be to achieve it, how long it might take, and whether we can achieve it at all. I remember starting out loving the game of pool, both 8-ball and 9-ball. It wasn't long before I thought I could go pro within a few years. So I practiced like no one's business, spending way too many hours in pursuit of this dream of mine, only to have it shattered years later when I realized the goal was far too elusive, especially at the age I started. I'm pretty good at these games now, yes, but there were a lot of other productive things I could've been doing that I didn't do, because I was pursuing such a will-o'-the-wisp goal. In the same way I want potential apologists to understand how daunting the task of apologetics will be for them. I want them to know *now*, not later, what it takes. So I'll articulate many of the problems they'll have to answer in the process of defending their faith.

In chapter three, I'll argue that the would-be apologist must be resolutely committed to being an honest life-long seeker of truth, wherever it can be found, no matter what the results. Given the vast amount of knowledge there is in the world today, no one should think he or she has landed on the truth, the whole truth, "so help me Jesus." Doing so requires a life-long diligence to courageously seek the truth, and if the evidence calls for it, changing one's mind. It requires adhering courageously, stubbornly, tenaciously, and persistently to the intellectual virtues.

In chapter four, I'll strongly suggest that students seeking to be apologists should get a good education by attending and graduating from a good university, in a good field of study for doing apologetics. Nothing less will do.

In chapter five, I'll write about apologetical methods. Since apologetics stands or falls with the issue of method, this is a very important discussion.

Which method is the one Christian defenders should use in defending their faith? There has been considerable debate among apologists themselves over method in defending the faith. My claim in this long chapter is that the only reasonable apologetical method is the evidentialist approach, as it's called—apologetics based on sufficient objective evidence. But as you'll see most Christian apologists don't accept this challenge. I'll argue that aspiring apologists must accept the challenge of defending the evidentialist apologetical method and then subsequently provide the requisite evidence for one's specific branch of Christianity.

I have personally studied apologetics with leading proponents of different methods. So I have a unique pedigree. I had several high-level classes with leading defenders of four different methods. At the master's level I studied apologetics with James D. Strauss at Lincoln Christian University, who argued along the lines of *Presuppositionalism* like Francis Schaeffer. Then I studied at Trinity Evangelical Divinity School with Stuart Hackett, the leading defender of what is called *Rational Empiricism*, Paul D. Feinberg, a leading defender of the *Cumulative Case Method*, and William Lane Craig, a leading defender of *Natural Theology* or the *Classical Method*. I also took a sympathetic learning class under Dr. Craig on the *Reformed Epistemology* of Alvin Plantinga. At the doctoral level at Marquette University I studied with Father Donald J. Keefe, S. J., who, even as a Catholic, defended *Fideism*, and Marc Griesbach, who, as a past president of the *American Catholic Philosophical Association*, defended *Natural Theology* or the *Classical Method*. Now I view myself as a counter-apologist. But don't let that bother you. I can teach you some tricks of the trade.

In chapter six, if I have not yet convinced budding Christian apologists of the need to present sufficient objective evidence, then this chapter should do the trick. I'll challenge you to be sure you start off being right. You need to be sure you are correct, that you have the true particular faith, the one that can be defended from all nonbelievers. Don't just assume the faith you were raised to believe is the true religious faith. You should first evaluate your faith, before defending it. Maybe a different faith is the true one, or none at all? In so doing I'll offer what I consider the only type of evidential apologetics that can actually convince reasonable educated nonbelievers, something I've called the *Outsider Test for Faith*. It's expressed in these words: "The only way to rationally test one's culturally adopted religious faith is from the perspective of an outsider, a nonbeliever, with the same level of reasonable skepticism believers already use when examining the other religious faiths they reject." Consider this chapter a sort of boot camp for training soldiers for intellectual battle. As the last chapter in Part 1, this chapter puts Part 1 all together. Consider it one of the most serious challenges to your faith, one that you should welcome if you are truly committed to seeking the truth. It should solidify the need for you to get a good education in order to defend your faith, for you'll be required to produce the sufficient evidence needed for nonbelievers to accept it.

In Parts 2 and 3 of this book, I'm going to show how Christian apologists have so far utterly failed to convince intelligent, educated nonbelievers. I aim to challenge potential apologists to do better than others before them. Of course, I don't think it can be done better, but maybe an aspiring apologist somewhere can learn from me and do a better job of it.

In Part 2, covering five chapters, I'll provide many concrete examples of how recognized and important Christian apologists defend their faith. Since they are the experts they must know how to "correctly" do apologetics. Using these examples I'll show budding apologists what to avoid doing if they want to become better than any of the expert apologists I'll be writing about. I'll offer some negative advice—lots of it—for what they should not do. I'll show that these experts engage in many fallacies of reason, and as such are not much help at all in convincing reasonable nonbelievers. Christian apologetics so far has been, at best, nothing more than special pleading and, at worst, intellectually dishonest. If they are doing apologetics "correctly" it likely cannot be done at all. Even so, this part of the book is instructive because it teaches aspiring apologists what *not* to do in defending the faith. When it comes to pool, I can learn how to play better by observing how others play—even first-timers. By doing so, I can learn what not to do, and that's a valuable lesson, even if I don't learn from them how the game is done right.

Finally in Part 3, covering five additional chapters, I focus on just one issue, the problem of suffering for a perfectly good, all-powerful, all-knowing God. I review several Christian attempts at dealing with this problem and show how miserably these arguments fare in defending their God concept from it. Since I don't think there is a sufficient answer to this problem, I only want to show why the answers provided don't work. I challenge potential apologists to find better ways of answering it, if that is even possible.

If this book helps aspiring Christian career apologists do Christian apologetics better than others have done before, then reading it will serve you tremendously. If, however, you realize you cannot do it better, you should not seek to be an apologist at all. And if you realize it cannot reasonably be done at all, then as an honest seeker of truth you should think about abandoning your faith.

* * *

I want to express my thanks to Lee Penya for his copyediting help with the first part of this book, but most importantly for suggesting I write chapter one.

* * *

Final note: Proof of plagiarism has destroyed the credibility of a few authors in the last few years. Keep in mind that plagiarism isn't just limited to the print media. A few video bloggers and podcasters should take note. If you get your main ideas from any authors or use their exact words then you should give them due credit. We'd appreciate this. It's considered to be common decency. You may be sorry if you don't.

I

The Most Important Question of All

In this chapter I'm going to address the most important question of all for would-be Christian apologists. It's the obvious elephant in the room, not seen by apologists because they don't have the eyes for it. My argument is that God, if he exists, failed to effectively communicate his will. He failed to provide the sufficient evidence we need to believe. Since he failed us, apologists have been given a tremendous work load, bigger than any one of them can bear up under. But if God had done a better job, there would be little, if anything, for apologists to do. In fact, God didn't even need to hire apologists at all for this most important job. He could have done all the work himself. Thus the most important question of all:

Why is it necessary to defend the Christian faith at all?

I'm going to do a job performance review of the Almighty. I used to believe in God. I used to defend his ways. Now I'm an atheist. I don't believe in him because his job performance rating is so poor he probably doesn't even exist at all. He could have done better, much better, if the goal was to save souls from the pits of hell. First I'll share why and then offer four other ways God could have done a much better job.

If God supposedly gave up Jesus to die on the cross for our sins, *which is the greater deed by far*, then why has he failed (and continues to fail) to do enough to reach nonbelievers, *which represents the lesser deeds*. I mean really, if God did the greater deed then why doesn't he also commit himself to doing the lesser deeds? Isn't that backassward for an intelligent being? It would be like preparing an extravagant delicious banquet, with enough food to feed all the starving people in a refugee camp, but not caring enough to send out workers to tell them about it—or hiring incompetent workers he knows won't do it. If you think God is doing the lesser deeds then read onward Christian soldiers.

Why has God given the most important task of them all to Christians, according to their own theology? They are still sinners on this side of heaven, lacking complete sanctification and consequently lazy, self-absorbed, greedy, lying, lustful, fallible, ignorant, finite human beings. Most Christians who attend church services are much more interested in networking with others, finding a mate, being entertained, or learning lessons from pop-psychology on how to be a good person (because for some reason they need reminding weekly), than in reaching out to people who, according to their own theology, are headed straight for an eternal conscious torturous hell.

Compared with an all-knowing God, even the best Christian defenders are bumbling idiots and incompetent fools. Compared with an all-loving God, even the best Christian defenders are utterly self-centered and completely unconcerned that people are going to hell. Compared with an all-powerful God, even the best Christian defenders are totally lacking any energy to help people believe. Surely it stands to reason that many people have not accepted Jesus as their savior because Christian defenders lacked the motivation, the energy, and the necessary smarts to do so. Christians who lacked the smarts haven't even known where to look for the needed evidence to believe, much less found it. This doesn't make any sense at all, especially if there's a flaming hell to pay for those who are not convinced to believe and be saved.

Surely a God like the one Christians believe in could have been more concerned for the lost than hiring the church to do this most important job, surely. If Christians have been incompetent with this task then God was incompetent in hiring them to do it. God should have cared for the lost more than that. As the CEO of his corporation his hiring practices are a failure. God should fire them and do the work himself.

The Problem of Divine Miscommunication

Not only are God's hiring practices poor. So also are his communication skills. If there is any miscommunication in a company, the kind that can bring a company to a halt, the kind that can lead people to do different things by pulling in different directions, the kind that that can cause a lack of overall purpose, then the buck clearly stops with the CEO. God is the ultimate CEO, so he is to blame for his company—the church—at least partially, if they cannot adequately defend the nature and purpose of the company.[1] I consider this problem, which I call *the problem of divine miscommunication*, to be a most serious one for a God worthy of the attributes ascribed to him, a God who is also believed to have revealed himself in the Bible. Christian apologists worthy of the name must deal with this most serious problem by defending God's lack of clear divine guidance.

A God worthy of the attributes ascribed to him should have prohibited certain kinds of barbaric behaviors and abuses in any given society. Here are five commandments God could have spoken, but for some failure of reason or malfunction of foreknowledge failed to do so:

> You should not torture or kill anyone for being a witch, or anyone with a different faith, or anyone with no faith at all.

> You should not prohibit the free expression of ideas, the free exercise of one's conscience, or the free assembly of peacefully organized people.

> You should never enslave or beat into submission anyone anywhere, anytime, under any circumstances for the express purpose of servitude, nor treat any person as less than a human being, ever.

> You should not treat women as inferior to men, but rather with equal respect and dignity as equally valued members of society.

> You should not abuse animals, trap them, raise them in factory farms, hunt them for their furs, or needlessly experiment on them.

This is just a very short list. The needless suffering that these five commandments alone could have stopped over the centuries is incalculable.

A God worthy of the attributes ascribed to him should have communicated better, so there would not have been as many doctrinal disputes that were a matter of life and death to Christian believers down through the centuries. Just the most basic knowledge of the human propensity for selfishness, greed, and lust should have been enough for God to foresee the need for a better revelation. The church, for instance, fought several wars in her history that were intended to be genocidal in nature against others who claimed to be Christians. This took place in the centuries after Emperor Constantine adopted Christianity as the state religion.[2] It also took place just after the Protestant Reformation, when eight million Christians slaughtered each other because God did not communicate the correct doctrine clearly to them.[3]

A God worthy of the attributes ascribed to him should also have known about vaccines and revealed that knowledge to us. That knowledge would have been very helpful during the most devastating outbreak of the Black Death plague, which killed a third of the population of Europe in the fourteenth century. This knowledge would also have been very helpful during the near worldwide pandemic of Spanish Influenza (1918–20), where between 50 and 100 million people died. Such a God should have known enough to reveal how to discover penicillin, anesthesia, and antibiotics. He should have warned us about the dangers of bloodletting, the failure to boil polluted water before drinking it, and lead poisoning. According to the Centers for Disease Control and Prevention, washing our hands "Save Lives." It "is one of the most important steps we can take to avoid getting sick and spreading germs to others."[4] But Jesus denied the need to do so in order to win a debate with the Pharisees (Mark 7:1-23). God didn't even warn us about eating poisonous plants, or the various poisonous species out there, whose bite or sting could kill us. A God worthy of the attributes ascribed to him should have warned us about building cities on or near the fault lines of the earth. These fault lines attract us like honey does to bees. From them we get our water and minerals as the earth opens up and grants us access to them. If he had warned about the dangers many millions of lives would have been saved from earthquakes, landslides, floods, tsunamis, and volcanic eruptions. Because such a God did not tell us these things, billions of people have died, sometimes torturous deaths.

God's Defense Lawyers in Retreat
If you believe God inspired the canonized Bible, ask yourself if God could've foreseen the problems that would surface in our modern era that have triply discredited the Bible as barbaric to democratic-minded people, superstitious to scientific-minded people, and unhistorical to historians and to an ever-growing number of biblical scholars.[5] The probability of the claim that the Bible is God's word is inversely proportional to the amount of work it takes Christian apologists to defend it from objections to the contrary (that is, the more work its defense requires, the less likely the Bible is God's word), and it requires way too much work to suppose that it is.

Consider the sheer number of books that have been published by the following Christian apologists/scholars: C. S. Lewis, Norman Geisler, William Lane Craig, Richard Swinburne, Paul Copan, Alvin Plantinga, N. T. Wright, Chad Meister, J. P. Moreland, Gregory Boyd, Gary Habermas, Steven Cowan, Douglas Groothuis, Peter van Inwagen, Randal Rauser, Michael Murray, William Dembski, Richard J. Bauckham, Michael Brown, D. A. Carson, Dan Wallace, G. K. Beale, Craig Blomberg, Craig Evans, Stephen Davis, Donald

Guthrie, Ralph Martin, Richard Hess, Dinesh D'Souza, and Timothy Keller, to name some of the more noteworthy ones. While some of these authors deal with the same issues, most of their material is unique to them. If we add in their magazine and journal articles we already have a small library of works. If we were to get and read the references they quote from we have a whole library of works in defense of the Christian faith, for a comprehensive case. That's what a comprehensive apologetic requires. The important question left unaddressed by them, as always, is why a defense requires so many books? Why does Christianity need such a defense at all? The fact that it takes so much work to defend Christianity is a strong indicator, all by itself, that the Christian God either does not exist, or doesn't care if we believe.

If God had done a better job of revealing his will, there wouldn't be much of anything for Christian defenders, or apologists, to do but share the gospel message like evangelists do. But since the God of the Bible didn't do his best, Christian apologists are forced to defend their faith against the multitude of objections raised against it. It's as if God gave Christian defenders permanent job security, forgetting that there are eternal destinies at stake, people who, on some accounts, will suffer conscious torment forever because of it.

When dealing with *the problem of divine miscommunication*, Christian defense lawyers seek only to get their divine client acquitted no matter what the intellectual or moral cost. Rather than face this evidence that shows their God to be nothing more than the product of ancient people, who didn't have a clue about civilized matters, these apologists use convoluted legalese to obfuscate and confuse the jury.

Typically they'll say we couldn't possibly know what an omniscient God is thinking, so we have no right to judge him and his ways. However, even if this is the case, it changes nothing. Millions of people died because God didn't correctly reveal the truth. Christians will further object by saying we just don't know if God did anything to help the people who died, to which the obvious answer is that this is my point. If God did something to help these people, then there is no evidence that he did! Think about it. There isn't any. This objection is based on faith, not evidence, the very thing reasonable people should reject if they want to honestly know the truth. And if God really wants us to believe in him and believe that he loves us, this is a strange way of going about things. For an omniscient God would have known that later generations of intelligent people would find him to be guilty of not doing what decent people would do if they could, and as a result, disbelieve in him and his love.

The best Christian defense lawyers are liberals who admit there are texts in the Bible that, to a great degree, are reflective of an ancient outlook rather than the rigid literalism of conservative believers. In their view, God's revelation is progressive, becoming better as humans grope to understand the divine. In other words, theology evolves. Liberals didn't come by this conclusion easily though. Down through the centuries, they came to it as the realities of life and the results of science forced them to accept it. Yet this view is exactly what we would expect to find if there is no truth to their theology. It's what we would expect if there is no divine mind behind the Bible or the church. If there is a God, then his so-called progressive revelation is indistinguishable from him not revealing anything at all, and, as such, progressive revelation should be rejected as an unnecessary theological hypothesis unworthy of thinking people.

Furthermore, such a view actually undermines their theology, for it leads to theological relativism, since there was no point in the history of the church when any theologian could say that a final, unchanging theology had been attained. So the theology of yesterday was true for Christians of the past, as the present-day theology is true for others, as the theology of tomorrow will be true for still others. So don't talk to me about an unchanging theological truth. Don't talk to me about an absolute standard for theological truth either. It doesn't exist. Never has. Never will. Liberals therefore cannot state any theological truth that is true for all time. As far as they can know, the end result of revelation could be the death of God, or the conclusion that we don't need God, which would make him effectively dead. As far as liberals can know, atheism may be the future of their theology. The only reason they won't accept the relativism of their theology is that they perceive a need to believe. They are playing a pretend game much like the people in M. Night Shyamalan's movie *The Village*. In my opinion, liberals should just stop pretending.

The bottom line is that the whole notion of progressive revelation is a "heads I win, tails you lose" strategy. If their God had revealed the truth from the beginning, then these Christians would use that as evidence he exists. Because he didn't, they have introduced the concept of progressive revelation, which betrays their desire to believe no matter what the intellectual cost. What they're doing is justifying their God "after the facts," rather than asking "before the facts" what they would expect of their God if he lovingly communicated to human beings.

Did God Do His Best in Providing Sufficient Reasons to Believe?
Apart from God's lack of communicative skills, in addition he did not provide good enough reasons for reasonable people to accept Christianity. If everything

about Christianity makes rational sense, then God could have created human beings with more intelligence so that Christianity's intellectual problems would be solvable. [6] He could have merely created us with a greater amount of intelligence. Or, he could have written the "mother of all philosophical papers" by answering such problems as why there is something rather than nothing at all, or why there is so much suffering. He could have provided reasonable answers to questions about the atonement, the trinity, divine simplicity, the incarnation, the relationship of free will and foreknowledge, and how it's possible for a spiritual being to interact with a material world.

Christians born into their faith within an already Christian-dominated culture may claim God has already explained the necessary things. But for most people in the world, he didn't explain enough. And because he has not done enough to help us understand these things, he is at least partially to blame for those who do not believe, especially if he knows in advance that people will refrain from believing if not provided with sufficient evidence to do so.

Short of helping us to understand these "mysteries," God needed to provide us with sufficient evidence to believe and less evidence to disbelieve. God could reveal himself to us in every generation in a myriad of ways: What better way to show us that he exists than what the book of Acts says he did for Saul of Tarsus on the road to Damascus! If God could convert Saul without abrogating his free will he could convert anyone without abrogating their free will. He could become incarnate in every generation and do miracles for all to see. He could spontaneously appear and heal people, or end a famine, or stop a war, or settle an important question like slavery. He could raise John F. Kennedy from the dead for all to see. He could restore an amputated limb in full sight of a crowd of people at the touch of a Christian faith healer. He could do any and all of the miracles he did in the Bible from time to time, including miraculously feeding 5,000 families. The list of things God could do in each generation is endless.

God could also have made this universe and the creatures on earth absolutely inexplicable to science, especially since science is the major obstacle to faith. He could've created us in a universe that couldn't even remotely be figured out by science. That is to say, there would be no evidence leading scientists to accept a Big Bang; nor would there be any evidence for the way galaxies, solar systems, or planets form. If God is truly omnipotent, he could have created the universe instantaneously by fiat and placed planets haphazardly around the sun, some revolving counterclockwise and in random orbits. God could have even created the earth as a flat disk, allowing for no plausible natural explanation at all. Then, when it comes to creatures on earth, God could have created us without any connection whatsoever to each other. Each species would be so distinct from every other species that no scientist would ever conclude natural selection was the process by which they arose. There would be no hierarchy of species in gradual increments. God could have created fish and mammals, but no reptiles nor amphibians. Then evolutionary theory could never have gotten off the ground. There would be no deposits of fossils that show this evolutionary process because evolution wouldn't exist in the first place. Human beings would be seen as absolutely special and distinct from the rest of the creatures on earth such that no scientist would ever conclude they evolved from the lower primates. There would be no evidence of unintelligent design. The existence of this kind of universe and the creatures in it would be inexplicable to science such that the existence of God would be the only viable explanation.

As far as the historical evidence goes, the all-powerful Christian God could have made it much more persuasive. Someone could have made a monument to Abraham that still exists and could be scientifically dated to his supposed time period. There could be overwhelming evidence for a universal flood that covered all the earth's mountains. Noah's ark could have been deposited exactly where the Bible says it landed, and it would be exactly as described in the Bible. Lot's wife, who was supposedly turned into a pillar of salt, would still be preserved and known by scientific testing to have traces of human female DNA in it. There could be noncontroversial evidence that the Israelites lived as slaves in Egypt for 400 years, conclusive evidence that they wandered in the wilderness for 40 years, and convincing evidence that they conquered the land of Canaan exactly as the Bible depicts. But there is none.

Furthermore, God could answer the prayers of Christians in such distinctive ways that even those who don't believe would seek out a Christian to pray for them. Scientific studies done on the prayers of Christians would meet with overwhelming confirmation. Had God created such a world, we wouldn't see the religious diversity that has divided the people of the world into distinct geographically located faiths.

If God has foreknowledge, he could have predicted certain events in history like the rise of the Internet, or the exact time of the 2004 Indonesian tsunami; he could have foretold the day that TV was invented, or the atomic bomb, using unambiguous language that would enable all to see these events as prophetic fulfillment. God could have predicted several things that would take place in each generation in each region of the earth so that each generation and each region of the earth would have confirmation through prophecy that he exists.

There could have been clear and specific prophecies about the virgin birth, life, nature, mission, death, resurrection, ascension, and return of Jesus in the Old Testament that could not be denied by even the most hardened skeptic.

The gospel accounts of the resurrection could have all been the same, showing no evidence of having been written incrementally over the years by superstitious people. The gospels could have been written at about the same time, months after Jesus arose from the dead. And these stories could have been free of implausibilites. Evidence like a Turin shroud could have been preserved and scientifically shown to be from Jerusalem and dated to the time of the Crucifixion; the shroud could contain an image that could be explained in no other way than that a crucified man had come back to life.

Christians will claim God has given us enough evidence to believe, but the existence of billions of sincere nonbelievers is strong evidence that God has *not* provided the evidence needed for all—or even most—of us to believe.

The bottom line so far: If God had much better communication skills and if he had provided good reasons to believe, then there shouldn't be anything for Christian apologists to defend about their faith, except to share it. Or, more precisely, to the degree that it takes to defend the Christian faith, then to that same degree the Christian faith is unlikely, and it takes way too much world to defend the Christian faith to think it has any likelihood to it at all.

What if Christians Went On Strike?

Christians should force God's hand to see what he would do if they stopped defending and sharing their Christian faith. They should all go on strike. [7] If they stopped all apologetical and evangelistic work, would their God step in and do something to save people from hell? Or would their God let the masses go to eternal damnation if his followers went on strike? If Christians stopped doing all the work we would learn whether God loves sinners more than his defenders do.

Workers go on strike when they are overworked and underpaid. So what would happen if Christians from around the world went on strike? This strike would be against having to do all of the evangelistic and apologetic work themselves. What if they stopped praying for others to be saved? What if they stopped telling others about Jesus? What if Christians stopped evangelizing and arguing on behalf of Christianity? What if all evangelists, missionaries, and apologists went on strike and instead let the Holy Spirit do the work?

I'm serious. What would happen? I know Christians believe they should do this work all by themselves, so this will never happen. Consider it a thought experiment instead, intended to force Christians to think about what God is doing now. Can God do this work himself? If he can, then why does he need Christians to do this work at all? If he cares, really cares for people, then he should do something himself. Would God step in and show he cares if they were to go on strike? Would he do what is right because it is the right thing to do regardless of whether Christians helped him? Would Christianity survive and even thrive into the future because God would be forced to get involved? Or would Christianity die out as God lets the world and its people go to hell?

If Christians were to go on strike there should be no cause for concern. If God is really inside the Christian faith then it cannot fail. The theme of the book of *Revelation* is God's victory in the end. So the faith response is to relax, since God's victory is assured.

My prediction if Christians all went on strike is that Christianity would soon afterward go out of existence. That's my prediction. This, of course, would be because God doesn't exist, just like all the other gods and goddesses that don't exist. The Christian faith needs people of faith who proselytize and defend it. This is true of every religion. So Christianity is no exception. You would expect it to be the exception though, if it were true. Without people of faith any given religion would die out because there is no deity behind any of them. That's what Christians think of other faiths. They should think of their own faith in the same way.

For those Christians who believe the Christian faith would not die out if they went on strike, they need to provide some objective evidence that God is doing something now that would help convert people even if they stopped defending and sharing the gospel.

God Could Have Done All the Work Himself

For Christians who must argue for the status quo, that given our present world this must be the best way for God to have run his company, I intend to show differently. I'll show how God could have done the work all by himself, and done it much better, guaranteed. I'll offer four different plans of salvation in what follows. If an all-knowing God had thought of them then a perfectly loving God would have implemented them. The fact that he didn't do differently, when he could have done so with much better results, presents a good case such a God does not exist.

With God, we're often told, "all things are possible." Christians believe this until an alternative divine plan is suggested that appears to be better than what God is believed to have done. Whenever someone suggests a better divine plan of action, then without even pausing to think about it, Christians argue God could not have done differently for a variety of reasons. So God can apparently do anything up until someone suggests he does something better. In other words, true Christian believers have no imagination at all. They unnecessarily limit their God by their utter lack of imagination.

Divine Plan One

If God exists he could have eliminated the middleman, so to speak, the prophets, apostles, and inspired authors who got God's supposed revelation wrong. He could have depended almost exclusively on revealing himself in the natural world alone. There would be no need for a book supposedly produced by inspiration or prophecy. I don't even need to offer any suggestions as to how the Christian God could have done this, because I have ideas based only on what is conceptually possible for an all-knowing, all-powerful, and all-loving God. An all-knowing God would know how to do this. An all-powerful God would have the power to do this (after all, he supposedly created the world from nothing). And an all-loving God would be motivated to do this.

However, I can indeed imagine how the Christian God could have done this, if he exists. Let's use just one example, that of George Washington, the first president of the United States. No serious person who is concerned with the truth doubts that George Washington was the first president of the United States. We would seriously question any person's integrity, or question whether his cognitive faculties were functioning properly, if after looking at the evidence he or she still refused to accept this fact. We don't need any special revelation from God to know this fact. The objective evidence shows us this, such that I don't even need to rehearse that evidence here.

If it's the case that God wanted us to accept as true every event we read about in the canonical Bible, then those biblical events should have the same historical evidence for them as we have for George Washington being our first president. Or, to say this more precisely, *the more important it is for God that people accept the historicity of certain biblical events, then the more important that evidence should exist leading reasonable people to accept the historicity of those biblical events, without the need for biblical revelation at all.* So I see no reason at all why God, if he exists and wants us to believe, needed human beings to write down any special revelations, or Scripture, at all. Everything written down would just be representative of the facts. This is what allows reasonable person to think George Washington was the first president of the United States.

How would this apply to the stories of Moses and Jesus, two of the key figures in the two testaments of the canonical Bible? In the case of Moses, the events we read about in the books of Exodus through Joshua, including the ten plagues, the wilderness wanderings, and the conquest of Canaan, would have been consistently reported in the ancient world by several different Mesopotamian cultures. Only with incontrovertible textual and archeological evidence that these events occurred, just as we find for George Washington's presidency, would people reasonably come to the conclusion that there is a God who loves the people of Israel and that the Israelites are a special people among others.

From these events alone, reasonable Israelites would have concluded that, as they are God's special people, he will send a redeemer when they are suffering prolonged hardship as a nation. God could also teach them about right and wrong through pain and pleasure, but mainly by pleasure. He could make sure they understood everything essential by what they experienced anyway. And guess what? This is *exactly* how we're told they learned truths from their God, so nothing else changes. God could teach them by experience, not by words, if he wanted to do so.

There are lots of nonessential lessons that could be dispensed with here, given the existence of the hard evidence I just suggested, like predictive prophecy and the whole animal and child sacrificial system. And given what I'm about to say about the life of Jesus, we wouldn't need any evidence from prophecy anyway. With regard to animal sacrifices, they were unnecessary and done away with in the New Testament, along with the need for circumcision. Anyone who thinks otherwise lacks an imagination.

The same standards of evidence would go for Jesus in the four canonical gospels. Everything in them would have overwhelming substantiation, from his sermons and teachings to his healings, and especially his death and resurrection. Jesus would write down his own story in his own handwriting. His disciples would take copious notes of his sermons, and they would all agree with what Jesus wrote down and with what the other disciples wrote down as well, with no discrepancies. Other key rabbis and Roman guards would do the same. There would be reliable trial manuscripts handed down to us in writing by eyewitnesses in Herod's and Pilate's courts. These texts would all be available as eyewitness accounts immediately after those events occurred, rather than as second-, third-, or fourth-hand accounts. The manuscripts they wrote would be preserved intact with the direct handwriting of the authors themselves, instead of as copies of copies of fourth-hand accounts that were then copied and recopied until the first full manuscripts we possess are from the fourth century C.E. There would be archaeological records of earthquakes at the death of Jesus, astronomical sightings from as far away as Rome, Egypt, and China verifying the sun turned to darkness, and records from King Herod and Pilate and many others that the saints of the Old Testament arose from the grave when Jesus did on the first Sunday. There would be other evidence, too, like a real Shroud of Turin that could be verified to have originated in Jerusalem at the time of a man described to be Jesus, who came to life from the grave. None of this would be considered special revelation. It would just be the verification of the events God would want us all to accept. Once we accepted this solid evidence, we would be Christians. Upon accepting this evidence, we would be saved from our sins. We would subsequently want to live in gratefulness for what Jesus did for us on the cross, and hope to be with him in heaven when we die. We would want others to know of this evidence so we would share it with others.

The essentials of Christian theology could be adequately deduced from the evidence to believe. Ethics could be taught by the trial-and-error experiences of life that would be built into the laws of nature themselves for rewarding good behavior and punishing bad behavior.

Divine Plan Two
If God exists, then he could just speak to everyone directly. He could be a voice in everyone's head. Why not? Why should God just speak to the prophets, apostles, or inspired authors? What makes them so special, the only ones to communicate God's voice to us? There would be no miscommunication about what to think, or what to accept, or what to do when it comes to the essential truths of Christianity. It would include any and all historical facts that support Christianity, like the death and resurrection of Jesus. There would be no need for a Bible. No need for natural revelation either, or evidence. Just grant everyone direct access to God in those essential areas, and those areas alone. Any sincere person who really wants to know what to think about God, or what to believe or do, would know. God would not force himself on anyone though. So he would never tell anyone who is not interested in his advice what to think or do, since any advice or counsel God offers could always be rejected.

This would be similar to what Christians already believe took place in the past anyway, except that in the Bible God spoke only to a limited number of prophets, apostles, and inspired authors. If he spoke to them why can't he speak to us all? If so, what's so problematic with people hearing actual voices in their heads, coming from God, voices that are communicating with everyone who wants to hear the truth? This would be a sure way to communicate to people. Only the truly disobedient would reject these voices. We might even call these disobedient people the insane ones. For in this different world, the people who listen to the voices in their heads are the sane ones!

Divine Plan Three

If anyone thinks having direct audible access to God is somehow bad, counterintuitive, or just plain crazy, then consider a somewhat different way. Let's say God wrote the truth about everything he thinks is essential to salvation on every person's mind from birth, to be understood better and better as we age throughout our lives. It would contain the knowledge of historical events that are essential to our salvation too, like the death and resurrection of Jesus in the first century C.E., along with theological and ethical truths based on the Pauline, Petrine, and Johannine epistles in the New Testament. We would truly have a full *sensus divinitatis*, or sense of divinity, along with all the essential theological truths irrespective of their rational merit, and irrespective of the evidence for or against them. It would be there. We would know it tacitly, subliminally, intuitively. We wouldn't need any Bible to have this knowledge. All we would need is to cultivate it by meditating on it, praying based on it, and acting on it.

This *sensus divinitatis*, as I just described it, would not be written in big bold permanent ink, so to speak. We could deny it if we wanted to do so, just by not thinking about it, ignoring it, not having it reinforced with like-minded people, not caring to accept it, or not acting on it for any number of reasons at all. Here then would be a propositional revelation without human prophets, apostles, inspired writers, preachers, or Sunday school teachers involved. And it would be accurate and convincing to anyone who has any propensity at all to accept that revelation inside their heads. Christians already believe the truth is written on everyone's hearts, and only by a willful rejection of that truth can anyone refuse to believe, so there should be no problem with this alternative divine plan either.

Divine Plan Four

If the evangelical God exists, then Theodore Drange argues as follows:

1. God wants all humans to believe in him before they die.
2. God can bring it about that all or almost all humans believe before they die.
3. God always acts in accordance with what he most wants.

4. If God exists, all or almost all humans would believe before they die.
5. But not all humans believe before they die.
6. Therefore, God does not exist.[8]

If we assume God exists and stop Drange's argument at the first conclusion, sentence 4, his argument entails that "all or almost all humans will believe and be saved before they die." Drange argues that if a person wants to know the truth, then "for God to directly implant true beliefs into his/her mind would not interfere with, but would rather comply with, the person's free will." Then whatever God did to help people believe would "not interfere with their free will." So God could perform private miracles for honest truth seekers. He could even take away the critical-thinking faculties of honest truth seekers, making them believe despite any problems with the unreasonableness of faith, and despite any lack of sufficient evidence to believe. If it complies with a person's desires there is nothing wrong with God doing so. It would be a much better plan to reach the world with the message of the cross.

Drange further argues that people really "want to know the truth. They want to be shown how the world is really set up." Now it's really hard for me to envision there are people who don't consciously want to know the truth. So his argument seems quite sound to me. God could do all the apologetical and evangelic work himself. Even if there are people who don't want to know the truth like that, God's involvement in this would make the rejection of Christianity a very rare thing in the world.

Conclusion

I have presented four alternative divine plans of salvation, where there would be no need for Christians to defend their faith, or evangelize, all of which are better plans than the one God supposedly instituted. I guarantee you if God had revealed himself in any of these four alternative ways, no one living under one of these alternative divine plans would ever suggest that the present world we live in is preferable, in which God gave Christians the task of defending the faith that was communicated poorly and failed to provide good solid reasons to believe in him. No one. It's only under our supposed divine plan of salvation in this present world that these alternatives seem strange, odd, weird, or impossible. If someone were to try to object that these alternative plans don't allow for free choices in matters of religion, Christians living under those alternative divine plans would respond by rhetorically asking how anyone can know what's best when compared to God? "God is all-knowing, so he knows how much truth to give people, and no more," they'd respond. "Who are we to judge God and his ways?" they would scold.

If any of these four plans were what God had done, rather than what Christians believe he did, there would be nothing for apologists to defend. There would be nothing much for Christian defenders to do at all, nothing! God would do all the work himself, and do it much, much better.

God's present job performance rating is poor, really extremely poor. He's lazy. He should not have chosen incompetent Christians to do work that he should have done. He's ignorant. He failed to communicate the knowledge that should have been communicated to us. He's incompetent. He failed in providing good solid reasons to believe, As Donald Trump would say to him, after just the very first episode of *Celebrity Apprentice*, "You're fired."

Part I

YOU MUST PREPARE
FOR THE TASK

2

Realize in Advance
the Monumental Challenges

I think it's fair to inform students what they're getting into when they choose a discipline of study leading to a particular career, don't you? Some students are not cut out for some careers. Some people should not be brain surgeons or rocket scientists because they lack the smarts. Others shouldn't be police officers or pastors because of ego problems. Somewhere along the line, preferably early on, responsible people—people who know—should try to steer some students away from particular careers for various reasons. But if we let some students go into some fields without advising them differently, we're likely setting them up to fail. Someone should tell these students what they're going to face in a given career before they pursue it, if possible. They might not listen to us but we should tell them anyway.

No one told me how tough it would be to defend the Christian faith, so I'm going to do you a favor here. Who knows where I would be if I had read a chapter like this one before pursuing apologetics? It's hard to tell. I still think my effort to lay out the monumental challenges will be worth it, so here goes. Hold on to your seat.

I should say from the start that no one can have a scholarly grasp of all the apologetical issues I'm about to summarize, certainly not me. Scholars specialize, sometimes on really minute issues. So the would-be apologist student can relax. You won't be called upon to defend your faith against all of the following arguments. You should still be aware of them. You should still think through them. I consider them to be important faith-destroying arguments you'll have to face. These are some of the issues you can see mentioned or argued for in greater depth in my other books. To get a full feel of the challenges you will face as a defender of the faith, get and read my other books.

So let's begin.

Arguments to God's Existence

There are two areas that are not up for debate, as far as I'm concerned. The first area concerns philosophical arguments that purport to show God exists. They are all such a failure that even discussing them is boring to me. That's right, they're boring because they've been reformulated and then defeated so many times by smarter people than I am that they're no longer worth bothering anymore. I know my readers may still disagree, but I cannot take them seriously anymore. The interesting debate to me is with the coherence of God- concepts, or lack thereof.

In 2010 atheist philosopher Dr. Keith Parsons announced he was done teaching philosophy of religion classes. According to him several atheists have "produced works of enormous sophistication that devastate the theistic arguments in their classical and most recent formulations," and as such, have "presented powerful, and, in [his] view, unanswerable atheological arguments." In his words:

> I think a number of philosophers have made the case for atheism and naturalism about as well as it can be made. . . . I now regard "the case for theism" as a fraud and I can no longer take it seriously enough to present it to a class as a respectable philosophical position—no more than I could present intelligent design as a legitimate biological theory. . . . I just cannot take their arguments seriously any more, and if you cannot take something seriously, you should not try to devote serious academic attention to it. I've turned the philosophy of religion courses over to a colleague. . . . So, with the exception of things I am finishing now I am calling it quits with the philosophy of religion.[1]

You can debate his conclusion if you want to, but you cannot ignore it, coming from such a heavyweight philosopher. I cannot rehearse his reasons here, only note them.

I most emphatically agree with Parsons, of course. In fact, due to the abysmal force of the arguments for God's existence I have called for the end of the philosophy of religion (PoR) discipline in secular universities.[2] I'm simply advocating the complete secularization of secular universities. My call has received some noteworthy attention and endorsement from Drs. Hector

Avalos, Jerry Coyne, Peter Boghossian, and James Lindsay. Avalos is a biblical scholar whose prior call for ending biblical studies is the model I'm applying to the PoR. Coyne is an evolutionary biologist. Boghossian is a philosopher and educator. Lindsay is a mathematician. I'm sure that as my call is heard by more atheists, more and more of them will heartily embrace it. There is no reason for the PoR as a separate discipline. Science departments should examine any evidence that exists about the origins of nature and the nature of nature, without reference to any ancient prescientific writings or the theologies built on them. We should transfer serious discussions about religion and its phenomena over to comparative religion departments. All religion should be treated the same. To have a separate philosophical department dealing with the parochial arguments of Western theistic religion, or Christian theism in particular, already favorably prejudices one religion out of the many global ones that exist.

There, I'll have nothing more to say in direct opposition to any of the philosophical arguments to the existence of God. I have no regard for them at all. I'm only interested in knowing whether there is any objective positive evidence for the existence of a divine supreme being and, lacking that, whether there is any objective positive evidence for his action in the world. Without this evidence, philosophers of religion are only constructing castles in the sky without any grounding to them. Only after we find objective evidence for God can philosophy help the believer. Specifically, it can help believers define their God after they produce the evidence that he exists. The only way Christianity can be defended is if it turns out there's positive objective evidence for the existence of God and they can come up with a coherent Christian God-concept. For even if there is some evidence that a god exists, without a philosophically coherent Christian God-concept, the Christian God probably doesn't exist, or at least, not the traditionally conceived one.

Implications of Evolution

The second area not of for debate concerns evolution. Evolution is a fact. Every scientist in every part of the globe knows it is a fact. It is not up for debate. The only thing left for would-be Christian apologists to do, based on the fact of evolution, is to deal with the implications of evolution honestly.

Richard Dawkins summed up the evidence for evolution in these words:

> Evolution is a fact. Beyond reasonable doubt, beyond serious doubt, beyond sane, informed, intelligent doubt, beyond doubt evolution is a fact. . . . It is

the plain truth that we are cousins of chimpanzees, somewhat more distant cousins of monkeys, more distant cousins still of aardvarks and manatees, yet more distant cousins of bananas and turnips. . . . continue the list as long as desired. . . . It didn't have to be true, but it is. We know this because a rising flood of evidence supports it. Evolution is a fact. . . . No reputable scientist disputes it.[3]

Evolution is based on so much well-founded evidence that it has convinced nearly all Catholic and mainline scholars to support or accept theistic evolution (not just old-earth creationism), including many Methodist, Lutheran, Episcopalian, Presbyterian, Unitarian, Congregationalist, United Church of Christ, American Baptist, and community churches. There are even a growing number of people who might be considered evangelical in their thinking (or considered former evangelicals) who have embraced evolution, like Bruce Waltke, a former president of the Evangelical Theological Society; Dennis Venema, a biologist at Trinity Western University; Kenneth R. Miller, professor of biology at Brown University; Denis Lamoureux of St. Joseph's College, University of Alberta; N. T. Wright, Anglican Bishop of Durham; Francis Collins, director of the National Institutes of Health and director of the Human Genome Project; Karl Giberson, scholar-in-residence in science and religion at Stonehill College; microbiologist Richard G. Colling of Olivet Nazarene University; Alister McGrath, professor of historical theology at the University of Oxford; and Timothy Keller, founding pastor of Redeemer Presbyterian Church in New York City. Then there are Ted Peters, Kenton Sparks, Conrad Hyers, Mark A. Noll, Keith B. Miller, Gordon J. Glover Howard J. Van Till, Pete Enns, Darrel Falk, Randal Rauser, Victor Reppert, and a growing list of others.

The reason why even some evangelical-inclined people are embracing the evidence is because of the evidence. As Jerry Coyne, professor of biology at the University of Chicago, says,

Every day, hundreds of observations and experiments pour into the hopper of the scientific literature. Many of them don't have much to do with evolution—they're observations about the details of physiology, biochemistry, development, and so on—but many of them do. And every fact that has something to do with evolution confirms its truth. Every fossil that we find, every DNA molecule that we sequence, every organ system that we dissect, supports the idea that species evolved from common ancestors. Despite innumerable possible observations that could prove evolution untrue, we don't have a single one. We don't find mammals in Precambrian rocks, humans in the same layers as dinosaurs, or any other fossils out of evolutionary order.

DNA sequencing supports the evolutionary relationships of species originally deduced from the fossil record. And, as natural selection predicts, we find no species with adaptations that only benefit a different species. We do find dead genes and vestigial organs, incomprehensible under the idea of special creation. Despite a million chances to be wrong, evolution always comes up right. That is as close as we can get to a scientific truth.[4]

For a book-length treatment of the implications of evolution, there isn't a better one than *Evolving out of Eden*, by biblical scholar Robert M. Price and Ed Suominen. Here are a few of the implications. The God-hypothesis for the creation of human beings is unnecessary at best. The Adam and Eve story is a myth. Human beings are not special nor even the highest creation. There was no original pair of humans, so there is no original sin. With no original sin, there is no need for redemption and no need for the second person of the trinity to die on the cross for our sins. With no need for an incarnation, there is no need for a resurrection from the dead either. When we die, we cease to exist, just like every other species does. Christianity itself becomes an unnecessary hypothesis at best.

There are other implications of evolution for Christianity. Apart from making its theology irrelevant and unnecessary, probably one of the most important implications is that we can trust science over the ancient scribblings of Bronze Age goat herders, who could not possibly have a clue as to the origins and nature of life and the cosmos. With such a monumental finding, it seems reasonable to wait on scientists to tell us the origins of life itself and of the cosmos as a whole.

Adam, Eve, Sin, and Free Will

I've written a lot about these topics in my previous works, where I argue that the Adam and Eve story is pure myth, and even if true, it's quite an illogical story, serving no reasonable explanation for the origin of suffering.[5] Having already argued those points, let me additionally argue something based on science. Science teaches us there never was a literal Adam and Eve. There was thus never a historic fall in the Garden of Eden either. That mythical story cannot be taken seriously by any scientifically literate person in today's world. Jerry Coyne tells us:

> There's one bedrock of Abrahamic faith that is eminently testable by science: the claim that all humans descend from a single created pair—Adam and Eve—and that these individuals were not australopithecines or apelike

ancestors, but humans in the modern sense. Absent their existence, the whole story of human sin and redemption falls to pieces.

Unfortunately, the scientific evidence shows that Adam and Eve could not have existed, at least in the way they're portrayed in the Bible. Genetic data show no evidence of any human bottleneck as small as two people: there are simply too many different kinds of genes around for that to be true. There may have been a couple of "bottlenecks" (reduced population sizes) in the history of our species, but the smallest one not involving recent colonization is a bottleneck of roughly 10,000–15,000 individuals that occurred between 50,000 and 100,000 years ago. That's as small a population as our ancestors had, and—note—*it's not two individuals*.

Further, looking at different genes, we find that they trace back to different times in our past. Mitochondrial DNA points to the genes in that organelle tracing back to a single female ancestor who lived about 140,000 years ago, but that genes on the Y chromosome trace back to one male who lived about 60,000–90,000 years ago. Further, the bulk of genes in the nucleus all trace back to different times—as far back as two million years. This shows not only that any "Adam" and "Eve" (in the sense of mitochondrial and Y-chromosome DNA alone) must have lived thousands of years apart, but also that there simply could not have been two individuals who provided the entire genetic ancestry of modern humans. Each of our genes "coalesces" back to a different ancestor, showing that, as expected, our genetic legacy comes from many different individuals. It does not go back to just two individuals, regardless of when they lived.

These are the scientific facts. And, unlike the case of Jesus's virgin birth and resurrection, we can dismiss a physical Adam and Eve with near scientific certainty.[6]

I think with the failure of philosophical arguments to the existence of God and the scientific fact of evolution and its implications, there is no longer any room for faith, especially the traditionally conceived Christian faith. These two nondebatable facts could end the apologetic task all by themselves. There are, however, ways around them, and good apologists, like good lawyers, seem to always find the smallest loophole in the evidence that still allows room for faith. You see, maybe we did evolve, but God chose two *Homo sapiens sapiens* to test in the Garden of Eden after all, even though the Genesis text says Adam was created without any ancestry and Eve was created instantaneously from Adam's rib. Where does the myth end? Where does it start? How do we tell where it begins and where it starts except as science progresses? If science tells us this, then why not just trust science in these matters, dispensing with the biblical texts entirely? Others might believe there wasn't an original sin in a Garden of Eden after all. Then where did sin come from? Have we always been infected with it? Then weren't we created as sinners, and if so, how could a good God create us already condemned to die? Or maybe instead, we all individually sin once we're born. But then how does God not get blamed for creating humans such that we all eventually sin? If an assembly line keeps producing flawed vehicles, something is wrong with that assembly line. If every human being who is ever born sins, then we are all condemned by virtue of being born, with no other reason to explain our sin except that we are born into this world. Just consider a teacher who gives the same final test to students throughout his or her teaching career and all students fail that test. The blame for their failure would be with the teacher who created the test. Something is clearly obvious, no matter how we look at it: The fault lies with the creator.

Science is also teaching us that sin and the need for salvation are quite likely based on the illusion of free will. We may not like the results of this science, but that is no reason to reject them. These concepts are very problematic given evolution. Humans share 50 percent of their DNA with bananas. Steve Jones, professor of genetics at University College London, noted this. Do bananas have free will? Can they sin? Can they ever make one single free-will choice? If they don't, then do human beings? Does adding more DNA change anything? What would that be?

In fact, neuroscience is destroying the notions of free will, sin, and the need for salvation. At the very least neuroscience is making it extremely difficult for believers to still claim that that we freely choose to sin, that we can freely choose to be saved, and that there is a wrathful God who will judge us on the last day. For a case in point, look at just one essay adapted from one book by the neuroscientist David Eagleman, "The Brain on Trial."[7] Eagleman writes:

> The choices we make are inseparably yoked to our neural circuitry, and therefore we have no meaningful way to tease the two apart. Many of us like to believe that all adults possess the same capacity to make sound choices. It's a charitable idea, but demonstrably wrong.
>
> People's brains are vastly different.
>
> Who you even have the possibility to be starts at conception. If you think genes don't affect how people behave, consider this fact: if you are a carrier of a particular set of genes, the probability that you will commit a violent crime is:
>
> 4 times as high as it would be if you lacked those genes.
> 3 times as likely to commit robbery,
> 5 times as likely to commit aggravated assault,
> 8 times as likely to be arrested for murder,
> 13 times as likely to be arrested for a sexual offense.

The overwhelming majority of prisoners carry these genes; 98.1 percent of death-row inmates do. These statistics alone indicate that we cannot presume that everyone is coming to the table equally equipped in terms of drives and behaviors.

And this feeds into a larger lesson of biology: we are not the ones steering the boat of our behavior, at least not nearly as much as we believe. Who we are runs well below the surface of our conscious access, and the details reach back in time to before our birth, when the meeting of a sperm and an egg granted us certain attributes and not others.

Genes are part of the story, but they're not the whole story. We are likewise influenced by the environments in which we grow up. Substance abuse by a mother during pregnancy, maternal stress, and low birth weight all can influence how a baby will turn out as an adult. As a child grows, neglect, physical abuse, and head injury can impede mental development, as can the physical environment. And every experience throughout our lives can modify genetic expression—activating certain genes or switching others off—which in turn can inaugurate new behaviors. In this way, genes and environments intertwine. We are each constructed from a genetic blueprint, and then born into a world of circumstances that we cannot control in our most-formative years. The complex interactions of genes and environment mean that all citizens . . . possess different perspectives, dissimilar personalities, and varied capacities for decision-making. The unique patterns of neurobiology inside each of our heads cannot qualify as choices; these are the cards we're dealt.

The upshot of this science, Eagleman informs us, is that "it is difficult to find the gap into which to slip free will—the uncaused causer—because there seems to be no part of the machinery that does not follow in a causal relationship from the other parts."

The Nature and Necessity of Conceptions of God
So far the evidence to believe just isn't there. But what of conceptions of God, do they fare any better? Julian Baggini and Jeremy Stangroom invite readers to create a do-it-yourself deity in their informative book, *Do You Think What You Think?: The Ultimate Philosophical Handbook*.[8] In two short exercises, they help readers see if their conceptions of God are rationally consistent. If you have never done an exercise like this, you should. Before we can even talk about the existence of the God you supposedly believe in, you must have an intelligible set of consistent conceptions of your God. This is not an optional exercise. It's required. Most Christians haven't even thought about this. When discussing any other subject, we must first have an understanding about what we're talking about, some definition of the terms involved.

What conceptions, characteristics, or attributes do you ascribe to the God you believe in? Most Christian theologians follow in the footsteps of Anselm, who asked us to conceive of the greatest being than which none greater can be conceived. This theology has become known as "perfect being theology," and Christians have struggled to exasperation in defending their conceptions of a perfect being from the charges of incoherence, inconsistency, and unintelligibility ever since. Those who don't adopt it are hamstrung by biblical depictions of Yahweh, the God of the Bible, the God of the Old Testament. Such a God is described by Richard Dawkins in this accurate manner:

> The God of the Old Testament is arguably the most unpleasant character in all fiction: jealous and proud of it; a petty, unjust, unforgiving control freak; a vindictive, bloodthirsty ethnic cleanser; a misogynistic, homophobic, racist, infanticidal, genocidal, filicidal, pestilential, megalomaniacal, sadomasochistic, capriciously malevolent bully.[9]

For anyone who thinks Dawkins was wrong to describe God in this way, Dan Barker, the co-president of the *Freedom From Religion Foundation* (FFRF), draws on the Bible's own words to document each of these qualities in a book titled *GOD! The Most Unpleasant Character in All Fiction.*[10] I've written a lot about the moral critique of the God of the Bible myself and I completely agree with this assessment.[11]

What we actually find in the Bible is an extremely not-so-good, very bad God! Yahweh, the part of the Godhead in the Old Testament, is exactly as Dawkins described. He's an embarrassment to all decent God-concepts. He's a God of war, a condemning bloodthirsty God of wrath. Christians want to focus our attention on Jesus instead. Jesus, the part of the Godhead we find in the New Testament, is representative of love, compassion, and redemption they tell us. The truth is not as they describe though. For according to Christian theology Jesus is one with Yahweh. This is not a good cop, bad cap routine. Yahweh is Jesus. Jesus is Yahweh, in mind, will, and purpose. What Yahweh said and did in the Old Testament, Jesus said and did. Jesus is not a kinder, gentler deity. He's a full-fledged member of the Godhead who shares responsibility for every word, every goal pursued, every action, and every decision of Yahweh in the Old Testament. If Yahweh, the first person of the trinity, is a moral monster, as the biblical evidence shows us, then so is Jesus, the second person of the trinity.

So it can equally be said that:

Jesus is arguably the most unpleasant character in all fiction: jealous and proud of it; a petty, unjust, unforgiving control freak; a vindictive, bloodthirsty ethnic cleanser; a misogynistic, homophobic, racist, infanticidal, genocidal, filicidal, pestilential, megalomaniacal, sadomasochistic, capriciously malevolent bully.

Starting with the God of the Bible, conceptions of God grew until he became the greatest conceivable being than which none greater can be conceived. James A. Lindsay delightfully and humorously described this trajectory as representing a schoolyard argument among children: "My god is bigger than your god; no, my god is twice as big as your god; no, my god is ten times as big as your god; no, my god is *infinitely* bigger, better, and more influential than any god you can imagine; yeah, well my god is even better than *that*; mine's that than which nothing greater can be conceived!" Lindsay concludes, "these omnis grow through time to the point of sheer ridiculousness. By that point the unfortunate faithful are left to incredible mental gymnastics to defend physical and philosophical impossibilities in a deity that exemplifies everything people wish it could be and yet that it cannot."[12]

In any case, ever since the widespread acceptance of perfect-being theology, Christian defenders have doubly struggled to defend their faith. For they now have two nearly impossible tasks. They must first harmonize the bloodthirsty, malevolent biblical descriptions of the God of the Bible with a perfect being, and then they must also defend conceptions of the perfect being from the charge of incoherence, inconsistency, and unintelligibility. One task seems quite impossible on its own, but both are now required, thus doubling the problem.

Christians have conceptual problems that other theists don't have for they must intelligibly conceive of a Trinitarian God. This triune God supposedly always coexisted as three persons in one (or, in other views, the Father God eternally created the Son and the Holy Spirit), who never had a disagreement within the Godhead, who never had a prior moment to choose his or her gender, or nature, who sent the second person of the trinity to earth as an incarnate God-man (even though no one has ever made sense of a person who is 100 percent man and 100 percent divine),[13] who somehow died on the cross to mollify the wrath (or offer satisfaction for the offense) of the first and third persons of the trinity for our sins (even though no one has mollified the wrath of the second person of the trinity, and even though there is no coherent correlation between the need to punish someone before forgiveness can be offered), who arose bodily from the grave (even though personal identity after death is quite problematic), who subsequently sent the third person of the trinity to lead his followers into "all truth" (yet fails in every generation to do this), who will also judge us based upon what conclusions we reach about his existence (paralleling the ancient barbaric thought police), and who will reward believers by taking away their freedom and punish the damned by letting them retain their freedom (lest the saints in heaven rebel, and lest the sinners repent in hell and thus no longer deserve their punishment). If you think this description is inaccurate, then read the literature I refer to in this book.

According to most conceptions of the perfect being, God is conceived to be all-powerful (or omnipotent), all-knowing (or omniscient), perfectly good (or omnibenevolent), omnipresent (present everywhere), transcendent (exists in a different realm, or dimension), immanent (exists in the material universe too), nonmaterial (or a spirit), and also a personal agent who both created the universe and acts in it. He's been conceived as immutable (that is, unchanging), impassible (i.e., passionless, without feeling), timeless (doesn't experience a sequence of events), eternally existing (with no beginning and no ending), and necessary (not dependent on anything else in any way).

Are these divine characteristics intelligible? Are they meaningful? Are they internally consistent? Are they consistent with other conceptions of God? Are they consistent with the facts of the universe? Graham Oppy has written a book titled *Describing Gods: An Investigation of Divine Attributes*,[14] which deals with the coherence and intelligibility of these conceptions of God. Any aspiring apologist needs to deal with this problem, and Oppy's book is a superior work on the topic. There are all kinds of conceptual issues to consider. There are severe problems in conceiving any single attribute of God as well as trying to harmonize them all together, and I only want to call attention to a few of these difficulties here, since the would-be apologist must grapple with them.

What are we to think of an omnipotent being? Can he ride a horse he's not riding? Can he create a stone so big he cannot lift it? This second problem is known as the paradox of the stone. It's not escaped too easily. The result of God not being able to do this task is that God ends up being an extremely powerful being, not an omnipotent one. An omnipotent being cannot exist.

What are we to think of an omniscient being? Is it possible for a being to know everything that can be known? Can he know everything about himself? Can he know what time it is now? Can he know the future? Can he know future human actions? If so, is the future fixed and unalterable? If it is fixed, can human beings be free if God knows the future? If it isn't fixed, can the past be changed? And if the past can be changed, why doesn't God start all over with a new creation? An omniscient being could not be ignorant of anything, so an omniscient being would not know something. He could not know ignorance.

Can God think? Can he weigh alternatives? If not, he cannot think. Can God know what it's like to have courage? If not, then how can he be considered virtuous, since enduring hardship is considered virtuous? Can God know what it's like to fear something or to worry about the future? If he knows everything, how can he know these things? Can a timeless God act within time? If not, how could he create time at a certain point in time? How could he act at all? How could he do miracles? In addition, how can God be a personal agent if he lacks the kinds of things we normally associate with being a personal agent? Can a timeless God be a person, an agent? Can an omnipresent being who exists in all dimensions have a centrality to the divine self, if by definition the divine self would be everywhere? But without a centralized self located in a place and time, how can God be described as timeless, omnipresent, and also a personal agent? Furthermore, how can an omnipresent God know what time it is everywhere since time is a function of matter in motion, speed, and location? How can God be unchanging or immutable if he is supposedly reacting to the events in the universe and the choices we make? A transcendent spiritual being without a body wouldn't know how to ride a horse, suffer a headache, play football, skate on ice, or run a mile.

One attribute of God is known as his simplicity. God is conceived of as a simple being who lacks separate characteristics, or attributes, which after everything is said and done is quite revealing of an admission. What it means is that all of the attributes of God boil done to just one. There is only one divine property, divinity itself, and this is identical to God. I kid you not! After all is said and done, God doesn't have the property of omniscience or transcendence or immutability or omnipresence or perfect goodness. Nope. We cannot conceptualize God, it's claimed, since he is beyond comprehension. All of the attributes we might normally conceive God to have are just ways to break up the divine into parts for our understanding. But the bottom line is that God is incomprehensible, according to the doctrine of divine simplicity.

Incomprehensible. That is, without a coherent definition, apart from the incomprehensible conception of divinity itself. Incomprehensible. That means something different than humanity itself. In other words, without a positive definition. It means not-humanity. Not-humanity is describing God in negative terms. Not this. Not that. As George Smith says, "if God is described solely in terms of negation, it is impossible to distinguish him from non-existence. . . .

God is not matter; neither is non-existence. God does not have limitations; neither does non-existence. God is not visible; neither is non-existence. God does not change; neither does non-existence. God cannot be described; neither can non-existence. And so on down the list of negative predicates."[15]

I have not argued here for the conclusion that Christians don't have a coherent, consistent, intelligible understanding of a greatest conceivable being. I'm merely informing the aspiring Christian apologist about the problems with conceiving God for further research. In the end, though, I agree with George Smith that the attributes of the Christian God "are merely a disguise, an elaborate subterfuge designed to obscure the fact that the Christian God is also unknowable. . . . When stripped of its theological garb, the Christian God emerges as the unknowable god of agnosticism." So Smith concludes, "the Christian, operating from a conceptual vacuum, is defending the rationally indefensible; he cannot even specify what it is that he believes in. Or, in more blunt terms, the Christian, when he asserts that 'God exists,' simply doesn't know what he is talking about. And neither does anyone else."[16]

Where's the Beef?

In a 1984–1985 Wendy's fast food commercial, a little old lady, played by actress Clara Peller, asked, "Where's the beef?" So let's finally ask where's the evidence, the sufficient objective evidence, the beef?

I've dealt with this plenty of times before in all of my books, so you should consult them if you're interested. From what I can tell, there are plausible natural explanations for every piece of evidence Christian believers use to defend their faith. Religious experiences? Consider wish fulfillment. Answered prayers and other paranormal claims? Read Theodore Schick Jr. and Lewis Vaughn's book, *How to Think About Weird Things: Critical Thinking for a New Age.*[17] Near-death experiences? Consider oxygen-deprived brains. Miracles? Read David J. Hand's book, *The Improbability Principle: Why Coincidences, Miracles, and Rare Events Happen Every Day.*[18] The resurrection of Jesus? Consider a legend based on visionary experiences that were common at the time. Intelligent design? Consider the problem of evil. You'd think there would be something, anything that would show that the believer has good, solid objective evidence to believe. There just isn't anything like that at all.

3

Become an Honest Life-Long Seeker of the Truth

Given that so many billions of intelligent people down through the millennia have been wrong, dead wrong, about so many important things, you should commit yourself to being an honest life-long seeker of truth. Given the extremely low odds of being right about everything important, this is the only reasonable intelligent position to take regarding knowledge of any kind. To be blunt, there are some important things you are sure about, things that you do not doubt, that you're probably wrong about. Let that sink in. You are probably wrong. We all are. Only intelligent or highly educated people know this completely, for the more we know then the more we know that we don't know.

Got that? You should. Daniel Dennett said, "One of the surprising discoveries of modern psychology is how easy it is to be ignorant of your own ignorance."[1] Recognizing one's own fallibility and ignorance is the inaugural point to any honest person's search for knowledge. You'll probably fail to completely realize this until later in life. It may take years or decades for this to dawn on most people. Others may never realize it. They may never be convinced they have been wrong about some important things. They just happened to get lucky to be raised to believe correctly about everything important, that's all. We should all be so lucky, or something!

This commitment to searching for the truth must be brutally honest and maintained throughout one's life. It must be there at the commencement of the would-be apologist's studies too. I think this commitment is of paramount importance. It's so important there should be an initiation ceremony for anyone deciding to be an apologist. Sort of like ordination services, where the ministerial candidate swears to preach the gospel truth, the initiation rite of the apologist candidate should be where aspiring apologists swear to become honest life-long seekers of the truth, no matter what the results may be. For only that kind of person with that kind of commitment has a chance to know what religious truth to defend, if any of them can be defended at all. Anyone lacking this kind of commitment should not aspire to become an apologist at all. You probably cannot get any better indicator of it than this. Don't pursue this goal. Drop out now before it's too late. Do something else in life. You are not the right kind of person for this kind of task. It says you are not really interested in the truth, come what may.

More often than not, when young college people first decide to become Christian apologists, they have not studied long enough nor plummeted deep enough into the range of issues needed to know which religious truth to defend. It's like getting married at the early age of twenty-one, the drinking age in the United States, and committing oneself to another person for life, not knowing how things will go in the future. It's just too early to expect most of these marriages to succeed in today's world (although it still is a worthy goal), and it's just too much to ask of would-be apologists to defend what is believed at the age of twenty-one too. So the better commitment is to become a life-long honest seeker of the truth, by far.

In this chapter I'm going to offer some sound advice for would-be apologists, or anyone for that matter. Since the goal of any apologist worthy of the title is to defend the truth, such a person should first of all be committed to an honest life-long search for the truth no matter what the results may be.

Don't Trust Your Brain

My first and probably most important piece of advice is not to trust your brain. It will deceive you if left unchecked. Does this sound like contradictory advice? After all, I'm trying to reason with your brain by telling your brain not to trust itself. No self-respecting brain would ever fall for that, right? If this advice is considered the cure then the cure is worse than the disease, correct? Any functioning brain will object to this advice, yes.

Not so fast. My advice is not contradictory at all. I should be more specific though. Your brain does not work that well at getting to the truth. It needs help. It needs better inputs, the objective inputs of science. Without these objective inputs it can easily be deceived. For the brain is a belief engine. It creates stories out of random data. It sees patterns where there are none by connecting random dots. It will "see" that which supports its own conclusions and ignore that which doesn't. Your brain will believe and defend what it prefers to be true and what is familiar, over evidence to the contrary. It can even justify what it concludes in the face of some incontrovertible evidence. In fact, when confronted with contrary evidence, the brain can and will dig itself deeper and deeper into the intellectual trenches of its own making, refusing to budge from what it has previously concluded. Once the brain latches onto an idea it can be extremely difficult to dislodge that idea from the grasp of the brain. The more important the idea is to the brain then the less likely it can be dislodged. There is a massive amount of solid research supportive of these undeniable facts.[2] Alvin Plantinga and others talk about cognitive faculties that are not functioning properly. Brain science shows that none of us have cognitive faculties that are functioning properly, or more specifically, they don't function correctly to a large degree.

Guy P. Harrison explains how the brain works when confronted with claims counter to its conclusions. If a skeptic disputes a psychic's readings, then "the believer's brain is likely to instinctively go into siege mode. The drawbridge is raised, crocodiles are released into the mote, and defenders man the walls." He goes on to explain, "The worst part of all this is that the believer usually doesn't recognize how biased and close-minded he is being. He likely feels that he is completely rational and fair. It doesn't happen just with fans of psychics. We are all vulnerable to this distorted way of thinking."[3] This process happens whenever the brain feels threatened by contrary data.

What Harrison says accurately reflects that current state of science on the brain. So don't trust you brain. Don't trust it when evaluating philosophical arguments without the hard evidence. Don't trust it when considering conclusions that are near and dear to your heart without the hard evidence. The nearer and dearer to your heart then the less you can trust your brain without the hard evidence. Even with the hard evidence the brain can and will deceive you. Your brain will even try to deceive you about what is to be considered evidence. It will try to trick you into thinking the lack of contrary evidence is positive evidence for what it wants you to conclude. Truth is, the lack of evidence is the lack of evidence. It neither affirms nor supports any conclusions, all by itself.

Your brain distorts and deceives. This we know. We know this without a shadow of doubt. We know this based on a whole host of recognizable cognitive biases, those annoying glitches in our thinking processes that produce dubious decisions and mistaken conclusions.

Here's what I mean with just two easily recognizable examples. I have seen intellectuals, extremely reasonable people, defend themselves, their family members, and their personal friends from personal attacks with such stupidity that it even makes a guest on the Jerry Springer show look good. The reason is that when people are emotionally engaged they usually cannot reason very well, even intellectuals. They are in a protective mode. They seek to defend themselves, their family, and their friends from being personally attacked at all costs, even if it means they must sacrifice their intellectual integrity to do so. They don't even see that's what they're doing. We see the same phenomenon when people are in love. It's really true that love is blind. Love is blind to the faults of the person loved. Others who are watching the lovers, who are detached objective observers, can see each of their faults. But people in love cannot, or perhaps more precisely, they do see the faults, but they are dismissed, disregarded, and rationalized away.

What I've just described is called motivated reasoning, something we all do as human beings. There are underlying motives for why we reason as we do—most of the time they are hidden. The brain does this. Most of the time. Again, we know this. Your brain operates on its own. There is no higher judge or arbitrator of how it thinks or what it concludes. While it's usually reliable there are many times it cannot be trusted. It just keeps on working, grinding out beliefs and justifying them without even caring if it's the truth. It deceives itself. The reason it's so incorrigible is because its primary purpose, if I can even speak this way, is in its own self-preservation. If left to itself your brain will try to fit all facts into a grid of self-preservation, a procrustean bed of its own making. Many times it doesn't care when coming into contact with reality. It only cares if what it concludes helps it to survive. For that's how the process of evolution works. And that's because the brain evolved to act this way.[4]

Given that the brain is such a deceiver, how is it even possible to be an "honest" seeker of the truth, as this chapter challenges? The brain doesn't think honestly in the first place. Its main function is to endure in a dog-eat-dog world where only the fittest survive. Coming to "honest" conclusions is not its main function. Yet there are ways to keep your brain honest. I hope to tell you how to train your brain. It can be done. The brain seems to find truths inadvertently through trial and error. Thinking like a scientist augments the truth-finding capabilities already in the brain.

Ask Lots of Questions

People who are truly seekers of the truth have their heads filled with questions on a daily basis. As they look around them at nature, at animals, at the sky above and the sea beneath, they are filled with wonder. The questions come just about as soon as one looks away from one object to another, from hearing one sound to the next, from touching something different, smelling something different, or tasting something different. Children have this natural curiosity. This curiosity is the desire to know, and it produces an astounding array of interesting and potentially fruitful questions.

Let's go back to a time before humanity had very many answers to the kinds of questions that honest truth seekers ask. At one time a child asked, "Why is the sky blue?" An adult answered, "Because God made it that way." "Why did God make it that way?" "Because he did." "Could he have made it red instead?" "Sure, but he didn't for a reason." "What is that reason?" "Only God knows."

Think about the perspectives of the child and the adult here. The child wanted to learn. The adult already had the answer. The child was seeking knowledge. The adult was not. In this scenario and many others, supernatural answers stopped the search for knowledge. If people had continued accepting those kinds of answers science would never have arisen. We would still be in the dark.

We know why the sky looks blue on a cloudless day. It's because molecules in the air scatter blue light from the sun more than they scatter red light. We know this because of science. We studied this because we first asked questions. Honest truth seeking begins with questions. All inquiry begins with honest questions. So ask questions about everything. Question to learn. Question to know. Question to grow.

Thankfully an ancient Greek scientist named Thales began our quest for knowledge by asking one simple question, "What is the source of all things?" His answer was "water" and he was wrong, given what we now know represented in the current Periodic Table of Elements. So we've learned people don't even have to answer questions correctly. We just need to ask them. If we cannot figure out the correct answers perhaps others will.

Socrates taught us to ask two questions over and over again in his search for the truth. In his day the Sophists were known as wise Greek educators who taught the youth in the fifth century B.C.E. They debated Socrates over such issues as piety, knowledge, politics, and beauty. Over and over Socrates would ask them to clarify what they were talking about. The first question he would ask is, "What do you mean by that?" He would also ask another question, "How do you know?" You should be asking these two questions several times a day in various contexts by using differing words and sentences. These two questions can lead us to truth. We must first clarify what we're talking about and then search for any evidence that will either confirm or deny a proposed hypothesis. The evidence will subsequently produce the range of probabilities. Go with them. Think exclusively in terms of the probabilities based on the evidence and reasoning about that evidence. Keep in mind there is little if anything human beings can know with certainty. So believers who claim to know with certainly that God exists are surely being deceived by their brains.

If you want to be an honest seeker of the truth you must develop the courage to question everything, if needed. We don't have to reinvent the wheel, so to speak. Some things we can take for granted, although even those things might deserve to be questioned, just in case we got it wrong before. We all hold to an integrated web of beliefs, as they're called. The beliefs located at the center of the web are the surest ones and the most difficult to question or doubt. Those beliefs at the rim or perimeter of our web of beliefs can be easily disregarded if shown false, without affecting anything closer to the center of the web. Probably very few of us ever question beliefs close to the center of our web of beliefs, or need to. But we should be willing to if we're honestly interested in the truth.

We need to develop a questioning disposition or attitude. A questioning disposition is a skeptical disposition. Honest truth seekers are therefore skeptics, reasonable skeptics. They seek reasonably good answers to honest questions. The term skeptic should not be seen as a pejorative or negative term at all. It should be a positive description of thinking people. Every reasonable adult should be a skeptic. We should all be skeptics, scientific skeptics. Skepticism is a virtue, probably the highest intellectual virtue of them all. One might need to distinguish this virtue from a radical skepticism if needed, but a healthy or reasonable skepticism based in scientific thinking weeds out the chaff of falsehoods from the flowers of truth.

Think Like a Scientist
If asking questions is the beginning of our quest for knowledge then thinking like a scientist is the way to gain that desired knowledge. Given that our brains deceive us we should think like a scientist. Many of us already know how to do that when it comes to bizarre paranormal beliefs of others. The problem is our brains won't allow us to fairly test our own paranormal beliefs, if we have them. Perhaps we should even consider ourselves to be trapped inside our brains and

in of need of escaping from its clutches if we want to know the truth. The brain can and does hinder us from knowing the truth if we don't train it to think correctly. We must therefore think like a scientist.

I had a friend that wanted to know more about me from my handwriting. She had a deck of handwriting sample cards by Bart A. Baggett, called "The Grapho-Deck Handwriting Trait Cards."[5] Unlike the science of handwriting where handwriting samples are compared to determine or exclude an author, Baggett's handwriting cards are supposed to determine one's personality. On the back of the deck it promised we were holding in our hands "the most accurate method for discovering someone's true personality." Yep, that's right. "Just by comparing anyone's writing to the sample on the card, you get a snapshot of the true personality in seconds!" I was writing a book at the time so I handed her a page I had just handwritten (I was without my computer). I first asked her the important question of how the cards could predict people's character traits based on their handwriting. "Where's the science in that?" I asked. "Where are the scientific studies showing these cards accurately can do this?" She didn't know any. A scientist would want to know how the samples and personality traits were determined in the first place. So all someone has to do is to ask to see these scientific studies. If they were not done there is no reason to trust these claims at all. End of story.

Anecdotal personal testimonials simply will not do here, nor would they do in similar cases like one's daily horoscope predictions, psychic readings, answered prayers, or claims of a miracle. Finding someone who says "I had a miracle" just does not cut it. We must test claims like these if we want to break free from a brain that will deceive us and hucksters and con artists who will fool us. We need scientific studies, clinical studies. They are probably the only way to find the truth given that the brain lies to us.

My friend proceeded anyway, by taking card samples out of the deck of cards to find my personality characteristics from any matches. On each card was an example of a handwritten letter or words along with a description of a personality characteristic. She proceeded to go through the deck and found no consistent matches, none. I was just as surprised as she was. There were a few that were close, but no cigar, as they say. For some reason when I was learning to write at an early age, I was not required to use consistent handwritten letters. I know that sounds strange. I write the letters L or T or B differently depending on the letter that precedes it, or the letter that comes afterward. Sometimes I'll start a word with cursive script and then abruptly stick in a block capital letter or two, or even end the word with block letters. My handwriting is a jumbled hodgepodge of inconsistent lettering, and the deck of cards didn't take into consideration that variable.

It turned out my handwriting sample was too large of a sample to use. It was only supposed to be one or two sentences, per the instructions. Because I submitted a whole page it was clear there was no consistent pattern of handwriting to discover, so no particular personality traits could be predicted either. That was big a flaw in the cards. People *should* submit a large handwriting sample, since the larger the sample the more accurate the results. Puzzled at this, she wondered aloud what a handwriting expert friend of hers might say about this odd result. That's when I made a prediction. I predicted that if she gave my handwriting sample to her expert friend, showing no hits or matches, then all bets would be off at that point. He could easily say any number of things that could not be verified. He could say I was an amazing one of a kind person unlike anyone else. Or, he could say I was a terrible person. Or that I was the funniest man alive, or the most intelligent. There would be no controls on what he could say.

It was then that she realized the card "experiment" was flawed, since she knew I was right. But I was just thinking like a scientist. I asked important questions that a scientist would ask. I asked for scientific evidence. I made a prediction that would surely have been realized, and she knew it.

There are plenty of ways to think like a scientist. Test everything important. Observe. Look for sufficient objective evidence. Consider alternative hypotheses. Include a null hypothesis in any experiment. Remember that correlation does not entail causation. Avoid any and all logical fallacies. Make predictions based on the evidence and see if those predications turn out to be true. Think exclusively in terms of the probabilities. If after testing an idea it passes muster, then assign a probability level to it and accept it into our brains as knowledge. Assign a lower probability to that which fails to pass sufficient muster. The process can be long, but it works best if we honestly want to know the truth. There are a few superior books that can help train your brain to think like a scientist, written by Carl Sagan, Michael Shermer, Joe Nickell, Guy P. Harrison, David J. Hand, Mike McRae, and coauthors Theodore Schick Jr., and Lewis Vaughn, that I highly recommend.[6] If you want to think like a scientist you need to read the books written by these authors. In fact, I'll say your search for the truth should begin with their books.

You should also get rid of the notion that scientists are out to destroy your faith. To think like a scientist is to intensely desire to get at the truth, period. As Guy P. Harrison said, "Thinking like a scientist is the gift that keeps on giving.

It's a never-ending process of discovery. New information is always coming in, or will if your brain is open to it."[7]

Become a Generalist

We live in an era of specialization. It seems as though every scholar must specialize in something if he or she wants to make a contribution to knowledge. Maybe that's true. Maybe it's not. I am a generalist. It's my specialty. I'm attempting to know as much as I can about all things Christian in related fields of study. No matter how much I read I cannot do it. So I limit myself to the important things one should know. Someone, some individual, must try to grasp as much about Christianity as humanly possible. That has been my goal. I know I fall short, as would anyone. But attempting to do this has greatly affected how I view the Christian faith. It has led me to become a nonbeliever. That's the result of my searching for the truth.

Regardless of where I've ended up in my quest for truth, if you really want to know the truth about your faith you should become as much of a generalist as you can. Christianity has way too many specialists who don't know that much outside their own specialty. And so one Christian scholar in philosophy may be almost totally ignorant about recent research in biblical studies, and vise versa. But each Christian scholar in his or her specialty will assume that other Christian scholars in their respective fields of study know what they are talking about when defending their faith.

This specialization within Christian biblical studies, theology, philosophy, and science helps perpetrate bad apologetics. Take for instance so-called scientific creationists (an oxymoron). They will read only evangelical commentaries on the Bible and then use their knowledge of science to defend creationism precisely because they are not biblically literate. If they were biblically literate they wouldn't think the creation stories are to be taken literally, but mythically instead. Their efforts in science are then used to reinforce the evangelical creationist biblical scholar's efforts to demonstrate that the Bible is literally true, even though they in turn are not scientifically literate.

Consider next the philosophical defense of evangelical Christianity by Alvin Plantinga. He is a brilliant thinker and philosopher. But he doesn't know much of anything about biblical scholarship, and not enough about the science of evolution. I've actually made the argument that Plantinga is an example of a brilliant person who is made to look stupid because of how he defends this faith.[8] He doesn't know that much in other disciplines of learning. He leans on other evangelical scholars who don't know that much about epistemology or the philosophy of religion, his expertise. They end up bolstering each other's arguments, even though they don't know that much outside their own areas of expertise. Plantinga, an evangelical philosopher, will argue his faith is rational, but it is rational only in the context of results provided by evangelical biblical scholarship—something Plantinga doesn't know much about, and vice versa. Dr. Jaco Gericke, however, who has PhDs in both the philosophy of religion and the Old Testament, calls Plantinga's philosophical defense of Christian faith little more than "fundamentalism on stilts." For as philosopher Stephen Law said: "Anything based on faith, no matter how ludicrous, can be made to be consistent with the available evidence, given a little patience and ingenuity."[9] Sometimes it takes a generalist to see bad arguments for what they are. A generalist can better evaluate the case for or against Christianity than a specialist can.[10]

Evangelical biblical scholars depend on evangelical philosophers even though they themselves are not philosophically literate. New Testament evangelical scholars are not experts in the Old Testament, and vice versa. But their scholarship reinforces one another. They read mainly inside the box of their given specialty and don't read widely outside of it. They simply trust each other's scholarship outside their own expertise. And on it goes. Where it stops no one knows. This is a viciously circular system. Christian apologetics itself needs to do better than this if it wants intellectual respectability. Don't just be a specialist then. Be one, yes. But strive to be a generalist too.

As a generalist you need to think outside the box. Read books and attend lectures that are outside the box of your comfort zone, outside of your specialization, written by liberals, skeptics, and atheists, but also by others defending other religions. Compartmentalization is the problem when it comes to arriving at the religious or nonreligious truth. One needs to read widely in areas related to science, philosophy, archaeology, psychology, Old and New Testaments, religion, and theology. Read outside the box in a wide assortment of areas. More than anything think outside the box, the box of your brain.

Fear Not, All Truth Is God's Truth
If your God is as you believe him to be you should not fear honestly searching for truth wherever it can be found. Don't let your brain fool you about this by instilling fear within you. Many Christian thinkers have argued that all truth is God's truth, so act on it. One of the best statements of this is found in a book by Arthur F. Holmes titled, *All Truth Is God's Truth*.[11]

Truth can be found everywhere that truth can be found. Since one never knows exactly where truth can be found we should not be afraid to search for it everywhere. If something is true it comes from God no matter where you find it, according to Christian theology. Whether it's found through science, philosophy, psychology, history, or experience itself, all truth comes from God because God is the creator of all truth, says Christian theology. Following this reasoning, there is no secular/sacred dichotomy when it comes to truth. There isn't even such a thing as secular "knowledge," if one means beliefs that are justifiably true. Neither sinful, nor carnal, nor secular "knowledge" exists because it isn't true, which is the prerequisite for calling something knowledge in the first place. If something is not true it is false, and there is no such thing as false knowledge. There is only true knowledge. To call something knowledge is to call something true. All knowledge is truth, and all truth is God's since he created it. All truth is therefore sacred, upon Christian assumptions, and it all comes from God, whether learned inside the pages of the Bible or outside of them in the various disciplines of learning.

Since one can find knowledge outside of the Bible, it follows that the Christian apologist must try to harmonize all knowledge. The defender of Christianity must argue that the Christian faith is what best interprets these other truths. The lessons learned outside of the Bible in other areas of learning must be harmonized with the best exegesis of the Bible it can allow. If a conservative understanding of the Bible must give way to the truths learned outside the Bible then so be it. Truth is still truth. Above all seek truth. Don't seek to defend anything less.

The perfectly acceptable Christian idea that "all truth is God's truth" was the middle ground that pushed me into finally accepting that the sciences can be better trusted to tell us the truth about life in this universe than God's so-called revelation in the Bible. The truths outside the Bible forced me to reinterpret the Bible over and over until there was no longer any basis for believing in the Christian faith. At some pivotal point along the way it became obvious that I should interpret the Bible through the lens of the sciences, rather than the other way around. In so doing I accidentally discovered how to circumvent my lying brain.

Practice the Intellectual Virtues
Aristotle discussed the kinds of virtues that led to knowledge, and they have been discussed ever since, with some additions. They are known as the intellectual virtues, which are good habits of the brain, leading it to become a better instrument for gaining knowledge. If anyone really desires to train the

brain he or she must adopt these virtues or habits. They include the virtues of intellectual *honesty*, *integrity*, *perseverance* in pursuing truth, *fair-mindedness* with the data, *humility* in recognizing one's limitations, *empathy* in putting oneself in the place of others to better understand them, *objectively* assessing arguments, and others. We need to train the brain to function properly. Never forget this. We need to force it to think correctly—to think rightly—which in turn will allow us to come to true conclusions. Nothing else will do.

In what remains in this chapter I want to focus on just two of these intellectual virtues. Then I'll conclude by mentioning a few intellectual vices, those habits of the mind that should be avoided because they thwart and hinder the truth.

Courage

By reading this book any would-be apologist has already shown some measure of courage. It takes some courage to entertain ideas that are outside one's comfort zone, so congratulations! I know of a woman who wanted to read one of my books so she said a prayer not to be deceived by Satan before every reading session! Okay, I guess. Is she to be congratulated too? Only a rare number of Christians would even consider reading non-Christian points of view with an open mind.

My guess is that most would-be apologists who read this book are not doing so primarily to learn from it, but rather to refute it if possible. That's two different intellectual attitudes, isn't it? One seeks to learn. The other seeks to rebut. If you're reading this book primarily to rebut it then you're not really seeking the truth. Your brain is in defensive mode, a mode of operation that has a proven track record of deception. You're not actually being courageous either. You're forgetting that everything should be approached as if it has something to teach you, since you're looking for the truth wherever it can be found, no matter what the result. Remember, if all truth is God's truth, you never know where the truth can be found.

I understand some ideas may seem just too far outside of your comfort zone. Some of them may sound bizarre on the surface, like atheism. However, there have been a great many ideas in the past that turned out to be true that were at one time considered bizarre. *So courage requires us to explore uncharted territory in hopes of finding the truth.* There would be no Columbus without courage, no Marco Polo either. The truth just may be there if we search for it, even if certain ideas sound strange. One thing is that since atheists are growing in numbers, atheism cannot be considered bizarre anymore. More and more scientific-thinking people are embracing it. It's a serious option for reasonable people. It's probably the wave of the future barring some environmental disaster, or large-scale war. Courage means reading this book with the primary goal of searching for the truth. If you disagree with it then argue against it. But the first question for honest seekers of the truth is to ask what can be learned from it.

It takes courage when considering ideas outside one's familial or social ties. Your brain will probably lie the most to you when it comes to these familial or social ties. One must have the courage to buck any and all peer pressure coming from family, friends, and church grouping. Truth for the courageous person is paramount. It must be if you want the truth. That doesn't mean you'll end up rejecting any person you love. It just means you really, honestly, sincerely, intensely, stubbornly, doggedly desire to know the truth and will pursue it regardless of what anyone else might think of your journey, or your destination. Since the fittest survive we have learned to depend on the closeness of our own species and our own people within our species to help us survive. We depend on people in our group to help fend off others in the out-group. We depend on close people in our lives during times of trouble or tragedy. So conforming to the opinions of our particular in-group keeps us within that group's safety net, with group assistance and privileges, rather than being ostracized or banned to fend for ourselves in a brutal red-with-blood predatory kill-or-be-killed world. So our brains trick us into accepting and defending whatever the group thinks. It's called "group-think" for a reason, and we all do it. But if you really want to force your brain into submission—if you really want to know the truth—you should be courageous enough to disregard what people close to you think. If it's required, and if this means disregarding what most people you know think, you should be courageous enough to think for yourself.

Open-Mindedness (or Doxastic Openness)
You must be the kind of person who is brutally honest by being willing to change your beliefs if, after considering the evidence for differing ideas, your beliefs are shown wrong. This takes a great amount of courage, so much courage that few people have it, especially when it comes to important beliefs like one's religion. As difficult as it is to do this, I would say you should be happy to be shown wrong. I know your brain won't like it one tiny bit. It prefers that you think you are right about everything. It hates being wrong. Even more than that, it hates having to admit it was wrong, with a passion. Psychologist Dr. Cordelia Fine tells us, "The brain evades, twists, discounts, misinterprets, even makes up evidence—all so that we can retain that satisfying sense of being in the right."[12]

But if you want to be unshackled from the dictates of your evolved brain, this is what you should desire. When examining some claim or debating with someone over an important issue, your attitude should be expressed in these words, "Show me I'm wrong, please! I'm stuck with this belief and cannot shake it. I want to know if I'm wrong." In many ways this is what the Socratic method of asking questions is all about.[13] Just like the TV detective Columbo, who asked questions to discover the truth by weeding out the bad from the good, you should also ask simple but penetrating questions. If the answers seem satisfactory you should be willing to honestly embrace those answers. If, however, you don't have the requisite knowledge to offer responses, then be genuine and authentic, as Peter Boghossian urges us.[14] Don't pretend to know more than you actually know. That's a sign your brain is lying to you, disingenuously defending what you think even though you cannot answer a question. An honest seeker of truth will be found to say "I don't know," rather than mindlessly quote mining a biblical text as an answer, or my personal favorite, talking about quantum mechanics as if one knows what is being talked about. Very few people understand quantum mechanics.

Now it's a fact that people think they're exactly the type of person I'm describing, courageously open-minded. If you think this of yourself then mentally say yes right now, before reading further. —This is a buffer sentence to remind my readers to first answer my question before proceeding.— If you said yes you are almost surely wrong. It is emphatically the case you are not an open-minded person. It's yet another bold-faced lie coming from your brain, which is naturally close-minded. Fine wrote a chapter in her excellent book, *A Mind of Its Own: How Your Brain Distorts and Deceives*, with the title, "The Pigheaded Brain." She tells us "research shows that our stubbornness is so pernicious that even the most groundless and fledgling belief enjoys secure residence in our brains."[15] Later, Fine tells us how bad the human brain really is when it comes to the truth-seeker advice I've given in this chapter. She tells us our problem "is that we are convinced that we are already doing this; it's simply that the other guy's view is absurd, his arguments laughably flimsy. Our pigheadedness appears to be irredeemable."[16] Boy, that's encouraging news, right?

The one thing everyone should acknowledge is that none of us are open-minded, none of us. Anyone who doesn't acknowledge this fact is either ignorant of the evidence, or closed-minded to it. But once we realize what our brain does, then we can become more and more open-minded. We can train our brain to ask questions and think scientifically once we learn that it deceives us. This isn't completely different from being convinced a particular teacher of ours cannot be trusted. For as soon as we realize this we will begin questioning what he or she teaches us. At that point we will seek to verify everything. We will study questions out for ourselves using the most reliable means possible, even doing the experiments ourselves, if needed.

Once we realize we have been led to accept some things that are wrong we'll also wonder what other things we're wrong about. That's the next obvious question. So this should help motivate us to consider new ideas, ideas that may seem absurd if encountered, rather than stay in a self-assured mental atrophy. And how did we first learn we're not open-minded in the first place? We learned this from science. So the natural place to start in our new open-minded quest for knowledge would be to pursue more science. It's the most reliable way to know the truth over a brain that cannot be trusted.

So whenever asked what makes a person open-minded, my answer is always the same. An open-minded person is someone who thinks like a scientist, someone who accepts science-based reasoning. Science changes minds. It always has and it always will. It has the potential to do this with reasonable people who are more open-minded to the truth than others, precisely because these people understand the value of science-based reasoning in the first place. Anyone who denigrates or denies the need and value for objective sufficient evidence coming from the results of science is not open-minded, no matter what their brain claims. Anyone who claims that an ancient prescientific book contains the secrets to the universe is clearly not open-minded to the truth of science either. The brain of a person like that is clearly lying to them. It's hiding the truth from them so they can live comfortably with their societal and familial delusions.

Conclusion

The enemies of truth involve attitudes such as fear, hate, xenophobia, intolerance, certainty, faith, and gullibility. The enemies of truth are all of the known cognitive biases—too many to even list—but I adjure you to look them up. The enemies of truth are all the formal and informal logical fallacies, also beyond the scope of this chapter, but look them up. The enemies of truth are pseudoscience, dogmatism, indoctrination, propaganda, rhetoric without substance, ignorance, specialization, and a lack of inquisitiveness. All of them serve the purposes of your evolved brain in one way or another. Do not embrace them if you want to know the truth. The brain lies. Never forget that. You must master your brain if you want the truth.

Training the brain by forcing it to obey reason and the results of objective science is the most important thing you can do in your search for the truth. Nothing less than training your brain to function properly, by forcing it to surrender to truth at whatever the cost, is going to significantly help you. Adopting the advice in this chapter and then disciplining your brain to doggedly follow the intellectual virtues wherever they lead is your best hope.

You must try to develop the olfactory sense of a bloodhound, sniffing through the libraries of the world in your search for the treats of truth wherever they can be found. You must try to develop the eyes of an eagle, looking for any available evidence in your search for the prey of truth. You must try to develop the taste buds of a catfish (which has 100,000 to 175,000 of them) in your search for any delicious morsels of truth, the sense of touch of a Manatee in detecting the smallest current of evidence, and the hearing of a greater wax moth (with hearing frequencies up to 300kHz) to detect the faint whispers of reason in an unreasonable world. You must do this to avoid the self-induced ignorance and lies perpetrated by your brain. That is, if you want to know the truth, to really know it, especially about that which is important.

4

Get a Good Education in a Good Field of Study

If you want to defend the Christian faith you must first become educated rather than indoctrinated. You must know where to get a good education and which fields of study to major in if you want to be a good apologist. All of this almost goes without saying. But I never considered any of it myself.

I studied at Great Lakes Christian College, Lansing, Michigan, graduating in 1977. It was part of the Christian churches and churches of Christ "non-denomination" that shared historical roots with the Disciples of Christ and the noninstrumental Church of Christ. While the institution calls itself a college, I can assure you I was not educated there. I was indoctrinated. I took Bible classes from a professor who would teach us how to "correctly" understand the biblical passages we were studying, rather than first informing us how scholars from different Christian perspectives interpreted those same passages. That's indoctrination! He taught us what to think, not how to think. He didn't teach us the exegetical tools needed for us to properly interpret a text. He gave us his conclusions without showing us how to properly arrive at the correct ones. He was the expert. We were supposed to accept what he said because he supposedly knew the truth.

There are at least three key indicators that indoctrination is taking place rather than education. This question will take up the first few sections of this chapter. Then later I'll deal with the questions of where to get a good education and which fields of study you should pursue to become a good Christian apologist.

Indicator One: Teaching against the Consensus

A key indicator that indoctrination is taking place rather than education is if you're being taught something that goes against the consensus of scholars working in their respective fields. Indoctrination is probably taking place if opposing scholarly viewpoints are not taken seriously, but are ignored, misrepresented, underrepresented, or even denigrated. This does not automatically mean indoctrination is taking place, but it is a strong indicator. The strongest indicator of them all is the consensus of scientists working in their respective fields. Anything taught that goes against the overwhelming consensus of scientists is an indoctrinating institution. Any sectarian college that denies the evidence of evolution is an indoctrinating institution with an agenda, even a hidden one. Stay far away from those colleges no matter what else they teach.

While it is quite easy to recognize indoctrination as a problem, it can be very hard to spot it when attending college. For in order to see indoctrination taking place, students must first be educated enough to see it taking place. Get it? This is a catch-22, just like the one the military pilots in Joseph Heller's 1961 novel *Catch-22* faced. If a pilot knew he was crazy and asked to be grounded from flying dangerous missions, then he wasn't crazy. The reason? A crazy person wouldn't be concerned enough about the danger of flying missions to ask to be grounded. So if he asks to be grounded he won't be grounded, but if he doesn't ask he won't be grounded either. In a similar manner, students must know enough to know they're being indoctrinated in order to know they're being indoctrinated. If they don't know enough to know this, then they cannot know they're being indoctrinated. In either case, they can't know they're being indoctrinated until they know enough to know they're being indoctrinated. You don't get it? I understand. Try this instead. It takes a con artist to spot a con artist, a liar to spot a liar, and a magician to know how a trick is being played on him. So it takes an educated person to know an educated person and what an education entails.

It won't do to object that all education is indoctrination. Only an ignorant indoctrinated mind would even think such a thing. Indoctrinated believers like that wouldn't even be reading this book. No one who has had a real education would ever say such a thing. There are undeniable facts. Mathematical facts. Scientific facts. Physical facts. Astronomical facts. Chemical facts. Geological facts. Meteorological facts. Biological facts. Biomedical facts. Genetic facts. Zoological facts. Neurological facts. Health facts. Medicinal facts. Historical facts. To be taught these facts is to become educated. To be taught how to discover these facts, test them for their facticity, and to distinguish them from nonfacts is to become educated.

Indicator Two: Not Reading Primary Sources

Another key indicator indoctrination is taking place is if you are not required to read any primary sources. When my Christian friend Dr. Dan Lambert was teaching for the evangelical college John Brown University in Arkansas, he used my book *Why I Became an Atheist* in several different teaching venues, including undergraduate- and graduate-level classes, and even at an adult study group for a church. He's not the only one. My friend Dr. Richard Knopp has used my book in his undergraduate- and graduate-level apologetics classes for Lincoln Christian University in Illinois. There are others, so I'm told. I applaud them all for doing their very best to educate rather than indoctrinate their students. This is probably the best we can expect of them. Maybe with the recent wave of atheist writers they have been forced to do this, I don't know. Their goal is to introduce their students to the arguments of the atheists so they won't lose their faith outside of the classroom after they graduate, when they encounter these same arguments. I can't really fault them for that.

Lambert is on record as saying "Christians should be reading John Loftus' books." Allow me to quote him:

> I first came across John Loftus more than five years ago [2008] while preparing to teach a new course at an evangelical Christian university. The class was called "Encountering Atheism, Skepticism, and Doubt." I was looking for a primary text to use that would help those very sheltered Christian college seniors understand that atheism has some important critiques of our faith and that would help them understand atheists' arguments against faith using the writings of atheists, not the writings of Christian apologists about atheism.
>
> When I found and read *Why I Became An Atheist*, I was impressed with the thorough scope and depth of Loftus' experiences and critiques of Christianity. I read all the best-selling books by all the popular atheist authors, but in my opinion, and for the purposes of my course, *Why I Became An Atheist* was the most thorough tome I found.[1]

Ya gotta love a guy like that!

At Great Lakes Christian College by contrast, I was never asked to read any atheist literature, and the books we were required to read were on some sort of unwritten approved list. We read conservative Christian books written, for the most part, by conservative Christians, some of which were written by our own Church of Christ authors. We were taught what to believe in my undergraduate years. Just coming out of high school we were taught the party line for the most part, or at least, in the classes I took during the years 1973–77. At Lincoln Christian University it was different of course. We read some liberal and atheist literature. But by that time the indoctrination process was already complete. That's a really good reason why you should not attend a denominational or sectarian undergraduate college. For doing so just after high school will continue the indoctrination you have already experienced from your upbringing and church.

If all you ever do in your college classes is read Christian apologetics books in response to the arguments of atheists like me, then you are not being educated, period. You are being indoctrinated. When no atheist author is used in a class on atheism, especially one that argues against atheism, you are being indoctrinated. Become educated by reading the primary sources. It's as if Christian professors are afraid you cannot think for yourself. They've put the blinders on you. "Just come this way, little horsey. Don't bother looking in any other direction so we can lead you into the indoctrinational stall we've built for you."

From reading Christian responses to my books I've discovered a woeful lack of understanding by the authors. I even wonder sometimes if they can read with comprehension. Yet they're written by potential professors of yours in Christian colleges. It isn't that these Christian apologists are stupid. It's because their brains are lying to them. The longer these apologists have studied their faith—the one they were indoctrinated to believe from birth—and the more they have had a vested interest in defending it, then the less they can be trusted. Their brains are blinding them more than others. The problem is that they're more intelligent with much more education than the average believer, so they can sound reasonable when defending the indefensible. And they do. To keep yourself honest make sure you study where professors require students to read the primary sources.

Indicator Three: Bucking the Trends
In Ed Babinski's book, *Leaving The Fold: Testimonies Of Former Fundamentalists*, published in 2003, there are testimonies from former fundamentalists who became moderates, liberals, and even "ultra liberals," like Dewey Beegle, Harvey Cox, Conrad Hyers, Robert Price (who now describes himself as a "Christian atheist"), and seven others. We could add other names like Howard Van Till, John Hick, Marcus Borg, John A. T. Robertson, James Wall, Andrew Furlong, and James Sennett. In another section of his book, there are testimonies of

former fundamentalists who became agnostics, like Ed himself, Charles Templeton, Farrell Till, and five others. We could add other names like Robert Ingersoll, William Dever, Bart Ehrman, and William Lobdell. In still another section of his book, there are former fundamentalists who became atheists, like Dan Barker, Jim Lippard, Harry McCall, Frank Zindler, and four others. We could add other names like Hector Avalos, Michael Shermer, Valerie Tarico, Marlene Winell, Ken Daniels, the late Ken Pulliam, Jason Long, Joe Holman, Paul Tobin, myself, and many, many, many others. If you read Ex.Christian.net, deconversion stories are posted there almost every day.

Here's what Ed wrote about this trend:

> Many professional scholars whose entire scholarly careers have consisted of studying and researching the Bible and whose careers began with a devout love of Scripture in a conservative Christian sense later abandoned their formerly conservative views after gaining knowledge of the full range of questions involved, and hence they changed from being religious conservatives to either more moderate or liberal or even agnostic standpoints. In fact entire seminaries founded originally as seminaries for conservative Christian denominations have changed over time into liberal arts colleges, and now entertain moderate to liberal to agnostic professors and views. (For instance the seminary founded by John Calvin later became filled with Deists. While in America, Yale was founded due to the "liberal theological excesses" of Harvard.) Even in our day look what happened to Fuller Seminary, or look at some of the professors and graduates of Wheaton College, Billy Graham's young-earth creationist and inerrantist alma mater. They seem to be stretching all sorts of boundaries these days, headed away from such conservatism and toward moderation, but not taking radical or huge steps all at once which would lose too many conservative donors. (Dr. Bart Ehrman, the agnostic Biblical scholar and bestselling theological author, graduated from Wheaton with extremely high honors.) Others who left the conservative fold of their youth after majoring in Biblical studies include well known and prolific biblical writers: Crossan, Goulder, Lüdemann, Borg, Cupitt, Bullock, Larson, Cunningham, Salisbury, Dever, Armstrong, and others listed at Steve Locks's *Leaving Christianity* website. Neither their stories, nor the stories of the host of seminaries founded as bastions of conservatism that grew more moderate and liberal, will be found in books sold at Evangelical Protestant or Catholic bookstores, nor highlighted on TV networks owned by those churches.[2]

This is true of Christian publishing companies too. They grow more and more liberal with each decade so that conservative ones are started to maintain the status quo, which themselves subsequently grow more liberal. This cycle repeats itself every few decades or so. We see this same trend in science. Why is there a need to start organizations and websites like *Answers in Genesis, Reasons to Believe, The Institute for Creation Research, The Discovery Institute, Creation Science Evangelism*, among many other examples? Why is it that Christians cannot just be scientists? If the evidence actually supported what conservative Christians believe, why does science gravitate away from creationism such that creationists must start separate organizations?

If you can't see this in the colleges themselves, then look at the Christian apologists teaching in the colleges. Many dedicated biblical scholars from a fundamentalist perspective are leaving that viewpoint and embracing anything but their initial stance. I'm happy to have lived long enough to see that evangelicals are now embracing Karl Barth. I've personally seen how theology evolves. Back in my seminary days one issue of interest was neo-orthodoxy, stemming from what most people think is the greatest theologian of the last century, Karl Barth. Wanting to be on the cutting edge, I did my master's thesis on his doctrine of the word of God. Barth had sparked a debate among evangelicals over inerrancy. Harold Lindsell's book, *The Battle for the Bible*, was heavily discussed among us. Evangelicals did not like Barth and neither did I. Due to the onslaught of nineteenth-century biblical criticism Barth was forced to deny natural theology. He argued that although the Bible contained myths and legends God still speaks through it. For Barth, the word of God was not to be located in the Bible itself. No. Rather, God speaks through it. God's word, his revelation, takes place when God speaks to his people, and he can do so through myths, legends, and even a Russian flute concerto. This idea was described as the new (or neo) orthodoxy. It was all Barth could do in the face of so much biblical criticism to maintain his faith. To read up on those good old days, see Robert Price's *Inerrant the Wind: The Evangelical Crisis in Biblical Authority*, where he made some predictions that have since proved to be true.[3]

After the dust settled the evangelical reaction to Barth became nuanced and mixed. Aside from the debates about the Bible, the main thing evangelicals came to understand was that the real issue is hermeneutics, or the science of interpretation. They argued that a text could be inerrant so long as it was understood according to its genre and context. So guess what? Evangelicals can now argue that the creation accounts in Genesis (1–2) are myths because they weren't meant to be taken literally after all, while still maintaining the Bible is inerrant. They can deny there is a hell since that too is considered mythical. They can even embrace universalism. See the mental gymnastics here? The floodgates were opened. Anything that seems nonhistorical in the Bible is just waved off as a mythical story with a point, somewhat like a parable. No contradiction here, you see.

So for a growing number of progressive evangelicals, the inerrancy debate has been rendered moot precisely because of the issue of hermeneutics. Evangelicals are embracing Barth and a number of other kinds of theologies once considered liberal. The thing is, this new evangelical orthodoxy is, well, the old neo-orthodoxy. A liberal is now the new evangelical, you see. These progressive evangelicals are embracing what was once thought of as reprehensible.

All one has to do is consider the writings of John Walton, Kenton Sparks, Peter Enns, and Christian Smith for starters.[4] There are others. When I was in seminary, I never dreamed evangelicals would ever debate the historicity of Adam, but they are doing it now.[5] Evolution is being embraced by these new evangelicals, as is feminist theology, homosexuality, and emergent Christianity. What's to stop evangelicalism from becoming liberalism? Nothing. So the old kind of evangelicalism can only be maintained by censoring and firing these progressive evangelicals, which is happening.[6]

Christians in every generation revise their theology just like I've watched evangelicals do in mine. And what's interesting to me is that younger evangelicals lack a historical perspective that the older progressive evangelicals are not telling them. The older progressive evangelicals are not telling their students how they arrived at their present theology. So the younger ones think this is what evangelicals have always believed. They have collective amnesia, and it's perpetuated by those who know but fail to pass this information on to them or, at a minimum, fail to communicate in a way that allows their students to get the message.

So when I critique the Genesis creation accounts, I'm met with some laughter, just as when I argue against hell. For these younger evangelicals think I'm arguing against a straw person no one believes anymore. They don't realize that they are the ones who have adopted a changing orthodoxy as if it's always been the evangelical orthodoxy. What they fail to understand, because they are young, is that their views would have caused them to be booted from the pulpits of churches and the lecture halls of seminaries across the land in the previous generation.

Where Can You Get a Good Education?
If you want to be a good Christian apologist, the best places to get a good education are at secular universities. If I say nothing else, you should agree with

me on this. Let me first speak in terms you might accept. Among Christian apologists and biblical scholars, the most marketable ones are graduates of secular universities, especially universities considered to have the best departments in their chosen fields of study. So if you want to be a professor, and if you want your manuscripts easily accepted for publication by top-ranked book publishing companies, then this is what you must do. The best of the best apologists will be the ones who studied in secular universities, heard the best that secular professors threw at them, and still believe. People will want to listen to you after that. There, glad we can agree on this even though this isn't all I have to say.

If you don't attend a secular university, then don't study in any Christian apologetics program, and certainly don't study where the professors must sign creedal statements of belief. Attend an accredited college where professors are free to pursue the truth based on the available evidence, one where the professors who teach there graduated from other colleges. Otherwise, you'll just be reinforcing what you were raised to believe rather than being an honest seeker of the truth. Let me explain all of this further.

Don't Study in an Apologetics Program

Do not study in an apologetics program, and certainly don't earn a degree in apologetics. There are a few reasons why I say this. The main reason is that apologetics programs are all sectarian programs taught exclusively at evangelical colleges. I don't know of any apologetics programs at more liberal colleges or universities. That's odd don't you think? A good education is one where the primary goal is the search for truth, whereas the primary goal of an apologetics program is to defend what is believed to be the truth. But how can students know in advance of getting an education what to defend as apologists, if they enroll in a college apologetics program that assumes it has the whole truth? Wouldn't these students just be signing their intellects away, trusting that their professors know the truth before they study it for themselves? *Having an apologetics program at all is a strong indicator, all by itself, that a college is not really interested in the search for truth, but rather in defending that which is believed to be the truth.* Let that sink in. Having an apologetics program prejudges the case in favor of whatever flavor of Christianity the founders of a college had tasted when they cooked it up. Colleges that are only or mainly interested in the truth are much better and more interesting to dine at.

By contrast there is no atheist apologetics program in any university. No one attends a university to earn a degree in nonbelief. There are atheist professors who teach their subjects of course. But there's no need to put it all together for atheist students who want to argue believers out of their faith. If Christianity stands above all other contenders there shouldn't be a need for any apologetics program. Period. Each intellectual discipline of learning should end up bolstering the Christian faith, if the evidence were there. *The fact that Christians need to have apologetics programs is a strong indicator, all by itself, that Christianity cannot win in the marketplace of ideas.* Let that sink in too.

An apologetics program is not teaching you to do serious scholarship anyway. An apologetics education is an oxymoron. An apologetics educational program is a sham, a farce, a chimera. It is a surrogate education. It is not geared for honestly searching for the truth. Its goal is to defend what professors in those programs already believe is the truth. This is as sure as one can get to an anti-intellectual educational approach that still retains the vestiges of an education. So if you want to be a scholar don't specialize in apologetics. These two processes are different in kind because seeking to discover the truth and seeking to defend what is already believed to be the truth are two different processes of the brain, and we know the brain specializes to a fault in defending what it already believes to be the truth.

Study to be a scholar instead. It's a much more rewarding enterprise filled with both wonder and discovery at the world and its workings. Refuse to allow professors to teach you how to fit the whole universe into a procrustean bed of their making. Learn to doggedly follow the evidence. Refuse to learn how to make evidence fit with your faith. There will be a great deal to relearn if you enter one of these programs and subsequently learn later in life they taught you how to do the wrong kind of thing with the available evidence. Learn how to follow the truth wherever it is found rather than learning how to defend what you were raised to believe. Learn how to follow the evidence wherever it leads. No one needs to justify a conclusion if the evidence is there. That's because no one needs to defend what the evidence shows. All anyone should have to do is simply present the evidence. So learn to be a scholar, to open your eyes to any new possibilities, and let the evidence do the talking. The whole idea of good scholarship revolves around doing good solid research, and then coming to solid conclusions (or results) based on solid evidential reasoning.

Don't Study Where There Are Required Creedal Statements

The last thing you should do is to study at a college where the professors are forced to sign a doctrinal statement. Even some students are required to sign them in order to graduate, or so I've heard. In order to teach in the Science

Department at Bob Jones University, all professors are required to sign a yearly statement of faith. Here it is:

1. Bob Jones University believes the account of origins in Genesis is a factual narrative of historical events; that is, God created the universe, including all original kinds of living organisms (including man), in six literal days.

2. We believe the genealogies recorded in Genesis 5 and 11 indicate a date for the creation week less than ten thousand years ago.

3. We believe the fall of man into sin and the consequent curse of God recorded in Genesis 3 had profoundly negative consequences for all of creation, including the introduction of death (1 Corinthians 15:21).

4. We believe the flood described in Genesis 6–8 was a historical event of approximately a year's duration, which was global in extent and biologically and geologically catastrophic in effect.

This institution is not an institution of learning, which teaches the Ken Ham literal creationist view of the world. The science professors must believe and teach that God first created the earth and then the universe of stars not that long ago, that there was a literal fall in the Garden of Eden, and that there was a universal flood.

Perhaps my readers can see how creedal statements like these hamstring the search for truth. What they might not see as readily is that others do so as well. Here is one from Wheaton College, home of the Billy Graham Center for Evangelism:

> WE BELIEVE that God has revealed Himself and His truth in the created order, in the Scriptures, and supremely in Jesus Christ; and that the Scriptures of the Old and New Testaments are verbally inspired by God and *inerrant* in the original writing, so that they are fully trustworthy and of supreme and final authority in all they say.

The word "inerrant" here means without error. Why would anyone interested in the truth require this of their professors? What if, upon studying the Bible, a professor at Wheaton discovered there were errors in the Bible after all? Why should he be censored if the goal was to find out the truth? If the truth can be defended, creedal statements like these shouldn't be necessary.

California's Biola University has a doctrinal statement where they deny that "humans share a common physical ancestry with earlier life forms." This sectarian institution is "fundamentally at odds with the entire direction of modern biology," noted Thomas Albert Howard and Karl W. Giberson. Why? Because "Common ancestry today is, quite simply, as well-established in biology as the motion of the earth about the sun is in astronomy. To attempt to exclude faculty who might hold this view is tantamount to closing one's eyes in the face of an encyclopedia of genetic information." [7]

Who would want to attend a backward school like this?

Not me. I would want a good education. This is not an education. This is indoctrination even at a higher level than others.

Who would want to teach for a backward school like this? Well, several important Christian apologists, that's who. The Biola apologetics faculty includes: Craig J. Hazen, William Lane Craig, Gary R. Habermas, J. P. Moreland, and Scott B. Rae, with visiting lecturers R. Douglas Geivett, Greg Koukl, Mark Mittelberg, Lee Strobel, Phillip E. Johnson, and Alvin Plantinga.

Why do they need creedal statements if the evidence for sectarian evangelical colleges is there in the first place? Why are they needed if the goal is the search for truth in a world of religious confusion? Professors in evangelical institutions are not allowed to be honest scholars. That is a fact. They are not allowed to think and write freely. If they step out of line, they are fired. But more and more of them are doing just that. More than a few evangelical scholars have been fired, suffered censorship, or incurred intense scrutiny because they tried to interact honestly with the wider scientific and scholarly communities. Dr. Bruce Waltke, an evangelical professor of Old Testament and Hebrew, is one such example. He had to resign his post from the Reformed Theological Seminary after endorsing evolution. Others, such as Drs. John Schneider, Tom Oord, Jim Stump, J. R. Daniel Kirk, Michael Licona, Peter Enns, Anthony Le Donne, and Christopher Rollston, have been forced out of their teaching positions for stepping outside of what was considered Christian orthodoxy.

Because of these and other censorings, I consider honest evangelical scholarship a ruse. There is no such thing. Why must the search for truth come up against a creedal wall that scholars cannot go beyond if the truth is worthy of seeking in the first place? Why must evangelicals need that wall? If evangelicalism has the evidence for it, then that wall is unnecessary. It's placed there because of the gradual trend, despite these creedal statements, toward liberalism. The trend does not work in reverse. You never see a liberal college gradually become a conservative one. It only happens by firings or by starting new colleges. The gradual trend toward liberalism takes place naturally as scholars interact with other scholars. The only way to stay conservative is to put up the wall of creedal statements or to cut yourselves off from the wider scholarship at large. But then you'll just be talking to yourselves and be ignored by others. Scholars cannot allow themselves to do this and still be recognized as scholars. They must interact with the wider scholarly community. So the choice is either to have scholars and risk upsetting your constituents, thereby being forced to fire them later, or basically be culturally irrelevant as a university. But what university worthy of the name can stand for that? None should.

While it's hard to convince conservative Christians they are wrong, just think for yourself what this all tells us about the evidence for their beliefs. Many dedicated biblical scholars from a fundamentalist perspective are leaving that viewpoint and embracing anything but their initial stance. It would seem that fundamentalists, conservatives, and evangelicals do not have a leg to stand on. Their ship is going down. All they're doing is rearranging chairs on the *Titanic*. That's why they need creedal statements in the first place, that is, because the evidence for their evangelical faith is not there. They cannot trust intelligent people to search for the truth, for their truth needs to be buttressed with creedal statements that have teeth to them. So to learn from these professors who are under the gun of a creedal statement is to perpetrate the same kind of thinking as they are forced to maintain. They are in defense mode. They will teach you to be in defense mode. They will not teach you to search for the truth. They will not teach you to be scholars.

Avoid these institutions like the plague, even if your parents don't want you to go to a secular college. Whether they realize it or not, they want to continue controlling your thoughts just as they did when teaching you which religion to adopt. You didn't know to believe differently. If you were raised in a Buddhist or Hindu or Muslim family or community, you would believe what is taught there too. So why do you think your evangelical faith has any more basis than the other faiths taught by other parents, who were taught by their parents, and so on stretching back for several generations and more. It's time to think for yourselves as adults. You will do so eventually. Why not start now? Let the first decision of your adult life be to go to a secular noncreedal affirming college. Say to college recruiters that, until creedal statements are abandoned, you will not attend an institution where the truth is suppressed. You want a good education from professors who are willing to pursue the truth wherever it can be found, who are not afraid of the creedal thought police.

Again, avoid these institutions like the plague, *even if you are in agreement with their creedal statements*. For even though you may be in agreement with these statements now, how do you know you'll still agree with them later in life? The search for truth should be yours from the very beginning. Life is short.

Begin now. Don't learn later in life that you started out defending something that was wrong. Don't be in defense mode at all. Follow the evidence. It's that simple. And since my Christian readers believe in God, then trust he will guide you. Why don't you have that kind of faith to trust him? You should if your God is good. Get a good education. You may end up an apologist after all. But you must start by learning how to search for the truth. You will not be taught that in any apologetics program, nor at an evangelical college where the professors must sign a creedal statement of faith. Then see what happens. If your faith is strengthened, then you will be a better apologist. If it causes you to become a liberal or nonbeliever, then follow the evidence where it leads. Be courageous.

I wish I had done this. Follow this advice and you'll be glad. I guarantee it.

A Note on Indoctrination and College Accreditation
Evangelical backward-thinking colleges and universities seek legitimization. Gaining accreditation is one way to do that. So accreditation should be denied to these colleges. Apply this retroactively to sectarian colleges that already have accreditation. No, I am not kidding. The principle to be used in denying them accreditation is that signing doctrinal statements disqualifies an institution of higher learning worthy of the name from accreditation. Why is college accreditation important? Several reasons:

> There are several reasons accreditation is important besides ensurance [sic] of quality and adherence to academic standards. Accreditation determines a school's eligibility for participation in federal (Title IV) and state financial aid programs, as well as eligibility for employer tuition assistance. Proper accreditation is integral for the acceptance and transfer of college credit, and is a prerequisite for many graduate programs. In addition, degrees attained from a school without regional accreditation may not be as accepted for professions that require licensure.[8]

Should something be done about this? I think so, and it has nothing to do with me being an atheist. I recognize private colleges have First Amendment protections. At the same time, accreditation agencies exist in order to insure the quality of education that students can expect to receive in U.S. colleges. So the best and only way to ensure the quality of education in institutions of higher learning is to withhold accreditation from them if they are sectarian in nature, if they have a doctrinal statement that forms the foundation of their colleges, and if they force their professors (or their graduating students) to sign a doctrinal statement.

I look to existing accreditation agencies to implement this new policy. Do it now, especially since there are accredited colleges that deny human-caused global warming, the single most pressing problem on our planet today, on the basis of scripture. Accreditation agencies cannot possibly be ensuring the quality of education for students who enter these colleges without taking this stand. Do it now for our future, for the students, for the truth, and for the planet.

Which Fields of Study Should You Major In?

If you want to be a good apologist do not major in the philosophy of religion. That field is dominated by Christian theists who argue for the claims of their faith in these classes. Some of them are no different than apologetics programs of study because of this, and as such, they fall under the same criticisms I made against studying in an apologetics program. I grant that the philosophy of religion programs don't discuss the full range of issues needed to defend the Christian faith. But on the relevant issues, they act like apologetics programs.

In 2009, David Chalmers of the Australian National University and David Bourget of London University surveyed professional philosophers and philosophy students on their philosophical views. The PhilPapers survey was taken by 3,226 respondents, including 1,803 philosophy faculty members or PhDs and 829 philosophy graduate students.[9] The question that interests me is what philosophers think about God:

God: theism or atheism?
Accept or lean toward: atheism 678 / 931 (72.8%)
Accept or lean toward: theism 136 / 931 (14.6%)
Other 117 / 931 (12.5%)

If we add in the "other" category, which would include New Age beliefs, deism, and agnosticism, then upward of 86 percent of respondents are not theists. Among those philosophers who are theists, I dare say most of them are probably not card-carrying evangelicals, since this includes Catholics, Muslims, Jews, and those who merely accept the so-called philosopher's god. William Lane Craig has gone on record as saying there is, at the present time, a renaissance of Christian philosophy in today's world. *Cough* Not so. Not so at all. Of the philosophers who took the PhilPapers survey in 2009, nearly three in four accept or lean toward atheism. Among philosophers of religion, meanwhile, nearly three in four (72.3 percent) accept or lean toward theism.

Why are so many philosophers of religion theists when others in the field of philosophy proper accept or lean toward atheism? It's because theists gravitate to the philosophy of religion field in the first place, according to a paper written by Adriano Mannino.[10] In fact, given that they do gravitate to that field, the fact that there aren't *more* theists working in it tells us something interesting about the philosophy of religion itself.

Over the years, I have similarly found that the philosophy of religion field has been a bastion for Christian apologists. It gives these Christian philosophers the appearance of having successfully defended their faith, but the reality is not there at all. Almost all of the philosophical arguments to God's existence that they wield could still be made if Christianity were not true. None of them are helpful in establishing any particular Christian sect or even Christianity as a whole. The same arguments are used to support Islam and Judaism. Even if successful, they do not privilege Christianity in any way. I'll deal with this later in chapter 5. Suffice it to say for now that the philosophy of religion cannot do the requisite work needed to defend the Christian faith. It doesn't even do the preliminary work needed, as I'll also argue later.

I've already said I have no regard for arguments to God's existence anyway. I don't even see the need for them if there really is a God who wants us to believe. Just as I argued that there should not be any need for apologetics in chapter 1, I see no reason for these arguments to God's existence. Why is it that a person's salvation depends on comprehending some of the complex philosophical arguments to God's existence and also agreeing with them, especially when there are plenty of good reasons to reject them? That doesn't make sense. What if everyone's salvation depended on accurately understanding what happened at Colonel Custer's infamous last stand, or why the Mayan civilization died, or who killed John F. Kennedy or JonBenét Ramsey? This just doesn't make any sense. I actually think argumentation in the Christian philosopher's toolkit serves as a substitute for positive evidence that God exists. When the evidence is not there, use an argument instead. Somewhere along the line, insert a non sequitur and hope nobody notices. Then *ka-boom*. God, my God!

So with that out of the way, I would strongly recommend any would-be apologist who chooses to study at a good university to major in one of the sciences. Since science has been beating down the door of faith for a few centuries, if you want to be a good apologist, become a scientist yourself. See what scientists do. See how they perform their experiments. Learn how to be one. Study geology, physics, biology, astrophysics, astronomy, cosmology, psychology, or, especially, neuroscience. I think a class on evolution should be a mandatory requirement in all universities, even for students majoring in disciplines like philosophy, business, food management, English, and so forth. Become an expert in parasites and viruses, since our world is chock-full of them. Become an expert in poisonous plants and creatures too. Ask and answer why any of these things exist if there is a perfectly good God who created the world out of nothing and could, if needed, perform *perpetual miracles.*

Other recommendations include becoming a biblical archaeologist by studying with Israel Finkelstein, William Dever, or Robert R. Cargill. Or become a biblical scholar by studying with Hector Avalos, Bart Ehrman, Andre Gagne, Jon D. Levenson, or Michael D. Coogan. Or, become an expert in comparative religion or cultural anthropology. Study with Peter Boghossian in philosophy at Portland State University. Do so at secular universities that have no creedal statements that professors are required to sign.

Basically, go study in fields that threaten your faith. If there is a discipline that threatens your faith, then go study it at a good university. Study under the major proponents of these threats to your faith, if possible. Get master's and doctoral degrees in these fields of study. If you want to be a good defender of the faith, you must learn the arguments and see the evidence for yourself. Study them until you know them better than people like me who seek to "destroy" your faith with them. Then defend your faith against what you've learned, if you can. My bet is you can't.

5

Accept Nothing Less Than
Sufficient Objective Evidence

The word "metapologetics" refers to the various apologetical methods used by Christians in defending their faith. Kenneth Boa and Robert M. Bowman Jr., put the matter this way: "While apologetics studies the defense of the faith, metapologetics studies the theoretical issues underlying the defense of the faith. It is evident, then, that metapologetics is a branch of apologetics; it focuses on the principle, fundamental questions that must be answered properly if the practice of apologetics is to be securely grounded in truth."[1] This present chapter will concern itself with metapologetics itself, that is, with apologetic methodology. I'll argue that apologists who seek to defend the Christian faith must accept and defend nothing less than the need for sufficient objective evidence. This is the only honest choice.

A Variety of Apologetical Methods
William Lane Craig has argued that in the last four decades there has been a "renaissance of Christian philosophy," and with it a resurgence of Christian apologetics. He traces this resurgence to a particular year, 1967, with the publication of Alvin Plantinga's *God and Other Minds: A Study of the Rational Justification of Belief in God*, in which Plantinga is thought to have shown how belief in God can be justified despite the arguments of those who argued God-talk cannot be verified, and despite those who argued God was dead following World War II and the horrors of the Holocaust.[2] Craig has triumphantly proclaimed:

In Plantinga's train has followed a host of Christian philosophers, writing in scholarly journals and participating in professional conferences and publishing with the finest academic presses. The face of Anglo-American philosophy has been transformed as a result. Atheism, though perhaps still the dominant viewpoint at the American university, is a philosophy in retreat.[3]

With the publication of the new atheist books by Sam Harris, Richard Dawkins, Christopher Hitchens, and Daniel Dennett in the aftermath of the militant Muslim attacks on 9/11, Christian apologists came out in force. Says Lee Strobel, the author of a few supposed investigative journalist books examining the case for Christianity: "There has been a resurgence in Christian apologetics as a direct result of the challenges Christianity has faced in the form of militant atheism in college classrooms, on the Internet, and in TV documentaries and best-selling books."[4] Christian apologists replied to the new atheist authors by saying they were not philosophically astute, theologically knowledgeable, or biblically literate. In other words, they didn't understand "sophisticated theology" enough to dispute the Christian faith. Whether that's true or not, these new atheist authors have broached important issues for Christians to debate, which in turn has changed minds, lots of them.

More than a decade prior to this "resurgence," however, it was already becoming clear that apologists themselves could not agree with each other on the proper method for defending their inherited faith. In 1953 Bernard Ramm was probably the first to call attention to these differences in his book, *Types of Apologetic Systems.*[5] The value of Ramm's important work was in categorizing three systems of apologetics, and in highlighting ten major problems of Christian apologetics.

Ramm asked the following ten questions: (1) "What is the relationship between philosophy and Christianity?" (2) "What is the value of theistic proofs?" (3) "Must the apologist work with some theory of truth?" (4) "What is the importance of the doctrine of sin for apologetics?" (5) "What is the character of revelation?" (6) "What kind of certainty does Christianity offer?" (7) "Is there a common ground between believer and unbeliever which forms a point of contact for conversation and argumentation?" (8) "What is the character of faith?" (9) "What is the status of Christian evidences?" and (10) "What is the relationship between faith and reason?"[6] As Ramm explained, every single question he asked was answered differently by Christian apologists. Ramm brought these types of metapologetical problems to the attention of a larger number of Christians, especially evangelicals.

Apologist James Beilby recently added another question to Ramm's list, "What is the task of apologetics?"[7] Apologists cannot even agree on their primary task. I would argue that the primary task of apologetics has been to help believers who are already in the fold of Christianity. Based on Anselm's "faith seeking understanding" dictum, the task of apologetics is to validate what Christians already believe. I'm arguing this should change if apologists want to reach out to reasonable nonbelievers, if possible. I've added another question to Ramm's list as well, in chapter one of this present book, one that no one seems to be asking, "Why is it necessary to defend the Christian faith at all?"

The next important book that looked in detail at these metapologetical issues was written by Gordon Lewis, *Testing Christianity's Truth Claims*.[8] In it Lewis explained the various apologetical approaches and offered criticisms of them while defending the *Cumulative Case* approach of Edward John Carnell above the others. In that same year Norman Geisler wrote the first apologetics book that began by discussing apologetical methodology in some detail (over about 134 pages). In his book, simply titled *Christian Apologetics*,[9] Geisler was the first evangelical to defend *Natural Theology* or the *Classical Method*, which was a staple of the Catholic tradition. In the decades that followed, most apologetics books contained at least a small section on methodology. There have been several additional books published on metapologetical issues, and there is a great deal of disagreement.[10] James Beilby informs us that, after decades of debate, "None of the traditional apologetic systems has received the endorsement of a substantial majority of Christian apologists."[11]

It's not just that Christian apologists disagree with each other on how to defend their faith. The problem is deeper than this and best described as a crisis. The problem is that the whole enterprise of Christian apologetics is doomed to failure if apologists cannot adequately defend a reasonable apologetical method for defending their faith. For Cardinal Avery Dulles notes, "The 20th century has seen more clearly than previous periods that *apologetics stands or falls with the question of method*."[12] There is a crisis of method because there is a crisis with apologetics itself.

Now, let's get on with the show. Several Christian apologists have offered differing classifications, or taxonomies, of apologetical methods.[13] I won't rehearse them here. Rather, I'll offer what I consider the best way to categorize metapologetics from my perspective, based on their primary approach in defending Christianity, using five headings: (1) Apologetics Based on Sufficient Objective Evidence; (2) Apologetics Based on Special Pleading; (3) Apologetics Based on Assuming What Needs to Be Proved; (4) Apologetics Based on Private

Subjective Experiences; and (5) Eclectic Pragmatic Apologetics Based on Prior Conclusions. The only method that has any merit at all is the first one. It's the one that proponents of subsequent methods reject or degrade to second-class status at best. Christians should find this troublesome. After all, we're talking about apologetics, defending the truth of Christianity. And it cannot be done without sufficient objective evidence. What else is there? What else is there by comparison?

1. Apologetics Based on Sufficient Objective Evidence
The first method of apologetics is based on the claim of sufficient objective evidence leading reasonable people to accept the truth of Christianity. This approach is called *Evidentialism* by apologists. When I first became a Christian believer I was an evidentialist. I had read Josh McDowell's evidentialist book, *Evidence That Demands a Verdict,* which confirmed my faith for me. There can never be enough evidence for something. The more the better. And I thought I had plenty of evidence to believe based on his book. Other noteworthy evidentialist apologists of the past and present are William Paley (1743–1805), Joseph Butler (1692–1752), Clark Pinnock (1937–2010), Wolfhart Pannenberg (1928–2014), John Warwick Montgomery, Gary Habermas, and John Feinberg. In Montgomery's words, the task of evidentialists, like himself, consists "of marshalling the full panoply of factual evidence to show that Christianity is true and its rivals false."[14] According to Habermas evidentialism "can be characterized as a 'one step' approach" to apologetics "in that historical evidences can serve as a species of argument for God. Instead of having to prove God's existence before moving to the specific evidences (the 'two step method'), the evidentialist treats one or more historical arguments as being able both to indicate God's existence and activity and to indicate which variety of theism is true."[15] Feinberg accepts this "one step" evidentialist approach in his apologetics book when explaining why he didn't include a chapter on the existence of God: "I don't hold a methodology that requires one to prove God's existence before anything else can be addressed."[16]

Given Montgomery's claim for the need of evidence in general, and Habermas's claim for the need of historical evidence in particular, all of which should lead reasonable people to accept Christianity, then what could possibly be wrong with this? Nothing. That's what I think. Nothing. Sufficient objective evidence must be there for Christianity, or else reasonable people should not accept it. Period. It supposedly convinced the early disciples so it should convince us too. What if Muslims or Mormons or Orthodox Jews or any other religious people of faith admitted their respective faiths did not have sufficient objective evidence for them? Well, I think we should all just take them at their word, and look elsewhere for truth. That should be the end of any inquiry into the truth of their claims.

Some of the first evidentialists were the deists, who are largely left out of this discussion among evangelical apologists. Deism began with Herbert Cherbury (1583–1648) in England. Deism is not a conclusion, as most people think, but rather a method based on reason and evidence. Deism is a natural religion as opposed to the Bible, or the church or "revealed" religion. Deism claimed people like Voltaire, Immanuel Kant, Baruch Spinoza (a deist in method but a pantheist in conclusion), David Hume, Thomas Paine, Ben Franklin, George Washington, and Thomas Jefferson (just consider *The Jefferson Bible*).[17]

Deism passed through several different stages in several different countries. With each successive stage deists began whittling away what they could accept by reasoning based on evidence. Initially deists believed God worked providentially in the world and that there was an afterlife. But as time went on more and more deists didn't see the evidence of providence or the afterlife. The final stage of deism is largely of French origin, where God is seen merely as the creator of the universe. God was viewed as an absent landlord who doesn't intervene in the world. The analogy for deists was the technological marvel of their time—the pocket watch. What should we think, deists would ask, if a watchmaker had to constantly repair the watch he made? We should think the watch was made by an inferior watchmaker. So if God created the world and had to regularly intervene with miracles then he didn't do a good job of creating it in the first place. Modern science has progressed past the original deist understanding of the Newtonian view of the world as a machine. But this didn't change anything. After the publication of Darwin's magisterial work, *On the Origin of Species*, in 1859, which accounted for the evolution of human beings from a common ancestor through natural selection, many deists became atheists, for that's where the evidence leads.[18]

As I studied to become an apologist I later became convinced the evidentialist approach was a failure precisely because there wasn't sufficient objective evidence to believe, even though it should be there. I thought the available evidence could not bring reasonable people to believe God exists. I was not alone. Most apologists agree, as we'll see, which explains why there are several other apologetical methods. It didn't dawn on me how serious this problem was for my faith until much later as I became a nonbeliever.

Evidentialist apologists who argue based on sufficient objective evidence have gotten their method correct. The other methods that denigrate it are wrong. It's not that other methods deny the value of evidence. It's just that differing methods are based on other things having a higher priority than the evidence itself, as we'll see. But why should any apologetical method not assign the highest priority to the evidence itself? Very odd is that!

The rejection of evidentialism as an apologetical method by most Christian apologists should be seen as a big flashing bright red light and heard as a loud annoying buzzer to warn Christians that sufficient objective evidence does not exist for their faith. For if the evidence did exist there would be no other alternative method of apologetics. *The very fact there are other methods is proof all by itself that Christianity does not have sufficient objective evidence for it*. All we have to do is picture a world where there is sufficient evidence for Christianity. If that were the case no Christian would ever propose any other method for defending Christianity. You know it. I know it. We all know it. So the fact that other methods exist means Christians themselves acknowledge there isn't enough evidence to believe. Their brains will even dispute the need for sufficient evidence it's so bad.

2. Apologetics Based on Special Pleading

This method is also called the *Classical Method*, or *Natural Theology*, because it's assumed to be the one used by most theologians in earlier centuries, especially Thomas Aquinas. Modern representatives include Norman Geisler, R. C. Sproul, John Gerstner, Peter Kreeft, J. P. Moreland, and, most notably, William Lane Craig. Unlike the evidentialist method which has only one step, this method has two steps. The first step is to defend the theistic proofs for the existence of God. The second step is to provide the evidence that Christianity is true. Apologists must first effectively argue for the existence of the God of theism, generally speaking, who created the universe. Then after successfully doing so, they must provide sufficient objective evidence that Christianity is the true theistic religion. If the first step cannot be done effectively their whole apologetic fails. Steven B. Cowan explains: "Before one can meaningfully discuss historical evidences, one has to have established God's existence because one's worldview is a framework through which miracles, historical facts, and other empirical data are interpreted. Without a theistic context, no historical event could ever be shown to be a divine miracle. The flipside of this claim is that one cannot appeal to alleged miracles in order to prove God's existence."[19] The reason why one cannot appeal to evidences for a miracle as evidence for God is explained by Norman Geisler: "The mere fact of the resurrection [of Jesus] cannot be used to establish the truth that there is a God. For the resurrection cannot even be a miracle unless there already is a God."[20]

I've already mentioned how little I think of the standard theistic proofs for God's existence. Not even Christian apologist John Feinberg thinks they work, for he wrote, "I wouldn't try to prove God's existence first, if at all, in that I am not convinced that any of the traditional arguments succeeds."[21] Richard Swinburne, one of the great Christian apologists of our generation, rejects the *Moral Argument* to God's existence, saying, "I cannot see any force in an argument to the existence of God from the existence of morality."[22] Listen, theistic arguments should at least convince Christians before anyone can expect them to convince others, right?

But both steps are essential to defend Christianity. If the first step isn't successful then neither is the second step, for the second step cannot be successful on its own. So if theistic proofs are shown to fail then classical apologists cannot show Christianity is true. This isn't just me saying this. Classical apologists themselves say this. With the collapse of theistic proofs the *Classical Method* is dead in the water. They just don't realize it yet.

More importantly, even if the first step is successful this does not show Christianity to be true. A lot more work needs to be done for that to be shown. Following David Hume, even if theistic arguments to God's existence succeed to some small degree, the remaining question is which god do these arguments point to? A wide diversity of theists such as found in Islam, Judaism, and Christianity all argue to the existence of God using the same exact theistic proofs. These arguments are mistakenly thought by adherents in these respective faiths to show their own particular God exists. For instance, I once skimmed through a set of intelligent design books that argued for Allah's existence. A Christian could lap up those two volumes and use them to defend Christianity. But wait just a minute. They were written by a Muslim scholar!

So various theists use the same arguments for the existence of God then mistakenly conclude these arguments lead to their particular parochial God. Upon concluding these arguments lead to their God they go on to argue that the particular miracles thought to be done by their God are more likely to have happened, than the miracles believed to be done by other deities. So in this way Christians argue for a natural theology to their particular God just as other theists do. However, there is no reasonable way to tell in advance if these theistic arguments point to their particular God. So believers cannot use them to establish their respective natural theologies either. For how do they know which God these arguments lead to in advance of looking at the specific historical evidence for their particular religion? They simply cannot reasonably approach their own miracle claims as having any more probability to them than other theistic miracle claims, even granting that theistic arguments work.

In other words, these arguments to God's existence simply do not grant theists any relevant background knowledge, or "priors," prior to examining the historical evidence for their own particular religious faith. Believers must still look at the evidence from the raw uninterpreted data to determine if a miracle took place, without using a potentially false presumption that their particular God performed the particular miracle under investigation. For even if there is a God of some kind, believers still have no reason to think their particular God did the miracle under investigation. So when investigating a supposed miracle claim it cannot be treated with any special favoritism. The investigation cannot be prejudiced in favor of one's own particular parochial deity. At best all that theistic proofs can show people is that there is a Supernatural Being who could do miracles if (and this is a big if) he or she decided to do them. These proofs don't show us such a Being did any miracle at all apart from creation. This line of reasoning destroys natural theology in one fell swoop.

To Christians who respond that the arguments to God's existence open up the possibility of miracles, I simply ask them if they would ever seriously consider the miracles of Islam, or those of believing Jews, or Catholics, or faith healers like Benny Hinn, or snake handlers for that matter? Theism does not entail that the particular miracles in your religious tradition have any more probability to them than others. I'm pretty sure Muslims and Jews, even as theists themselves, are no more open to the foundational Christian miracle claims than I am as a nonbeliever. Christians shouldn't be either, not if they are reasonable anyway. So natural theology ends up specializing in special pleading, even if we assume the arguments to God's existence work, which they don't.

Christians leap over what's known as *Hume's Stopper* without a pause, jumping to the conclusion that if these arguments work their miracle traditions have been granted a higher, better status than others.[23] But given that there is nothing in these arguments that lead a reasonable person to accept a specific sect's god out of the many other supernatural beings or forces, they open your mind up to almost any possibility. You cannot reasonably favor any one religious tradition's miracle claims. You must consider them all. Every supernatural claim would be, strictly speaking, on the boards without any way to determine which god is actually doing them, if they're being done at all.

Natural theologians who rejected evidentialism because evidentialism cannot convince nonbelieving outsiders, end up falling back into the laps of the evidentialists. They now face the same problems evidentialists face. They must now present sufficient objective historical evidence for the existence of the God who supposedly raised Jesus from the dead anyway. They must do this apart from leaning on any view of which deity exists prior to looking at the historical evidence. The classical approach ends up being nothing less than a dressed-up evidentialism. Unwittingly they have ended up back where they started from, embracing the evidentialist position that they had previously rejected.

3. Apologetics Based on Assuming What Needs to Be Proved

This method for doing apologetics is known by the standard nomenclature of *Presuppositionalism*. It's a relatively new apologetical approach most associated with Cornelius Van Til (1895–1987), Gordon Clark (1902–1985), Francis Schaeffer (1912–1984), Greg Bahnsen (1948–1995), and John Frame. I'll include a very brief discussion of *Reformed Epistemology* in this section too, since it suffers similar criticisms.

The presuppositionalist approach considers Christianity as a whole worldview and pits the rationality of its presuppositions against other world-views. Presuppositions are defined as beliefs people presuppose prior to any argument or evidence. It's argued we all have them. A consistent set of presuppositions makes for a whole worldview. The goal of the presuppositionalist is to show the nonbeliever's worldview is inconsistent or self-defeating within itself. The presuppositionalist argues that nonbelievers who use reason and logic to defend their worldview cannot do so without assuming the Christian worldview. Only Christianity can justify the use of reason and logic. So it's argued nonbelievers must therefore presuppose Christianity even as they argue against it.[24]

This apologetic strategy is reasoning by presupposition. It's admittedly circular reasoning because presuppositions are not inductively known by evidential reasoning, nor arrived at by deduction from premises to a conclusion. They are assumed to be true from the start without evidence. For instance, presuppositionalist John Frame wrote: "are we not still forced to say, 'God exists (presupposition), therefore God exists (conclusion),' and isn't that argument clearly circular? Yes, in a way. But that is unavoidable for any system, any worldview. One cannot argue for an ultimate standard by appealing to a different standard. That would be inconsistent."[25]

Presuppositionalists, just like classical apologists, reject the evidentialist method. They admit there isn't sufficient evidence to convince nonbelieving outsiders for Christianity. In the presuppositionalist's mind, unless the evidence is viewed through Christian presuppositions, it's not considered evidence at all. The task of the Christian apologist is to destroy false presuppositions so nonbelievers can adopt the presuppositions of Christianity and believe.

According to presuppositionalists the evidence for the resurrection of Jesus can only be seen as supportive of what they already believe through the lens of Christian assumptions, not before. And then it's not the evidence that convinces them Jesus arose from the dead. It's the presuppositions that make the evidence for the resurrection seen for what it is. It's no wonder William Lane Craig accused presuppositionalists of committing a very serious informal fallacy, in these words:

> Presuppositionalism commits the informal fallacy of begging the question, for it advocates presupposing the truth of Christian theism in order to prove Christian theism. It is difficult to imagine how anyone could with a straight face think to show theism to be true by reasoning, 'God exists, therefore God exists.' A Christian theist himself will deny that question-begging arguments prove anything.[26]

Gary Habermas accuses presuppositionalist John Frame of committing another serious informal fallacy, saying:

> He argues that rationalists must accept reason as an ultimate starting point, just as empiricists assume sense experience, and so on. So the Christian may begin with Scripture as a legitimate starting point. But these are not analogous bases. While the rationalist uses reason and the empiricist uses sense experience as tools from which to construct their systems, Frame assumes both the tool of special revelation and the system of Scripture, from which he develops his Christian theism. In other words, he assumes the reality of God's existence, his personal interaction with humans, plus a specific product: Scripture. Does Frame not realize that, in the name of everyone needing a presupposition, he has imported an entire worldview when others have only asked for tools?[27]

One other major criticism of presuppositionalism I find persuasive was written by Thomas Morris about Francis Schaeffer's apologetics. Morris showed us that although Schaeffer attacked the nonbeliever's epistemology and stressed the absurdity of living life without God, Schaeffer just assumed that by doing so the only viable alternative was his own conservative Calvinist Christian theology.[28] Other theistic alternatives seem well-equipped to justify reason and logic, like Judaism, Islam, and even deism. After the deconstruction why didn't Schaeffer just presuppose Christian liberalism instead, if we grant his arguments succeeded?

Where does evidence come into play for presuppositionalists if evidence is seen in light of circular presuppositions? Well, the evidence comes into play when presuppositionalists need it to come into play, not before, thus highlighting a third informal fallacy, the fallacy of ad hoc rationalization. This occurs when someone grabs some type of explanation, no matter how improbable, to save an argument from being refuted. The result is an explanation that may not be very coherent, does not explain much at all, and probably has no way of being tested. Contrary to presuppositionalists, reasonable people need evidence from the very beginning. Apologists simply cannot presuppose the truths of disputable historical events in an ancient world prior to investigating whether or not those events actually took place if they want to be taken seriously.[29]

With regard to the *Reformed Epistemology*, Alvin Plantinga seeks to show Christians can be entirely rational in having a "full-blooded Christian belief"[30] in the "the great truths of the gospel."[31] But his conclusion is only correct if his Christian God exists. That's a big *IF*! All he's doing is arguing it's reasonable to believe in God, if God exists. Don't think so? Then listen to Richard Swinburne, who correctly argues that Plantinga's conclusion in his 500-page book in defense of reasonable Christian belief, *Warranted Christian Belief*, is "of little use." For Plantinga

> works up to the conclusion that 'if Christian belief is true, it very likely does have warrant.' But this conditional is of little use to anyone without some information about the truth of the antecedent (whether Christian belief is true); and on that, Plantinga explicitly acknowledges in his final paragraph, he cannot help us. For he writes there that on the really important question of 'is Christian belief true,' 'we pass beyond the competence of philosophy.'"[32]

Not only is this the case but Plantinga says something else every Christian apologist should take note of: "I don't know of an argument for Christian belief that seems very likely to convince one who doesn't already accept its conclusion."[33] Now that's quite the admission, isn't it, from someone who is a bit revered among evangelicals.

What an apologetical method should do is engage in *positive apologetics* by presenting sufficient evidence for the truth of Christianity. *Reformed Epistemology* doesn't even pretend to do this. Plantinga is defending the reasonableness of Christianity against objections brought against it, known as *negative apologetics*. But engaging in this activity without first presenting sufficient evidence for the truth of Christianity is like having the gas without having a car. Still, *negative apologetics* is not nothing. At least one might have gas.

Plantinga challenges the idea that belief in God needs any evidence at all. He says "the believer is entirely within his epistemic rights in believing, for example, that God has created the world, even if he has no argument at all for that conclusion. His belief in God can be perfectly rational even if he knows of no cogent argument, deductive or inductive, for the existence of God—indeed, even if there is no such argument."[34] He argues there are countless things we believe (and do so properly) without proof or evidence—for example, that other persons (or minds) exist; that the world continues to exist even when we don't perceive it; that we have been alive for more than twenty-four hours; that the past really happened; that we aren't just brains in a vat; that we live in an ordered universe; that we can trust our minds and our senses about the universe; that cause and effect are universal laws of nature; that nature is uniform and intelligible; and so on. He further argues by analogy that people can also believe in God (and do so properly) without proof or evidence—in particular, since believing there are other persons is rational without evidential support, so also is belief in God.

I have come to the conclusion that all of these scenarios are disanalogous to believing in God. For with God there is no empirical experiential evidence he exists—such as gained from seeing, hearing, or touching him—since he's conceived as a spiritual being. Nor does anyone see God do a miracle either. Even if an extremely rare unexplainable event took place we don't see him doing it.[35] By contrast, when it comes to experiencing life twenty-four hours ago we have the artifacts of yesterday, like a photograph, a dirty pair of pants, a friend who remembers what we talked about during lunch, and perhaps a paycheck showing we worked that day, etc. So these scenarios do not apply to God. Other hypothetical scenarios that are far-fetched, including the possibility there isn't a material world, or that we're living in a Matrix, or the Cartesian demon hypothesis, are not good defeaters of the demand for sufficient evidence either, as I've argued at some length.[36] The major problem with them is that possibilities don't count. Only probabilities do if we're thinking like scientists. It may be remotely possible that we're living in the Matrix right now, or dreaming or being deceived by an evil demon. But I'm not changing anything I do or anything I think based on a possibility. We must think exclusively in terms of the probabilities.

Now I unwittingly accept some things without objective evidence for them, like my own subjective experience of being me. However, I can easily offer concrete examples where it would be irrational not to have the needed objective evidence for them. Consider the nature of nature and the workings of nature, studied in disciplines like geology, chemistry, astronomy, neurology, biology, zoology, and so forth. In these concrete examples rational people need sufficient objective evidence before coming to any conclusions. They are the kinds of examples mathematician W. K. Clifford (1845–1879) surely had in mind when discussing the ethics of a shipowner who had stifled his doubts about a ship's seaworthiness by trusting in God's providence, rather than in patiently investigating the evidence for himself. Clifford may have claimed too much when he stated, "it is wrong always, everywhere, and for anyone, to believe anything upon insufficient evidence."[37] But Plantinga failed to properly and charitably understand him, for he focused on Clifford's *statement* rather than on his *concrete example*. We most certainly do need sufficient objective evidence for almost everything. So his ship of arguments sailed right past Clifford's ship in the middle of the night without a good skirmish.

The most I could grant for the sake of argument—as loathe as I am to do even this—is that it might be rational to believe in a Supreme Being without evidence. But even if I grant *that*, the belief in a particular triune God who created the universe from nothing, who tested Adam and Eve in the Garden, rescued the Israelites from Egyptian slavery, sent an incarnation of himself to earth who was born of a virgin in Bethlehem, who did and said the things we read about in the canonical Gospels, who was crucified as a substitutionary sacrifice for our sins, who bodily arose from the dead, and who ascended into the sky with the promise of coming again to judge the world *is simply not a god-belief it's rational to believe without evidence!* There's just way too much belief going on there.

Plantinga surely believes there is historical evidence for his fundamentalist "full-blooded Christian belief," even though bizarrely he argues it's reasonable to believe without any of it. Speaking for sixteeenth-century reformer John Calvin—and agreeing with him—Plantinga says the great truths of the gospel found in a self-authenticating scripture are evident in themselves: "[W]e don't require argument from, for example, historically established premises about the authorship and reliability of the bit of Scripture in question to the conclusion that the bit in question is in fact true; for belief in the great things of the gospel to be justified, rational, and warranted, no historical evidence and argument for the teaching in question, or for the veracity or reliability or divine character of Scripture are necessary."[38]

Upon what basis does Plantinga say this? He believes we all have a sense of divinity (or *sensus divinitatis*, if you prefer the Latin) within us, and a (holy) *spirit guide* who guides us to know "the great truths of the gospel" when reading the scripture. This is the same kind of thing psychics claim they can do by reading tea leaves and tarot cards. He's effectively saying the spirit world gives Christians these same kinds of psychic abilities! So if we were to ask a Christian if Jesus died as a substitutionary atonement for our sins, which is one of the great truths of the gospel that Plantinga believes, just have him or her open the Bible to any page and start reading. They don't need to bother studying the Bible, or in reading good commentaries (although they can). They certainly don't have to be properly trained to study the Bible. We might also want to know if we should be baptized to be saved. That's an important truth of the gospel, one way or another, right? For if we need to be baptized God should tell us. So just ask a Christian what God says. "No," might be the answer. "How do you know?" we might ask. "Because God told me so." There, that settles it, except for the fact that I personally came from a Christian tradition that concluded otherwise. Any other questions about "the great truths of the gospel" would be met with this same answer, "Because God told me so." We might as well ask Christians to tell us what happened at Custer's last stand, or who killed JonBenét Ramsey, or solve any other unsolved crimes. We might ask them to read palms and contact the dead like psychics supposedly do. Why would God limit this knowledge to just the great truths of the gospel?

Lest anyone think I am too harsh on Plantinga, I assure you I'm not trying to be, although in describing and criticizing such a large body of work in such a small space my descriptions contain within them my criticisms. I just disagree, strongly. Pay close attention to what Plantinga says: "Faith involves an explicitly cognitive element; it is, says Calvin, knowledge. . . . and it is revealed to our minds. To have faith, therefore, is to know and hence believe something or other." And Christian beliefs come "by way of the work of the Holy Spirit, who gets us to accept, causes us to believe, these great truths of the gospel. These beliefs don't come just by way of the normal operation of our natural faculties, they are a supernatural gift."[39] If this is not claiming to have psychic abilities then I don't know what is. And if anyone thinks psychic abilities are incompatible with Christianity then just think of the Christians in Haiti who embrace both Catholicism and voodoo.

It is one thing to have a warranted belief that we are reading the Bible, so long as we're reading it with cognitive faculties functioning properly in the right kind of cognitive environment. It is something entirely different to be reading the Bible and claim "God is speaking to me." That additional claim is miles and miles away from what any rational person can conclude from the actual experience of reading the Bible itself. For that additional claim depends on the rationality of believing that the ancient documents in the Bible are truly God's word, that what they say about God, the nature of nature, and its workings are true, and that how one interprets them when reading them is correct. Since the rationality of claiming "God is speaking to me" depends on the rationality of accepting these other claims, it should be shown that it's rational to accept these other claims before one can rationally claim "God is speaking to me." Until then the rational conclusion when reading the Bible is "I am reading the Bible," not "God is speaking to me."

Old Testament scholar and philosopher of religion Jaco Gericke has written a devastating criticism of Plantinga's epistemology based on these concerns:

> [P]ast critiques of Plantinga have tended to focus almost exclusively on problems in the philosophical "superstructure" of Reformed Epistemology with little real attention being paid to the biblical-theological "base structure" of his arguments. And yet it cannot be disputed that the latter is ultimately foundational to the former—its raison d'être, if you will. But if this is indeed the case, it means that whatever the merits of Plantinga's sophisticated philosophical rhetoric, if it can be shown that his biblical foundations are both mistaken and/or nothing of the sort, the entire modus operandi of Reformed Epistemology will have been fatally compromised.[40]

One of Gericke's main criticisms concerns the particular belief in God that Plantinga thinks is properly basic. Plantinga's view of Yahweh, the God of the Bible, is

> radically anachronistic and conform[s] more to the proverbial "God of the Philosophers" (Aquinas in particular) than to any version of Yahweh as depicted in ancient Israelite religion. This means that the pre-philosophical "biblical" conceptions of Yahweh, the belief in whom is supposed to be properly basic, [are] not even believed by Plantinga himself. His lofty notions of God in terms of "Divine Simplicity," "Maximal Greatness," and "Perfect-Being Theology" are utterly alien with reference to many of the characterizations of Yahweh in biblical narrative (e.g., Genesis 18).[41]

In sum, presuppositionalists, including Plantinga, simply assume what needs to be proved, way too much. This is not an acceptable way for reasonable people to argue on behalf of Christianity, or most things. Anyone who argues this way, or who thinks this is acceptable, ought to pay closer attention to their lying brains.

4. Apologetics Based on Private Subjective Experiences

Søren Kierkeegaard, Karl Barth, John G. Stackhouse, Myron B. Penner, and others are roughly all representatives of this, uh, apologetical strategy as I'm loathe to call it. This is not a reasonable method for convincing nonbelievers at all. It's also called *Fideism*, or faithism since this "method" concedes the whole argument, that there just isn't sufficient evidence to believe. Myron B. Penner, author of the book, *The End of Apologetics*, says his book is "against apologetics,"[42] that is, modern rationalistic apologetics, saying it "is no longer valid. It tends toward an unbiblical and unchristian form of Christian witness and does not have the ability to attest truthfully to Christ in our postmodern context." Of course it doesn't, as we've seen. The reason is because apologists have simply not found the sufficient evidence to believe. Indeed, Penner and his cohorts all agree there isn't a sufficient amount of evidence to believe. In place of evidence, Penner proposes the biblical concept of faithful witness. "Our task as Christians," he says, "is not to know the truth intellectually but to become the truth."[43] James K. Beilby tries to explain by saying, "Proponents do not hold that the truth of Christianity must be presupposed, but rather that it must be experienced."[44]

Okay then, not to be too blunt, but how does someone experience the story of the Israelite Exodus out of Egypt? How do we experience the story of Jesus turning water into wine in Cana of Galilee? Even if someone were to magically experience biblical stories in a dream-like state, what difference does it make if there is no evidence for their truth? The same would go for the resurrection of Jesus. How is a private subjective experience of Jesus' resurrection any indicator of the truth of that story? *A private subjective experience is only evidence of a private subjective experience and nothing more.* How does an experience of love in a Christian community mean anything either? A lot of people within other religious and nonreligious communities, communes, and social clubs experience love and acceptance.

There cannot be an apologetical method based on private subjective experiences if we want to know the truth. The only thing that can be done with subjective experiences is to place oneself in a position whereby these experiences can be had to produce faith, presumably through prayer, saying the rosary, going to church, becoming under the influence of a Christian friend's "witness," or reading the Bible. One doesn't need apologetics or a method to do this. Basing one's apologetics on subjective experiences that supposedly lead to faith is to adopt a nonmethod, since it can produce many irreconcilable, different, and bizarre conclusions. To test whether subjective experiences can produce religious truth all we have to do is watch as Catholics, Fundamentalists, Hindus, Muslims, Orthodox Jews, and Mormons perform similar religious activities from their perspectives, to see if they come away with the same or similar conclusions and faiths afterward. Hint: They won't. Then too, if people accept subjective experiences as objective truths then every crackpot purveyor of a dubious new religion who wants to sleep with your daughter and take all your money would have an extremely easy day of it. So this is a nonmethod. I should have excluded a discussion of this *cough* method from the outset since I'm focusing on a discussion of reasons to believe. None are offered here, just lots of hugs and kisses, and warm fuzzies. It abandons rational apologetics and is proud of it, which is absolutely bizarre.

5. Eclectic Pragmatic Apologetics Based on Prior Conclusions

Representatives of this approach include Edward Carnell, Basil Mitchell, C. S. Lewis, Richard Swinburne, Paul Feinberg, John S. Feinberg, Kenneth Boa, Robert M. Bowman Jr., Douglas Groothuis, and others. Usually it's called the *Cumulative Case Method*, or the *Integrative Approach to Apologetics*. It supposedly takes the best of each method and combines them all together into one. It's instructive from the start to note that Kenneth Boa and Robert M. Bowman Jr. excluded from their own integrated approach the fourth method we discussed above based on private subjective experiences, because this method abandons rational apologetics. That's fine as it goes, but if they're coming up with an integrated Christian approach to apologetics they should include it. Otherwise what they have is a selective approach to Christian apologetics, for they aren't integrating all Christian approaches.

Cumulative or integrative apologetics is what apologists eventually get when they reject evidentialism. It's the final stop on a journey with an evidential beginning. It's the slippery slope they eventually slide into. This method is best described as eclectic or pragmatic. An eclectic or pragmatic method is one where the conclusion largely dictates the method. Christianity is the conclusion. Now use whatever method needed to reach that conclusion. The pragmatic motto is this: "We'll use whatever works." If the available evidence doesn't work, then first use the theistic proofs. If the theistic proofs don't work, then switch back to presupposing what needs to be proved. If presuppositionalism asks way more than any reasonable person should accept, then switch to the need for private subjective experiences of God somehow someway someday. If none of these methods work separately, then pragmatically choose to use something, anything that has the persuasive power to convince nonbelievers of the correct conclusion. Just ignore the fact that a cumulative method is no method at all, but rather a pragmatic adoption of ineffective and eclectically chosen methods that themselves have many holes in them.

So the adoption of an eclectic or pragmatic method is a clear indicator, all on its own, that Christian apologetics is in a serious crisis primarily because of what this says about the lack of evidence. Either apologists think the evidence will lead a nonbeliever to Christianity or they don't. Only one method outlined above says yes, that Christianity stands or falls on the evidence. All of the other methods try to fix the problems with evidentialism because sufficient evidence simply is not there. They cannot sugarcoat this inside the good-ole-boys bakery before dishing out their half-baked treats to the hungry crowds. There are roughly five overarching major apologetics methods. If we grant that an equal number of Christian apologists defend these respective approaches, then any given one of them is rejected by 80 percent of all Christian apologists. Since evidentialism is the only method that accepts the need for sufficient evidence, and it only has 20 percent support among apologists, then 80 percent of all Christian apologists do not think there is sufficient objective evidence to believe. If that's not a crisis then what is?

We see this eclecticism and pragmatism among supposed representatives of the other methods. Just carefully read through the debate book edited by Steven B. Cowan, *Five Views of Apologetics*, where five Christian apologists debate each other over the proper apologetical method. After debating each other William Lane Craig notes in his closing remarks that, "What we are seeing in the present volume is a remarkable convergence of views, which is cause for rejoicing."[45] Craig, a defender on the *Classical Method*, astoundingly admitted he and presuppositionalist John Frame "do not have any substantive disagreements."[46] Craig said this even though he had just accused Frame of arguing in a viciously circular manner. Craig also astoundingly admitted that he and evidentialist Gary Habermas are in agreement "on virtually everything."[47]

So if we take Craig at his word, his views are in substantial agreement with two opposing views represented by Frame and Habermas. Habermas chides Craig for admitting this, saying Craig must now include himself "among the evidentialists" because "he does not take the classical position of the classical apologist!"[48] Habermas adds, "I have no problems with Bill Craig. I simply welcome him back to the evidentialist fold!"[49] For his part, John Frame acknowledged in the book that other presuppositionalists would not consider him to be "a pure presuppositionalist," for what he defends "is not clearly distinct from the other methodologies.[50] So okay then. Neither Craig nor Frame are true representatives of the positions they purport to defend. Habermas himself doesn't have a position different than the *Cumulative Case Method*, for he says, "I have said repeatedly, evidentialists are eclectic in their methodology."[51] Habermas admits he "has no major disagreements with Paul Feinberg,"[52] who in turn also admitted his approach was "eclectic" in nature.[53]

Whew! Did you get that? From reading that debate book it's confusing to know where these apologists stand. John S. Feinberg's discussion of these issues is also confusing. In his own apologetics book he discusses just two apologetic methods in two separate chapters, *Presuppositionalism* and *Evidentialism*.[54] Feinberg tells us in one chapter that many current presuppositionalists "have so modified some of its main ideas that at times it is hard to detect much difference between their form of presuppositionalism and some forms of Christian evidentialism."[55] Right that! Then in the other chapter he defends the merits of "three varieties of evidentialism," which include *Evidentialism*, the *Classical Method*, and the *Cumulative Case Method*. Feinberg ends up defending an eclectic pragmatic cumulative approach, except that he simply calls it all "evidentialism."[56] His kind of evidentialism is one where he's "most drawn to a cumulative case approach to defending Christianity."[57] But how can Feinberg truly adopt a cumulative case approach that in turn includes the classical approach? He's already admitted the classical approach fails since the traditional arguments to God's existence all fail?

If we take the apologetic methods at face value in their purest forms, it should be clear they cannot be integrated without changing what each one stresses. It's like mixing oil with water. Furthermore, since each of these methods are indeed separate methods, then proponents of them have disputed key planks in the other methods. If each of these separate methods has holes in them, as the different proponents themselves point out, then putting them together won't solve these separate problems. Neither will putting together a few leaky buckets completely stop the leaks.[58]

At the present time James Beilby acknowledges there are no clear lines to be drawn between apologetical methods. Instead there is "a dizzying diversity of approaches to apologetics."[59] And "there are many contemporary apologetic methodologies whose work is best labeled 'Eclectic.'"[60] True that! In their apologetics book, *Reasons for Our Hope*, H. Wayne House and Dennis W. Jowers openly acknowledge the pragmatism of their method after discussing various approaches to apologetics. In the conclusion they say:

> Several approaches are available to apologists, from classical to evidential to presuppositional to fideist. Each has strengths and weaknesses, and each presents valid and useful apologetics. The Christian apologist, then, needs to understand each approach thoroughly and glean the best from each of them. Further, the apologist needs to be able to employ different approaches in different contexts. Every person will react and be reached differently, so there is *no one approach that will work every time* [emphasis mine]."[61]

So let's rehearse what we've found using the standard nomenclature Christians themselves use:

- Evidential Method: Admitted failure by 80 percent of apologists.
- Classical Method: At best no more than a dressed-up evidentialism.
- Presuppositionalism: Question begging and presumes way too much.
- Reformed Epistemology: Requires psychic abilities!
- Fideism: Simply abandons rational apologetics.
- Cumulative Case: Plainly shows apologetics to be in a serious crisis!

6

How to Know
Which Religion to Defend

As a would-be Christian apologist you cannot just assume your faith is the one true one, the one you should rightly defend. Most Christians in their particular denominational sects were raised to believe, by far, within a largely Christian culture. Others were raised in different religious cultures. Now that you are a young adult, one who is about to get a real education in a real university, or already there, you need to become an *adult*. Passage into adulthood means reexamining the faith you have inherited from your upbringing and culture. If you are committed to being an honest life-long seeker for the truth (chapter 3), then let's start here. If you want a good education (chapter 4), you must start here. If you demand solid objective evidence for what you can accept as true (chapter 5), you need to start here. This is a must-obey, "Do Not Pass Go, Do Not Collect $200" Monopoly game card. You cannot pass "Go" without doing this, by not fairly testing your own inherited faith. Skipping this test for your faith would be an indicator that you're really not honestly seeking the truth, but rather only interested in defending what you have been taught to believe.

I inherited my religious faith, first from my father and then later from my mother. This is not surprising in the least. It's what we would expect. As children, we were all raised as believers. Whatever our parents told us we believed. If they said Santa Claus or the Tooth Fairy or the Easter Bunny existed, then we believed what they said until we were told otherwise. If they had told us Allah or Zeus or Baal or Poseidon or Thor or Odin existed, we would have believed them. We learn our religion on our Mama's knees, so to speak, usually surrounded by a culture of people who believe in the same religious tradition.

So Catholics will raise Catholics. Evangelicals will raise evangelicals. Pentecostals will raise Pentecostals. Orthodox Jews will raise Orthodox Jews. Mormons will raise Mormons. Muslims will raise Muslims. Pantheists will raise pantheists. Polytheists will raise polytheists. Scientologists will raise Scientologists. Wiccans will raise Wiccans. At some point along the line, as we become adults, we need to critically examine what we were taught to believe as children. We must learn to question. As we do, we eventually become thinking adults. But the strange thing is that even as adults, we don't usually question our religious faiths. They just seem too obvious to us. They have become too ingrained within us. We see no need to question them.

But we know that religious faiths cannot all be true. There are just too many of them spread out over the globe believed by people with the same level of certainty as other believers. Many of them are mutually exclusive to each other.

What Is the Outsider Test for Faith?

When I speak to groups about this test for faith, sometimes I start by asking the audience this question: "How many of you know which religion is true?" Hands are raised. I continue, "How sure are you that your religion is true?" The overwhelming response from the people who had previously raised their hands was "100 percent." It's the typical response when it comes to religious faith because faith is basically immune from testing. It offers no method for determining truth. With faith anything can be believed or denied without any evidence at all. No wonder there are so many mutually exclusive religions in the world. Testing one's religious faith is anathema to the minds of overwhelming numbers of believers since faith pleases their imagined gods. Faith pleases the gods because the gods cannot allow testing. They cannot allow testing because the gods are all made up by kings, priests, prophets, philosophers, gurus, shamans, witchdoctors, and so forth who only want blindly obedient followers. In some cases, the gods do ask believers to test them (see Malachi 3:10), but those tests are not real ones given the plethora of cognitive biases human beings have to count the hits and to discount the misses.

For believers who want to know which religion is true, if one is, I have proposed the *Outsider Test for Faith* (OTF). How we test a truth claim has a great deal to do with the kind of claim we're testing. Sometimes a poll can settle one type of claim. Other times we can settle a different claim by traveling somewhere. Counting spoons can test a certain type of claim, while sitting on a fluffy pillow can test a different one. Logic and math can test other types of truth claims. In testing some types of claims we rely heavily on one discipline of learning, while in testing other claims we rely heavily on other disciplines of learning. Some claims demand testing from several different academic disciplines. The type of claim we're testing determines how we test it.

I argue there is no better alternative to the OTF. If readers think there is one, then what is it? It's the type of test geared to test religious faith just as geologists test the age of the earth with rock samples, just as neurologists test brain states with CAT scans, and just as economists test economical theories with the results of economical policies. You cannot test the age of the earth with a CAT scan, nor can you test economical theories with rock samples. We develop appropriate tests for each different truth claim being tested. It's that simple.

I find that people who disagree with a reasonable non–double standard test for religious faith cannot be reasoned with, for obvious reasons.

The OTF is based on the following progression of four steps, precursors of which stem back in time to many thinkers, including Antony Flew, Robert Ingersoll, David Hume, and even Socrates:

1. People who are located in distinct geographical areas around the globe overwhelmingly adopt and justify a wide diversity of religious faiths due to their particular upbringing and shared cultural heritage, and most of these faiths are mutually exclusive. This is the Religious Diversity Thesis (RDVT).

    The sociological facts are easy to come by. If we were raised in Thailand, we would probably be Buddhists. If we were raised in Saudi Arabia, we'd probably be Muslims. If we were raised in Mexico, we'd probably be Catholics. The main thing religious diversity shows us is that not every religious faith can possibly be true. In fact, given the number of mutually exclusive religious faiths in the world, each of which claims exclusive access to religious truth, it's highly likely, given the odds alone, that the one we inherited in our respective culture is false. This is a problem that believers must take seriously. It cries out for a good explanation.

2. The best explanation for (1) is that adopting and justifying one's religious faith is not a matter of independent rational judgment. Rather, to an overwhelming degree, one's religious faith is causally dependent on brain processes, cultural conditions, and irrational thinking patterns. This is the Religious Dependency Thesis (RDPT).

    From brain biology we know that humans have inherited from our animal ancestors an innate capacity for detecting patterns (like faces) in random data, and for seeing personal agency behind random forces in nature. In the animal world, where any hesitation in fleeing from a predator could lead to being eaten alive, these senses of patternicity and agenticity (as they are called by Michael Shermer) are beneficial for survival. Human beings transformed these survival mechanisms into seeing divine beings active behind the scenes, orchestrating such natural and human-made phenomena as thunderstorms, droughts, victory or defeat in war, births of sons, bumper crops, and so forth.[1]

Anthropological data have shown us that we overwhelmingly adopt what our respective cultures teach us and that we are unable to see our own cultural biases because we are completely immersed in our inherited culture. Culture has an overwhelming impact on what we think and believe.[2]

From conclusive psychological studies we have learned that people, all of us, have a very strong tendency toward believing what we prefer to believe and toward justifying those beliefs. Once our minds are made up, it is very hard to change them. We will even take lack of evidence as evidence for what we believe. Almost shockingly, these studies have shown us that encountering information that goes against our point of view can actually make us more convinced that we were right to begin with.[3]

From (1) and (2) it follows that:

3. It is highly likely that any given religious faith is false and quite possible that they all could be false. At best there can be only one religious faith that is true. At worst, they could all be false. The sociological facts, along with our brain biology, anthropological (or cultural) data, and psychological studies, lead us to this highly likely conclusion.

Which leads us to the OTF itself:

4. The only way to rationally test one's culturally adopted religious faith is from the perspective of an outsider, a nonbeliever, with the same level of reasonable skepticism believers already use when examining the other religious faiths they reject. This expresses the Outsider Test for Faith.

The OTF is based on the same kind of data that cultural relativists use when arguing that, because moral practices and beliefs do in fact vary from culture to culture as well as at different times in history, morality is not the result of independent rational judgment but rather is causally dependent on cultural conditions. All we have to do is insert the phrase "religious faith" in place of the word morality, with one caveat. I'm not arguing that all religious faiths are false because of religious diversity or that they are completely dependent on one's cultural upbringing. I'm merely arguing that believers should be skeptical of their own culturally inherited faith because it is overwhelmingly the case that one's faith is dependent on one's cultural upbringing.

The OTF is a self-diagnostic test to aid honest believers in examining their inherited religious faith. It is for believers who, upon becoming adults, wish to test their inherited faith. Learning a religion upon mama's knee is an unreliable way to gain the "correct" religious faith, since a wide diversity of religions are taught to children in the same exact way, only one of which, at most, can be true. The odds are that the religious faith you were taught to believe is false, given the number of faiths handed down by parents in separate geographical regions around the globe.

I want people to see the OTF as a solution to the problem of religious diversity, a problem that needs a solution. No other methods have worked before. If people cannot find solutions to problems within a business, they hire solution specialists who offer ways to solve them. Mediators find ways to bring people together by offering ways they can see their differences in a better light. That's what the OTF does. The goal is to offer a fair test to find out which religion is true, if one is. To be a fair and objective test, it must allow that any conclusion could result, and the OTF does just that. The OTF grants that a religious faith can be reasonable and asks believers to test their faith with it, just as it grants that nonbelief can be reasonable and asks nonbelievers to consider the religious options available. It grants the possibility that one particular religious faith could pass the test, just as it grants the possibility that none of them might pass it. It offers the only objective non–double standard for doing so.

Believers can respond to the OTF in four ways: (1) object to (or mitigate) the facts of the RDVT and the RDPT that form the basis for the test; (2) object to the OTF by arguing that it is faulty or unfair in some relevant manner; (3) along with objections (1) and (2), provide a better alternative to reasonably judge between religions; or (4) subject their religion to the test, as it has been described here, in which case it either (a) passes or (b) fails intellectual muster. It's that simple. If, in the end, believers can neither find fault with the OTF nor propose a better alternative, and if they find that no religion can pass the test, then that's not the fault of the test itself. Rather, the problem is with the religious faith(s) being tested.

I suspect that if believers are willing to take the challenge of the OTF, they will find that their faith fails the test, and they will be forced to abandon it like I did mine. I argue that religious faiths do not pass the OTF. I argue that, by its very nature, faith cannot pass the OTF because faith is always unreasonable. I argue that the problem is *faith* itself. If not, then what is the problem? With faith as a foundation, anything can be believed, so informed people should reject faith altogether. Faith-based reasoning is belief in search of the facts. Faith, as I argue, is an irrational leap over the probabilities. Probabilities about such a matter are all that matter. We should think exclusively in terms of them.

When believers criticize the other faiths they reject, they use reason and science to do so. They assume these other religions have the burden of proof. They assume human, not divine, authors to their holy book(s). They assume a human, not a divine, origin to their faiths. Believers do this when rejecting other faiths. So the OTF simply asks believers to *do unto their own faith what they do unto other faiths*. All it asks of them is to be fair and consistent.

The OTF asks why believers operate on a double standard. If that's how they reject other faiths, then they should apply that same standard to their own. Reason and science, rather than faith, should be their guide. Assume your own faith has the burden of proof. Assume human rather than divine authors to your holy book(s) and see what you get. If there is indeed a divine author behind the texts, it should become known even after that initial skeptical assumption. The OTF uses the exact same standard that believers use when rejecting other religions. It is how believers already assess truth claims. For it should only take a moment's thought to realize that if there is a God who wants people born into different religious cultures—who are outsiders—to believe, then that religious faith *should* pass the OTF.

If Christians want to reject the OTF, then they must admit they have a double standard for examining religious faiths, one for their own faith and a different one for others. Or, they must admit their faith cannot pass the OTF in the first place. In either case, all of their arguments against the OTF are based on red herrings, special pleading, begging the question, denigrating science, and an ignorance that I can only attribute to delusional blindness.

The Perspective of an Outsider
What does the OTF require when it comes to reasonable skepticism? Every rational adult knows what it's like to be a skeptic or to doubt something. Since we all know how to be skeptics, we must distinguish between two types of skepticism, only one of which is a reasonable and informed one. There is a

kind of skepticism that is born of faith. Faith-based skepticism causes believers to doubt other religious faiths simply because they believe that theirs is the true one. Since theirs is the true faith, the others must therefore be false. This same type of faith-based skepticism causes believers to doubt scientific findings whenever those findings undercut or discredit their faith in some way. This type of skepticism caused many believers to doubt that the sun was the center of the solar system in Galileo's day. It also causes Mormons to doubt the DNA evidence showing that Native Americans are not descendants of Semitic peoples.[4]

This type of faith-based skepticism should be avoided if believers really want to know the truth about their religion. Faith-based skepticism, because it refuses to question its own premise (i.e., faith), cannot help us solve the problem of religious diversity. It has a proven track record of not helping people reasonably examine their respective faiths. It has a proven track record that runs counter to the progress of science itself.

The other type of skepticism is born of science. It's a reasonable skepticism that demands sufficient evidence before accepting some claim as true. Even people of faith utilize scientific findings in every area of their lives (except those rare findings that directly undercut or discredit their respective faiths). So we all know how to be skeptics and we all know what it's like to trust science, too. At the very minimum, reasonable or informed skeptics acknowledge that the scientific findings supportive of the RDVT and the RDPT are trustworthy, even though this means they should be skeptical of their faith. The reasonable or informed skeptic is therefore someone who understands the force of the RDVT and the RDPT, and, at a very minimum, initially presumes when examining one's own religious faith that it is probably false.

This informed skepticism becomes the default adult attitude when examining any religion, including one's own. It's an attitude, a skeptical attitude. It's a reasonable attitude that reasonable people should adopt. The extent of skepticism warranted depends on (1) the number of people who disagree, (2) whether the people who disagree are separated into distinct geographical locations, (3) how their faith originated, (4) under what circumstances their faith was personally adopted in the first place, (5) the number and nature of extraordinary miracle claims that are essential to their faith, and (6) the kinds of evidence that can be used to decide between the differing faiths. My claim is that, precisely because of these factors, a high degree of skepticism is warranted about religious faiths when compared to the objective results of science.

Informed skepticism is an attitude expressed as follows: (1) it assumes one's own religious faith has the burden of proof; (2) it adopts the methodological-naturalist viewpoint by which one assumes there is a natural explanation for the origins of a given religion, its holy books, and its extraordinary claims of miracles; (3) it demands sufficient evidence before concluding a religion is true; and, most importantly, (4) it disallows any faith in the religion under investigation.

Believers should begin by asking themselves how they first adopted their religious faith. Ask yourself who or what influenced you to believe? Under what circumstances did you adopt your faith? Did you seriously investigate your faith before adopting it? Did you consider other religious and nonreligious options? Or, like most believers, did you just adopt the beliefs given to you by your parents? If you merely adopted your faith for this reason, then it doesn't matter if your faith originated with people who had sufficient evidence to justify the beliefs they passed on to you. You don't know if they did until you examine the evidence for yourself with the OTF.

It also doesn't matter if you feel certain that your religious faith is true. Most all believers feel this way. Neurologist Robert Burton explains this misplaced sense of certainty in this way: "Despite how certainty feels, it is neither a conscious choice nor even a thought process. Certainty and similar states of knowing what we know arise out of involuntary brain mechanisms that, like love or anger, function independently of reason." Burton says that the "feeling of knowing," or certainty of conviction, should be thought of as one of our emotions, just like anger, pleasure, or fear. This feeling is unrelated to the strength of the evidence for what we believe. The feeling of "knowing" can be extremely powerful—so much so that our feeling of certainty wins despite contrary evidence that should mitigate it. Not only this, but our brain prefers to make up reasons to justify this feeling of certainty rather than follow the evidence to its reasonable conclusion.[5]

Believers may object that if they assume the skeptical attitude it will automatically cause them to reject their religious faith, since doing so unfairly presumes its own conclusion. But I think not. So long as there is sufficient, objective evidence for one's religious faith, even an informed skeptic should come to accept it. Many people are convinced every day of the truth of claims when the evidence suggests otherwise. If God created us as reasonable people, then the correct religious faith should have sufficient evidence for it, since that's what reasonable people require. Otherwise, if sufficient evidence does not exist, then God counterproductively created us as reasonable people who would subsequently reject the correct faith. It also means that people born as outsiders to the correct faith (perhaps because they were born in remote geographical locations or during a time before the correct faith was revealed) will be condemned by God merely because of where or when they were born. This doesn't bode well for an omniscient, omnibenelovent, but wrathful kind of god.

When Christians examine the claim that Muhammad rode on a flying horse, they should do so by way of a reasonable and informed skepticism, just as they should when considering claims such as levitating Buddhists or the magical properties of Mormon holy underwear or the existence of the Scientologists' evil Thetans that supposedly infest our bodies. Christian believers should examine the specific extraordinary claims of Christianity using the same kind of skepticism. The OTF calls on people to do unto their own religious faith as they do unto the faiths they reject. It is a Golden Rule for testing religious faiths: "Do unto your own faith what you do unto other faiths." It calls on believers to subject their own faith to the same level of reasonable skepticism they use when rejecting other faiths, which is the skepticism of an outsider, a nonbeliever.

Liberal believers will bristle at this. They don't reject other religious faiths altogether. Rather, they incorporate the best elements of other faiths by embracing a commonly shared understanding in an ecumenical dialogue. Liberal believers include the most enlightened Jews, Muslims, Catholics, and Protestants, who all share the common understanding stemming from Paul Tillich's notion of "ultimate concern." To liberals, I say that the rejection of faith-based reasoning can be seen on a continuum. Faith is much more prominent in some religious sects, most notably the conservative ones that, for instance, reject outright the overwhelming evidence for evolution in favor of a straightforward literal reading of the Genesis texts, and who embrace a literal understanding of hell as eternal conscious torment in an everlasting fire. So the OTF will be more helpful and more important to members of these conservative kinds of faith. The more conservative, exclusivist, and pseudoscientific the religious faith is, the more helpful the OTF will be. The more liberal, inclusivist, and accepting of scientifically based reasoning the religious faith is, the less important the OTF will be. But it is important for all types of religious faiths, to varying degrees.

If nothing else, liberals are not off the hook. For faith-based reasoning should be rejected by all scientifically informed people. At best, if liberal believers conclude that a god does exist, then, based on their ecumenical beliefs, it follows that such a god doesn't care which religion we accept. They end up believing in a nebulous god with no definable characteristics, perhaps a deistic god or the "god of the philosophers." This god is quite different from the God of full-blown Christianity or any specific revealed religion though, and can safely be ignored. For a distant god is no different than no god at all.

Precursors to the OTF

I don't claim to have invented this test for faith, since it has been bandied about for millennia wherever there were skeptics who didn't believe. They didn't believe precisely because they were outsiders, nonbelievers. I do claim to have brought it to the attention of people in our generation, and that I have defended it better than anyone else.

The great Catholic apologist G. K. Chesterton argued for something like the OTF in his book, *The Everlasting Man* (1925), which contributed to C. S. Lewis's conversion to Christianity. Chesterton wrote, "The point of this book . . . is that the next best thing to being really inside Christendom is to be really outside it. . . . It is the contention of these pages that while the best judge of Christianity is a Christian, the next best judge would be something more like a Confucian." Chesterton goes on to say, "that when we do make this imaginative effort to see the whole thing from the outside, we find that it really looks like what is traditionally said about it inside. It is exactly when the boy gets far enough off to see the giant that he sees that he really is a giant. It is exactly when we do at last see the Christian Church afar under those clear and level eastern skies that we see that it is really the Church of Christ."

In our own day, evangelical Christian apologist Josh McDowell takes this one step further. He travels around the country challenging Christians to refute their own faith. That's right! Try to refute it, he challenges. I think that is a noteworthy thing to say. I could only wish more Christians would take up his particular challenge. I agree with this sentiment. People who were raised to believe due to cultural influences, especially upon our mama's knees, *should* try to do this. What happened when Dustin Lawson, McDowell's former protégé, took him up on his challenge? Lawson did just what McDowell challenged him to do. He took him seriously. As a result, Lawson no longer believes.

Christian Responses

Christians have responded by attacking the science that the test is based upon, by claiming the test is self-defeating, asserting that the test has hidden faith assumptions, and that the test unfairly targets religion. All of these objections are red herrings thrown in the path in a dishonest effort to sidetrack us from getting at the truth, something I address at length in my book on the topic. Earlier in chapter 3 of this book I had discussed the intellectual virtues, showing that a person who is open to science-based reasoning is a person who is more open-minded than others, someone willing to search for truth wherever it's to be found. Now with this non–double standard reasonable test for faith I maintain that believers who reject it are being lied to by their brains. They are not open-minded people but rather closed-minded people who really don't want to know the truth. They have allowed their brains to lie to them. Let this test also be a test for those who want to be an honest open-minded person. Those who reject it are not. Period.

Critics of the OTF either do not understand the perspective of an outsider, or they grossly misrepresent it in favor of faith. In my book *Why I Became an Atheist*, I contrasted the insider's perspective (IP) with the outsider's perspective (OP), which can be explained like this: The insider believes in a particular religious sect. The outsider does not. The insider has faith. The outsider doubts. The insider makes extraordinary claims. The outsider makes no claims. The insider has a belief in search of data. The outsider looks at the data to determine the probability of a claim. The insider takes a leap of faith beyond the probabilities. The outsider doesn't claim more than what the probabilities can show. The IP represents a person who has faith. The OP represents a person who does not have faith. The IP represents faith-based reasoning. The OP represents science-based reasoning.

That is the contrast between the IP and the OP. It is the perspective of science, which is the same standard believers use when rejecting other religions. Now, ready for the kicker? The IP has no method for settling which religion is true. The OP does.

If anyone thinks the OTF is unfair or faulty in any way, then propose a better alternative. I've examined all of the ones I know, and by comparison, they all fail, sometimes miserably.

The OTF One More Time for Clarity
This time in short numbered points for the reading impaired:

1. We are all raised as believers. As children, we believed whatever our parents told us, all of us.

2. We were raised in our respective families and cultures to believe what our parents told us about religion.

3.   Psychological studies have shown that people have a very strong tendency to believe what they prefer to believe. Cognitive bias studies show this.

4.   Psychological studies have shown that most of us, most of the time, look for that which confirms what we believe rather than that which disconfirms it, even though the latter is the best way to get at the truth. This is known as confirmation bias.

5.   Neurological studies have shown that people have a sense of certainty about the beliefs they have that is unrelated to the strength of the actual evidence, as Robert Burton argues in *On Being Certain: Believing You Are Right Even When You're Not*.

6.   Skepticism is not usually an inherited characteristic. We must acquire the capacity to doubt what we are raised to believe. Skepticism is the adult attitude.

    Full stop. There are a lot of books on these subjects. This data is undeniable, noncontroversial, and obvious. We must think about the implications of what these undeniable facts tell us about who we are as human beings. If we were raised as Christians, then we seek to confirm what we were raised to believe because we prefer that which we were raised to believe. If we were raised as Muslims, then we seek to confirm what we were raised to believe because we prefer that which we were raised to believe. If we were raised as Orthodox Jews, then we seek to confirm what we were raised to believe because we prefer that which we were raised to believe. If we were raised as Scientologists, then we seek to confirm what we were raised to believe because we prefer that which we were raised to believe. If we were raised as Hindus, then we seek to confirm what we were raised to believe because we prefer that which we were raised to believe.

7.   When there are billions of people who are certain of an inherited faith they all learned in the same manner, who live in separate geographical locations around the globe, who all prefer to believe what they were raised to believe, and who all seek to confirm that which they were raised to believe, it should cause them to doubt what they were raised to believe.

8.   All believers who are certain of their faith will fallaciously argue that this data applies to atheists, too. If that were the case, then which faith should atheists adopt—all of them? You see, this argument does nothing to solve the problem of religious diversity, since believers still have not come up

with a method that can solve their own differences. Atheists are doubters. We are skeptics. Knowing this data causes us to require hard, cold evidence for that which we can accept.

9. Skepticism is a filter that adults use to help sift out the wheat of truth from the chaff of falsehood. We cannot doubt that filter! There is no other alternative.

10. *The Outsider Test for Faith* is the best and only way to get at the truth if you want to know the truth. Examine your own faith with the same level of skepticism you use when examining the other religious faiths you reject. We cannot merely say to people that they should be skeptical without offering a standard of skepticism. Why? Because if we ask believers who are certain of their faith to test it with doubt then, to a person, they will say they have, and that their faith is sure. But ask them to test their faith with the same level of skepticism they use when examining the other religious faiths they reject, and that will get their attention.

A Few Questions
If anyone disagrees, I have five sets of questions to be answered:

1. Do you or do you not assume other religions shoulder the burden of proof? When you examine Islam, Orthodox Judaism, Hinduism, Scientology, Mormonism, Shintoism, Jainism, Haitian Voodoo, the John Frum Cargo Cult, Satanism, or the many African or Chinese tribal religions, do you think approaching them with faith is the way to test these religions, or would you agree with the OTF that a much fairer method is by assuming they all have the burden of proof, including your own?

2. Do you or do you not think that a consistent standard invoking fairness is the best way to objectively come to know the correct religious faith, if one is? If not, why the double standard?

3. Do you or do you not think that if Christianity is true, it should be supported by the sciences to the exclusion of other, false religious faiths?

4. Do you or do you not admit that if you reject the OTF, then your God did not make Christianity such that it would lead reasonable people who were born as outsiders to come to believe it, and, as such, they will be condemned to hell by virtue of where they were born? If not, and if

outsiders can reasonably come to believe, then why is it that you think the OTF is faulty or unfair?

5. Do you or do you not have a better method for us to reasonably settle which religious faith is true, if one is? If so, what is it?

Let the Debates Begin
If religious believers accept the OTF and claim their faith passes the test, then at that point we have an agreed-upon standard for debating the merits of faith. If the test does nothing else, that is a good thing.

Let the debates begin.

Part 2

HOW TO DEFEND
THE CHRISTIAN FAITH

7

You Must Specialize
in Special Pleading

All apologetics is special pleading. If you want to be a Christian apologist you must perfect this art. It's what you'd be taught in any college or seminary apologetics program. However, if you want to be a *good* Christian apologist you must avoid doing so entirely. But if you avoided doing so entirely you wouldn't be an apologist at all. The risk here should be clear. If you didn't special plead your case you wouldn't be an apologist at all.[1]

Someone is special pleading "when applying standards, principles, and/ or rules to other people or circumstances, while making oneself or certain circumstances exempt from the same critical criteria, without providing adequate justification. Special pleading is often a result of strong emotional beliefs that interfere with reason."[2] It is to adopt double standards, something the *Outsider Test for Faith* disallows if one is honestly searching for the truth.

When Christian apologists special plead their case they usually do so to solve a puzzle of faith. Indeed, all apologetics is puzzle solving too. They already believe their faith is true, so they seek to solve the problems that come from believing. It doesn't even occur to them this is what they're doing, solving problems based on faith, not arguing to their faith. In this part of the book you will see how special pleading is used to defend the faith. It's done by punting to possibilities rather than by sticking to the probabilities. It's done by gerrymandering districts like politicians do to gain seats of power over others for God. It's done by mischaracterization. And it's done by lying for Jesus, at least by some.

The Special Pleading of Randal Rauser

As I see it, the wave of the future for evangelicals is to morph into moderates and even liberals in the coming years. Dr. Randal Rauser represents the future of evangelicalism as somewhat of a liberal when it comes the Old Testament, but a conservative when it comes to the New Testament, a clear double standard. At his invitation I cowrote a debate book with him titled, *God or Godless? One Atheist. One Christian. Twenty Controversial Questions.*[3] If you want to see special pleading raised to an art form then read what Rauser wrote. Even if you're not a moderate evangelical the lesson from him is clearly seen on almost every page.

In that book Rauser proposed ten chapter topics to debate, and I chose ten. Although all of Rauser's chapter topics are examples of special pleading, we can see what he's up to from the titles themselves in most cases. Consider the following: (1) If There Is No God, Then Life Has No Meaning; (2) If There Is No God, Then Everything Is Permitted; (3) God Is the Best Explanation of the Whole Shebang; (4) If There Is No God, Then We Don't Know Anything; (5) Love Is a Many Splendored Thing, but Only If God Exists; (6) God Is Found in the Majesty of the Hallelujah Chorus; and (7) God Best Explains the Miracles in People's Lives. Unstated in every one of these chapter titles is the question of which God he's talking about. In every case Rauser assumes that if I cannot explain something, then his God solves it, that his God gets a free pass around "Go" to collect the $200 in Monopoly money. Why not Allah, or the Jewish Orthodox Yahweh? People in those different religions use the exact same arguments and conclude that their God is the solution, and yet they cannot convince each other that their God is the solution to the mystery needing solved. Rauser is special pleading a case for his particular God. He has a great deal more work to do before concluding his God is the correct solution.

More importantly, if science cannot explain something then the proper conclusion is that science cannot explain something, nothing else. Of course, science does explain quite a bit even though it's still considered to be in its early stages. To expect science to explain most or nearly everything, especially in its early stages, is asking it to do too much. Science may not be able to explain everything anyway, for as science progresses it constantly opens up new fruitful questions to explore. Science is our best bet given that we each have a deceptive lying brain.

I became frustrated with Rauser's special pleading so I wrote a rebuttal to what he was doing in the book itself:

> Nearly all of Randal's chosen debate topics, if shown correct, would not present the slightest problem for most of the people on the planet. They have

no force at all against non-Christian theisms that disagree with his particular type of Christian faith, which includes biblical theisms such as Islam or Orthodox Judaism, and nonbiblical theisms such as Hinduism, polytheism, and Deism. Nor do they have any force against nonnaturalist atheisms such as Buddhism and Taoism. He still must argue for his specific trinitarian, virgin-born, incarnational, biblically centered faith.

Continuing, I said:

The only reason Randal cares about this issue is because he believes the God who exists is the same one who sent Jesus to die for him and with whom he will spend eternity. But the actual source of these additional Christian beliefs is the Bible and the theology he has built on it. What I'm doing here by contrast is showing why we cannot believe the Bible or the supposed good God it speaks about. If we have no good reason to believe the Bible or its God, then the question of whether there is a supernatural force (or being) out there is an uninteresting academic one for people only interested in that sort of thing as a curiosity. For if that's all we can conclude, and there is no way to know what this force (or being) wants us to do, why we're here, or where we're going when we die, then it ends up being an unnecessary hypothesis even if it's true. No one who believes in such a nebulous supernatural force (or being) would even care to engage in writing a book like this one.[4]

The one topic in our book that gets to the heart of what Rauser believes was on the resurrection of Jesus (chapter 19). I don't think the brain of an apologist like him can appreciate the impact of what I'm about to say, but here goes. Jesus may well have been raised bodily from the grave by his God. Fine. I can grant that for the sake of argument, even though I don't think this Easter "event" happened at all. The problem is that there just isn't a reasonable way to know if he did, and the only tools we have to determine if he did, are the tools of the historian. I wrote a whole important chapter on this topic.[5]

Here is how a historian must look at the miracle of the resurrection of Jesus, as explained by New Testament scholar Bart Ehrman: "All that historians can do is show what probably happened in the past. That is the problem inherent in miracles. Miracles, by our very definition of the term, are virtually impossible events," so "miracles, by their very nature, are always the least probable explanations for what happened."[6] And he gives us this example:

Suppose . . . that Jesus was buried by Joseph of Arimathea . . . and then a couple of Jesus' followers, not among the twelve, decided that night to move the body somewhere more appropriate. . . . But a couple of Roman legionnaires are passing by, and catch these followers carrying the shrouded corpse through the streets. They suspect foul play and confront the followers, who pull their swords as the disciples did in Gethsemane. The soldiers, expert in swordplay, kill them on the spot. They now have three bodies, and no idea where the first one came from. Not knowing what to do with them, they commandeer a cart and take the corpses out to Gehenna, outside town, and dump them. Within three or four days the bodies have deteriorated beyond recognition. Jesus' original tomb is empty, and no one seems to know why.

Is this scenario likely? Not at all. Am I proposing this is what really happened? Absolutely not. Is it more probable that something like this happened than that a miracle happened and Jesus left the tomb to ascend to heaven? Absolutely! From a purely historical point of view, a highly unlikely event is far more probable than a virtually impossible one.[7]

Even Christian professor Dale Allison admits, with regard to the pivotal claim of the resurrection of Jesus, that

the accounts of the resurrection, like the past in general, come to us as phantoms. Most of the reality is gone. It is the fragmentary and imperfect nature of the evidence as well as the limitations of our historical-critical tools that move us to confess, if we are conscientious, how hard it is to recover the past. That something happened does not entail our ability to show that it happened, and that something did not happen does not entail our ability to show that it did not happen. . . . Pure historical reasoning is not going to show us that God raised Jesus from the dead.[8]

Christian professor James McGrath said the same thing about the historian's dilemma, that

all sorts of fairly improbable scenarios are inevitably going to be more likely than an extremely improbable one. That doesn't necessarily mean miracles never happened then or don't happen now—it just means that historical tools are not the way to answer that question.[9]

The bottom line is that the tools of the historian are inadequate for the task of detecting miracles. But the tools of the historian are all we've got to know if an extremely improbable miraculous event like a resurrection happened. There is no other method. So even if the resurrection of Jesus did happen we cannot know that it did. That's the point of Ehrman. That's the point of Allison. That's the point of McGrath. To claim anything beyond what the tools of the historian lead us to conclude is special pleading one's case.

Troeltsch's Principle of Analogy

One of the tools of the historian is Ernst Troeltsch's *Principle of Analogy*. Troeltsch was an important German theologian (1865–1923) who argued that the laws of nature operate the same for the past as well as for the present. So when investigating the past for what happened historians must assume the present is the key to the past, and that the laws of nature were the same for people in biblical times as they are for our present day.[10] The consequence of his principle is that if miracles do not happen in the present then they did not happen in the ancient past either. That's because the laws of nature have not changed. Pieter Craffert said of it:

> The principle of analogy which is one of the basic principles of all social scientific study, is not restricted to the skeptical historian, but applies to all historiography as well as to everyday life. There is no other option but to apply it to present practical standards of everyday life to determine whether the decision of the historian to reject the claims of some events narrated in ancient sources, is valid.[11]

I find there to be nothing controversial about this principle at all. It's obvious. We must assume this about the past. Christians can argue that it's possible the world behaved differently in the past all they want to, but it's not possibility that matters. Only probability does. If God expects us to believe based upon a mere possibility that the world was different in the past than in our own day, then he's not expecting us to be the reasonable people he supposedly created us to be.

How believers respond to Troeltsch is characterized by both Michael Licona and Alvin Plantinga. Licona questions the antecedent probabilities that show us miracle claims in history always turn out to be false (or to be very generous, almost always). That's the probabilities given Troeltsch's principle. Licona argues that in order to empirically establish these probabilities it would require investigating all miracle claims. But since that would be impossible, he asks how we can really know uniform experience is always against the occurrences of miraculous events. Licona: "Investigating every miracle claim would be a seemingly impossible task, thus rendering [the] assertion that the uniform experience of reality supports the non-existence of miracles equally impossible to support."[12]

However, we emphatically don't need to investigate all miracle claims to establish the principle of analogy—just enough of them to show it to be very probable. We're not looking for certainty, nor do we need it. So any possible loophole seems fair game to Licona. Maybe some miracles have actually occurred. The tools we have to determine whether miracles took place don't lead us to that conclusion. When historians investigate miracle claims on our behalf by doing it correctly, they always conclude *there isn't enough evidence to turn an improbability into a probability.* In fact, it's precisely because we cannot investigate all miracle claims that we must come up with some sort of conclusion about the antecedent probabilities when assessing if any particular one of them took place. There is no other alternative. When historians do this, miracle claims always turn out to be false.

Because Licona doesn't think uniform experience is against miracles, he argues we "must consider miracle-claims on a case-by-case basis"[13] rather than adopt the antecedent probabilities showing that miracle claims in history always turn out to be false. Licona suggests we should dismiss the antecedent probabilities and investigate miracle claims in isolation from each other. He does this so he can proceed to investigate the evidence for the resurrection of Jesus without factoring in the antecedent probabilities that miracle claims in history always turn out to be false. In fact, Licona says that "by placing too much value on antecedent probability in historical judgments, the historian is many times forced to make conclusions that are incorrect."[14] Well then, when it comes to miracle claims in history, which ones, other than Licona's belief in the resurrection of Jesus, does he think historians have gotten wrong when they reject them all as improbable? He doesn't say. Presumably based on his evangelical faith he thinks most all of the miracles reported in the Bible took place as reported. What reasonable basis would he have for concluding this if historians with their tools don't conclude the same thing? That is the question.

Licona says, "historians should neither presuppose nor *a priori* exclude the possibility of God's intervention in human affairs."[15] This is fine as it goes. Many historians are themselves believers. But once again Bart Ehrman tells us the problem: "Since historians can establish only what *probably* happened in the past, they cannot show that miracles happened, since this would invoke a contradiction—that the most improbable event is the most probable."[16] Ehrman explains,

A historical occurrence is a one-time proposition; once it has happened, it is over and done with. Since historians cannot repeat the past in order to establish what probably happened, there will always be less certainty in their conclusions. . . . And the farther back you go in history, the harder it is to mount a convincing case. For events in the ancient world, even events of earth shattering importance, there is often scant evidence to go on. . . . This is what makes alleged miracles so problematic. On one level of course, everything that happens is to some extent improbable. . . . As to events that defy all probability, miracles create an inescapable dilemma for historians. Since historians can only establish what probably happened in the past, and the chances of a miracle happening, by definition, are infinitesimally remote, historians can never demonstrate that a miracle *probably* happened.[17]

By arguing that miracle claims "must be judged on an individual basis,"[18] Licona simply dismisses the antecedent probabilities that force him to reasonably shoulder the burden of proof when it comes to the resurrection of Jesus, since those probabilities show that miracle claims in history always turn out to be false. He wants to examine the resurrection of Jesus in isolation from any antecedent probabilities since in order to succeed he must do that. *He wants to make the resurrection of Jesus out to be a special case deserving of special treatment by virtue of special pleading without a special justification for doing so.* He ends up opening up a gaping hole in the dam for other religionists to float their own miracle claims through it, who can now demand the same consistent kind of special pleading. Then nothing will stop believers from arguing their miracle claims are exceptions too, rendering the antecedent probabilities null and void, even though the antecedent probabilities still tell us the rule, that miracle claims in history always turn out to be false. Just think of what Bart Ehrman argued:

> To agree with an ancient person that Jesus healed the sick, walked on water, cast out a demon, or raised the dead is to agree, first, there were divine persons (or magicians) walking the earth who could do such things and, second, that Jesus was one of them. In other words, from a historian's perspective, anyone who thinks that Jesus did these miracles has to be willing in principle to concede that other people did them as well, including the pagan holy man Apollonius of Tyana, the emperor Vespasian, and the Jewish miracle worker Hanina ben Dosa. The evidence that is admitted in any one of these cases must be admitted in the others as well.[19]

I cannot help but be reminded of the Egyptian magicians in the story of Moses and the Exodus out of Egypt. When Aaron threw down his staff in front of the Pharaoh it became a snake, we're told. When the Egyptian magicians threw down their staffs they also became snakes, we're told (Exodus. 7:10–12). The magicians were able to do this feat, plus turn water into blood (Exodus 7:19–22), and duplicate the plague of frogs (Exodus 8:18), just as Moses did. *One cannot believe Moses did these feats unless one also believes the Egyptian magicians did, since the same story tells of them both.*

Alvin Plantinga, for his part, argued that the whole reason for "Troeltschian" biblical scholarship is because "the very practice of science presupposes rejection of the idea of miracle or special divine action in the world."[20] But Troeltsch only said we must assume the laws of nature were the same for the people in biblical times as they are for our day. It just so happens that in our day miracles don't happen. It could have turned out differently had the Christian God continued doing miracles, but it didn't. That is most emphatically not a problem with Troeltsch's principle. It's the fault of a God who apparently stopped doing miracles as we became more and more scientifically literate. Why did miracles stop as science progressed? A reasonable person could conclude miracles "stopped" because they never took place at all.

Plantinga goes on to say Troeltschian biblical scholarship is "elitism run amok," in that it "presupposes the philosophical and theological opinion that there isn't any other epistemic avenue to these matters; it presupposes that, for example, faith is not a source of warranted belief or knowledge on these topics . . . that traditional Christian belief is completely mistaken in taking it that faith is, in fact, a reliable source of true and warranted belief on these topics."[21] Faith? How is it possible that faith can be a reliable source for anything? A Mormon or Jehovah's Witness, Muslim or Jew, could say the exact same things. *Faith is the excuse apologists make when special pleading.* Faith has no method and is promoted by a lying brain.

What about Miracles in a Religious Context?

To help neutralize the impact of Troeltsch's *Principle of Analogy* Christian apologists have arbitrarily introduced the concept of a "religious context" for miracles, hoping this can eliminate the burden of proof that is rightfully theirs by virtue of the antecedent probabilities. They argue that the probability of a miracle happening is increased when an extraordinary event occurs in a "religious context." Michael Licona argues:

> We may recognize that an event is a miracle when the event . . . occurs in an environment or context with religious significance. In other words, the event occurs in a context where we might expect a god to act. The stronger the context is charged in this direction, the stronger the evidence becomes that we have a miracle on our hands.[22]

Comparing David Hume's hypothetical example where Queen Elizabeth comes to life after dying with the example of the resurrection of Jesus, Licona says, "A significant difference exists [because] the historical matrix in which the data for Jesus' resurrection appears is charged with religious significance . . . whereas the life of the queen enjoys no such context."[23] What is he talking about? Licona offers two analogies. If a fifty-year-old atheist who has been blind from birth recovered his sight on a Saturday for no apparent reason, this is merely an anomaly, an unexplained fact. It might be a miracle, but who can say for sure. There just isn't anything that offers us a clue as to why this happened.

But if instead this same atheist recovered his sight right after a Baptist preacher visited him out of the blue, prayed, and recited the words to "Amazing Grace," —"I once . . . was blind, but now I see"—then that is a religious context. In such a context, Licona argues, a physician is justified in thinking a miracle has truly occurred.[24]

Licona's analogies are interesting because they reveal his bias. Please note, Licona didn't suggest an analogy where the atheist bathed in the Ganges River in India and was subsequently healed of his blindness; nor did he propose one involving a witchdoctor's spells, or a Catholic nun praying for him in the sanctuary of Our Lady of Lourdes, in France. These analogies involve a religious context too. Besides, even though these are just analogies, from what I can tell, sick, blind, and paraplegic people in charismatic and Pentecostal churches are prayed for every worship service to no avail, sometimes under the same circumstances of this hypothetical story. So even if such an event might actually happen someday I still would want to ask why so many others are not healed under the same circumstances.

Nonetheless, does a religious context add anything significant to the probability that a miracle took place? If it does then Christian miracle claims in history still have no more probability to them than any others. I could cite an almost endless number of claims of healings and miracles coming from many other religious traditions. Just think of the pagan holy man Apollonius of Tyana, the emperor Vespasian, and the Jewish miracle worker Hanina ben Dosa. Do any of these and other miracle claims in history have any more probability to them because they took place in religious contexts? If a religious context increases the probability that a miracle occurred then this doesn't help Christian apologists, since most all miracle claims come from specific, not always Christian, religious contexts. Neither Licona, nor any other apologist who uses this line of reasoning, can claim anything special with regard to their faith.

But more to the point. If a religious context adds anything significant to the probability that a miracle took place, it only does so if an extraordinary event took place. First things first, as they say. One cannot merely hear a faith healer say "be healed" and conclude anything until it can be established that the person was sick or infirmed and then instantly healed. But that doesn't happen. No faith healer does a long-range clinical study on his subjects. They come in the door, pay their money, get smacked down with the "power of the Holy Ghost," fall backward, claim to be healed out of faith, and leave the stage with no follow-up.

The fact is we're talking about miracle claims in history. We cannot just take the narrator's words that Jesus came up to someone and said, "Be healed," upon which the person was healed. We must judge the whole story as we find it since we were not there to hear Jesus utter these words. What Licona would have us believe is that the "religious context" of a biblical miracle *story* adds any probability to the miracle story itself. Well, no. Consider the miracle stories about Jesus. They spread orally from person to person before being written down in a different language decades later by anonymous authors with agendas who didn't agree with each other. These gospels were then copied and collected into full manuscripts that are three centuries removed from the supposed events. So does a "religious context" add to these stories as we find them? No.

The bottom line is that in my world miracles do not happen. What world are apologists like Licona living in? The odds of a resurrection, from my experience, are zero. I must judge the past from my present knowledge. I cannot reasonably do otherwise. Christians cannot believe based on the raw uninterpreted historical evidence apart from how they were raised. The only way they can reach this faith conclusion is by special pleading, and that's it. If in our world miracles do not happen then they probably did not happen in first-century Palestine either. They must approach said evidence from our present-day perspective where miracles like virgin births, resurrections, and ascensions into the sky do not happen. And that should be the end of it.

The Minimal Facts Approach to the Resurrection

Gary Habermas and Michael Licona, just like William Lane Craig in his debates, all stress the facts that most scholars agree on in assessing the case for the resurrection, and then they seek the best hypothesis that explains all of these agreed-upon facts. They do not want "to be saddled with the task of first showing that the Gospels are, in general, historically reliable," writes Craig.[25] Instead, Craig merely has to establish "that the Gospel accounts of the discovery of Jesus' empty tomb can be shown to be historically reliable without first showing that the Gospels are, in general, historically trustworthy."[26]

Habermas and Licona tell us about their own "minimal facts approach" in these words: "This approach considers only those data that are strongly attested historically that they are granted by nearly every scholar who studies the subject, even the rather skeptical ones. . . . We present our case using the 'lowest common denominator' of agreed-upon facts. This keeps attention on the central issue, instead of sidetracking into matters that are irrelevant."[27] What is *irrelevant* according to them? The general trustworthiness and inspiration of the Bible:

> One of the strengths of this approach is that it avoids the debate over the inspiration of the Bible. Too often the objection raised frequently against the Resurrection is, "Well, the Bible has errors, so we can't believe Jesus rose."

We can quickly push this to the side. "I am not arguing at this time for the inspiration of the Bible or even its general trustworthiness. Believer and skeptic alike accept the facts I'm using because they are strongly supported. These facts must be addressed." To them these topics are "separate issues."[28]

It should be obvious what is wrong with their approach. Habermas and Licona had previously quoted from Annette Gordon-Reed, a law professor of New York Law School, when she said of historical and legal cases, "The evidence must be considered as a whole before a realistic and fair assessment of the possible truth of [any] story can be made."[29] What Habermas and Licona are doing is isolating a few so-called minimal facts and treating them separately from the general trustworthiness of the Bible.

Nonbelievers don't agree to this approach since the trustworthiness of the Bible is indeed relevant to the case for the resurrection of Jesus. What are the so-called agreed-upon facts that Habermas and Licona are referring to? That (1) Jesus died by crucifixion, (2) his disciples believed he arose and appeared to them, (3) the church persecutor Paul was suddenly converted, (4) James, the brother of Jesus, who was formerly a skeptic, converted, and (5) the tomb of Jesus was empty.[30] Craig, Habermas, and Licona are looking for the best explanation of their isolated minimal facts based on isolated miracle claims and isolated historical tools.

The first thing to note is that not everyone agrees with all of their "facts." Muslims, over one billion of them, along with skeptics Hugh J. Schonfield (*The Passover Plot*, 1965) and Robert Price disagree with the first one.[31] It's also not agreed that James, the brother of Jesus, was a skeptic at the time Jesus died, or that he was converted as the result of Jesus appearing to him. A number of scholars on both sides of the issue doubt the empty tomb, including Dale Allison and many liberal Christian scholars, something Habermas and Licona admit. Yet they include the empty tomb as an agreed-upon fact anyway, thus revealing that theirs is not a minimal facts approach after all.[32] They feel justified in including it because Habermas discovered that "roughly 75% of scholars on the subject accept the empty tomb as historical fact."[33]

This argument from consensus includes a preponderance of evangelical tomes written on the subject due to the fact that evangelicals are more interested in it than others. Did Habermas include Muslim scholars in his survey? As far as I know he still has not produced a list of the authors included. Richard Carrier did an exposé of this claim in 2013 and says Habermas

doesn't give any numbers, or name or date any of the items in his sample that are being set in ratio to each other. . . . Habermas doesn't release his data (still to this day; even after repeated requests, as some of those requesting it have told me), so his result can't be evaluated. That makes his claim uncheckable. Which is a perversion of the peer review process. That basically makes this bogus number propaganda, not the outcome of any genuine research methodology.[34]

Apologists look at what nonbelievers have proposed as alternatives to the resurrection and find them all improbable, thus declaring their faith in Jesus' resurrection to be a better explanation than what nonbelievers offer. What they fail to realize is that nonbelievers do not have to propose an explanation of these isolated facts at all. We're first and foremost arguing that the New Testament is so riddled with discrepancies and evolved layers of religious tradition from a superstitious era that it leaves a great deal of room for doubt—that it's much more likely no one can know what happened, if we take the New Testament at face value—which means Christians have little basis beyond blind, irrational faith for believing Jesus rose from the grave. That's what we're saying.

Our conjectures only come after arguing that reasonable people must doubt a straightforward reading of the tales in these texts. Habermas and Licona ignore the fact that a miraculous resurrection is always going to be more improbable than any improbable speculation about what may have happened instead. Improbable things happen all the time. People get struck by lightning. People win contests against overwhelming odds.[35] So nonmiraculous explanations of the resurrection might all be improbable and yet be better candidates for explaining the evidence, since a miracle is still less likely to be true than those other improbable explanations. Unless Christian scholars can show that these "improbable" explanations are more improbable than a miracle (and they never do), their argument can't even get off the ground.

Methodological Naturalism

Another tool of the historian, not completely unlike Troeltsch's principle of analogy, is to proceed along the lines of methodological naturalism, which would, in the case of the Bible, treat it like one treats any ancient document. Methodological naturalism (MN) is a proven method whereby scholars assume there is a natural explanation for any event rather than a supernatural one. Scientists and historians limit their research to the study of natural causes. They assume for the sake of fruitful and productive research that all causes are natural ones, not supernatural ones.

About the use of methodological naturalism professor James McGrath comments:

> I don't see how historical study can adopt any other approach, any more than criminology can. It will always be theoretically possible that a crime victim

died simply because God wanted him dead, but the appropriate response of detectives is to leave the case open. In the same way, it will always be possible that a virgin conceived, but it will never be more likely than that the stories claiming this developed, like comparable stories about other ancient figures, as a way of highlighting the individual's significance. And since historical study deals with probabilities and evidence, to claim that a miracle is "historically likely" misunderstands the method in question.[36]

When there is a crime do investigators assume a natural cause? Or, do they assume Allah did it? Isn't it more productive to assume a natural cause? And doesn't assuming a natural cause lead to solving crimes? What if we cannot solve that crime? Then what? Should we leap to Allah as the cause? Or, should we simply suspend judgment? Now it might be that Allah did the "crime." The method doesn't preclude that possibility. It's just that with MN we cannot come to that conclusion. So using it might not allow us to solve a supernaturally caused crime. I get this. But if assuming a natural cause cannot help us solve the crime what other method do we have? As far as I can tell faith has no method, solves no crimes, and leads to dead ends. If Yahweh exists and did the "crime" instead, then MN itself doesn't allow us to conclude he did. Therefore, if Yahweh exists he must convince reasonable people by other means, and I indicated how he could have done so in chapter 1 of this book.

Believers have criticized the use of MN since it places their faith conclusions outside the research of scientists and historians. Christian apologist Dr. Victor Reppert objects, saying, "Methodological naturalism would rule out a supernatural explanation in any event." Continuing, he says:

What is needed is a defeasible version of methodological naturalism that allows for some point at which it is no longer reasonable to apply it. What you have to say is that we have good reason to apply MN to the actual evidence, but there are some possible pieces of evidence, which, if we had them, we would have to give up MN and admit the supernatural. But when someone says there is no method for detecting the supernatural, then I take it they mean what they say. If supernatural activity were to occur, we would be obliged to overlook it no matter what. Even if you argue that that's the only reasonable thing to do, you have to face up to the consequences of what it says.[37]

Reppert is concerned that the use of MN might exclude supernatural explanations and miraculous events before even examining them. His assumption, like other Christian apologists, is that it would be unreasonable to exclude supernatural explanations since those explanations might be the best ones for some kinds of unexplainable events.

Let's first consider the possibility Reppert is correct, that utilizing MN would in principle exclude miraculous explanations and miracle claims from consideration. What if MN cannot detect God's handiwork? If that's the case then believers must bite the bullet. Just admit MN cannot detect God's handiwork. If it's reasonable to adopt MN when honestly searching for the truth about nature and history, and if this means scientists and historians must suspend judgment rather than conclude "god did it," then so be it. Believers like Reppert should just admit that scientists and historians cannot find God. Whose fault would this be, if so? It would be God's fault for setting up the universe such that in order to gain objective knowledge about the nature of nature and history, scientists and historians must adopt MN. It would be God's fault for not doing miracles today to convince us that he exists. It would be God's fault for providing an incompetent revelation in the superstitious past that lacks sufficient evidence to convert outsiders, a revelation that got so many things wrong in the first place.

So there is nothing about MN that is unjustified even if it excludes supernatural explanations. Christian believers use MN every single day. They do not assume there is a demon behind every tree, like many did during the infamous witch hunt period. Today's Christians are "enlightened Christians," unlike them. They just use it selectively, in every area except those rare areas that conflict with their prescientific sacred book.

But in fact, Reppert is incorrect about MN. MN does not prohibit supernatural explanations when investigating the historical claims of the Bible. It doesn't, most emphatically. It doesn't prohibit testing stories in the Bible with the science of archaeology, whether investigating the Exodus, or the wilderness wanderings in the desert for forty years, or the Canaanite conquest reported in Judges, nor does it prohibit testing whether there was a census at the time Jesus was born, nor does it prohibit testing the language styles used by the writers of the Bible to see if there is more than one writer for Isaiah, or if 2nd Peter was a forgery. It doesn't prohibit tests on petitionary prayer to show whether there is a supernatural deity, nor does it prohibit testing so-called prophecies. In fact MN is the method used to test all of these claims and more. If the results were positive for faith, those results would show us these claims are true, despite MN. Now that's not the problem for MN. It's a problem for faith-based claims. If the method of MN successfully showed these claims to be true believers would change their tune and crow about it. Because the results turned out differently they must find some loophole to attack the method. Heads I win, tails you lose, right?

MN by itself may not help tell us everything about the nature and workings of the universe. It is *only* as reliable as that method works. It seeks natural causes for everything. So it is a limited method. However, what other method exists that can do a better job? We can rely upon MN to produce the goods. It is overwhelmingly probable, almost virtually certain given its past record.

So where are we? God supposedly created a world that is best explained by a method that looks for natural causes if we want to learn about it. He did that, on the Christian view. That method has gradually jettisoned supernatural explanations by scientifically literate people and by historians. And believers find themselves arguing against it. So they must argue against what their God did in order to believe in him. Don't you find that strange? That their God would put something in place that undermines their faith whereby they must selectively deny it to believe? And what is it they think excludes its grasp? An ancient prescientific barbaric superstitious unhistorical set of selected canonized sacred books as they interpret them in today's world? This does not make sense to me.

Reppert's God has failed him on two counts. First, he created the world such that MN obtains if scientists want objective knowledge about the world and if historians want to know what happened in history. But the utilization of MN to investigate the world and history undercuts knowing that God created and acted in history. Second, even though MN does not exclude knowing that God acted in the world and in history, God has failed to provide the evidence that he did act or has acted. Some God that is!

Methodological naturalism works so well it's very probable that nature is all there is. We must think exclusively in terms of the probabilities. We may misjudge the probabilities, but we should never go against them. MN has given us that knowledge. Faith has been wrong so many times it should be obvious it cannot be relied upon to produce any knowledge. Faith adds nothing to our probability calculations.

So Let's Recap

Christian apologists arbitrarily isolate the miracle claim of the resurrection of Jesus and exclude from consideration the antecedent probabilities that miracle claims in the ancient world always turn out to be false. Then they isolate miracle claims that have a "religious context" as having higher probability to them than other unexplained or extraordinary events, even though most all miracle claims have a religious context to them. Next they arbitrarily exclude from discussion everything but the minimal facts that believers and nonbelievers both accept, especially the overall trustworthiness of the Bible. Finally they unreasonably exclude two important tools of the historian, the principle of analogy and methodological naturalism.

Okay? Got it! So *that's* how it's done! That's a whole lot of isolating and excluding going on! But this is how it's to be done folks. It's nothing more than special pleading in favor of Christian faith, pure and simple. It's a lot of empty rhetoric meant to bamboozle the uniformed and the logically impaired.

These kinds of arguments only convince the already convinced though. That's the nature of special pleading. It only has the appearance of defending the faith for people who already believe it.

8

You Must Punt to Possibilities

Most Christian apologists believe that a fall into sin in the Garden of Eden damaged our rational cognitive powers to some degree. I think a much better explanation for how badly human beings reason relates to how our brains evolved. Nonetheless, even if our cognitive powers are damaged because of a fall in the Garden of Eden, this does not negate or diminish the need to present sufficient evidence to believe. Apologists must still present the evidence to believe regardless of the state of our rational cognitive powers. The task doesn't change.

In this chapter I intend to show how many times Christian apologists punt to the mere *possibility* that their faith is true rather than consider the probabilities. My claim is that the more often Christian apologists resort to this defense, the less likely their faith is true. For the more often they use it, the more often they're admitting the evidence is not on their side. If the evidence were on their side they would not have to defend their faith by repeatedly suggesting it is still *possible* their faith is true despite overwhelming evidence to the contrary. I will go farther to suggest that *at several crucial points* in the defense of their faith, some of the best Christian apologists have resorted to punting to the possibilities. The problem with this defense is obvious. When we are assessing the truth claims of the Christian faith (or any other religious faith), *probabilities* are all that matter. We should think exclusively in terms of them.

Possibility arguments are not necessarily wrong to use in defense of a claim, since there are many cases where anomalies persist and need to be explained. My claim is that the crucial arguments on behalf of Christianity are based on possibilities not probabilities. They are based on *ad hoc hypotheses* utterly unrelated to the strength of the evidence. To be a Christian is to believe against the overwhelming evidence to the contrary. Because of this I must show the Christian faith is nearly impossible before Christians will consider it to be improbable, which is a reversal of how reasonable people should evaluate their faith. However, that being said, if you want to be an apologist you must punt to possibilities since so many of the best apologists do. If you want to be a *good* apologist, you shouldn't do this at all. But then if you didn't do it at all, you wouldn't be an apologist at all.

It's *Possible* That . . .

Let's start with creationism. This is not the place to argue on behalf of evolution.[1] Evolution is a fact. The evidence for it is overwhelming and convincing, even to most believers. The implications for the Christian faith are enormous. The God-hypothesis for the creation of human beings is unnecessary at best. The Adam and Eve story is a myth. There is no original sin, so there is no need to atone for it. Human beings are not special nor even the highest creation, if for no other reason than we are still evolving. When we die, we cease to exist, just like every member of every other species.

Nonetheless, believers still try to argue that evolution is guided by God— that is, it is still *possible* that God exists even though all life evolved. To see this, all we need to do is look at dog breeders who manipulate the breeding habits of their dogs to produce new breeds all the time. Some kind of god could act like these dog breeders by manipulating the environment and breeding habits of the various species on earth to produce new ones. Doing so would not violate the evolutionary process, it's argued. It would merely inject purposeful direction into it. But how reasonable is it to suppose this scenario is the case? Not very. Such a scenario is *possible*, but what we want to know is if it is *probable*. It is also possible that the Loch Ness Monster exists but escapes all of our attempts to detect it.

The first question we need to ask is: Where is the evidence for such a claim? I don't see any god doing anything. Who does? The second question is: Why, if a good, omnipotent creator exists, did he made the law of predation one of the centerpieces of his creative handiwork? Evolution works through the survival of the fittest. Nature is red in tooth and claw. This evolutionary process has forced animals to kill or be killed. Nearly 99 percent of all species that ever existed are extinct because the evolutionary process is extremely wasteful. This is surely not a good way for an omnipotent creator to create. If there is some supernatural force (or being), it is *not* the God of Christian theology.[2] A third question is: How does it benefit believers to say there is a supernatural force (or being) if that is all they can claim? Such a god is no different to none at all. Such a force would be a distant god, irrelevant to life and our pursuit of knowledge and happiness. He/she/it can safely be ignored. A fourth question is: Where did this supernatural force (or being) come from? It doesn't explain anything to say it is a *necessary* being. Perhaps the universe (or multiverse) is the necessary being. I see no reason to suppose it isn't. In any case, while it is *possible* God exists, this is such a slim possibility, given evolution, that the more reasonable position by far, is that such an entity is an unnecessary hypothesis that we can do without.

If the "God did it" explanation is to be taken seriously, then modern science should not be able to offer so many viable alternatives to that explanation. Either Christians argue from the mysterious gaps in scientific knowledge to their particular God, or they don't. If they do, then they're arguing from ignorance, a well-known informal fallacy. If Christians *don't* argue from the gaps by claiming their God is merely the sustaining creator of the universe, then what we end up with is a universe that is indistinguishable from one without God at all. *The probability that the Christian God-hypothesis is the best explanation for the universe is inversely proportional to the amount of reasonable alternative scientific explanations there are (i.e., the more that science can explain, the less probable it is that God is the best explanation), and too many scientific explanations exist to suppose that the Christian God-hypothesis explains anything at all.*

Let's turn to miracles. Christian apologists John King-Farlow and William Niels Christensen argue that just because we don't experience miracles today doesn't mean that throughout the history of mankind God hasn't done a plethora of them and won't do so again when the time is right in the future. Their exact words are, "an irregularity relative to a limited sample of our experiences might really be a regularity relative to a vastly larger sample."[3] They are asking us to believe against the overwhelming present-day experience of nearly all modern people that things might turn out differently than we now experience. Is this impossible? No, not at all. But again, it's not probable. Take as but one example among many the story that Balaam's ass spoke to him. The problem is not that Balaam *thought* his ass spoke to him. The problem is that someone believed him and wrote it up in the Bible. If today's Christians lived back in that superstitious era, they wouldn't believe this happened since all they had was Balaam's testimony. Back in Balaam's day they themselves would not have believed it until Balaam made his ass talk in their presence.

What Christians must first show is that a miracle could not have happened within the natural world because it was nearly impossible (or else it's not to be considered miraculous at all). Then they must turn around and claim such an impossible event probably took place anyway. *So the probability that a miracle really did take place is inversely proportional to the probably that it could take place (i.e., the less probable it is considered to be, then the more probable it didn't happen at all).* The improbability that a miracle took place defeats any attempt to show it probably took place. Furthermore, as we saw in chapter 5 when discussing Classical Apologetics, when evaluating the evidence for a miracle, someone cannot presuppose any given particular god performed the miracle in question, since only the evidence of the miracle itself can give us good reason to think such a god exists in the first place. After all, non-Christian theists reject the evidence that Jesus was raised from the dead even though they are theists.

There are many other misfiring guns in the apologist's arsenal. It is still *possible* that petitionary prayers are efficacious even though scientific studies have shown they work just about as well as chance. It is still *possible* that even though the tools of the historian cannot detect miracles in the distant past, miracles took place in the past anyway. It is still *possible* that evangelical Christianity is true even though it is a late historical development to Christianity in general. It's still *possible* that, even though Christians trust science in an overwhelming number of areas, they can still distrust it when it conflicts with what some ancient, prescientific people wrote in a set of books believed to be sacred. Sure, all of these things are possible, but probabilities are all that matter. If we're going to talk about what is *real*, then we must think exclusively in terms of probabilities.

The Problem of Religious Diversity and Hell
Consider why the Christian God will send people to hell who don't believe the right kinds of things, even though what people believe is overwhelmingly based on when and where they are born. William Lane Craig calls this the "soteriological problem of evil" and provides the answer by saying, it "is possible that God has so providentially ordered the world that those who fail to hear the Gospel and be saved would not have freely responded affirmatively to it even if they had heard it."[4] Or, in a different place he talks instead of creation itself, that it "is possible that God has created a world that has an optimal balance between saved and lost, and those who never hear the gospel and are lost would not have believed in it even if they had heard it."[5]

In his argument to this effect he uses the word "possible" in one section of a chapter twenty times on my count.[6] Take, for instance, lines from two back-to-back paragraphs when defending the traditional view of hell:

> it is entirely *possible* that God is all-powerful and all-loving, and that many persons hear the gospel and are lost. . . . As a good and loving God, God wants as many people as possible to be saved and as few as possible to be lost. His goal, then, is to achieve an optimal balance between these, to create no more of the lost than is necessary to attain a certain number of the saved. But it is *possible* that the actual world has such a balance. It is *possible* that in order to create this many people who will be saved, God also had to create this many

people who would be lost. It is *possible* that had God created a world in which fewer people go to hell, then even fewer people would have gone to heaven. It is *possible* that in order to achieve a multitude of saints, God had to accept a multitude of sinners.[7]

Following this Craig offers "possible" answers to three different questions, and claims afterward: "These are *possible* answers to the questions we posed. But so long as they are even possible, they show that there is no incompatibility between God's being all-powerful and all-loving and some people's never hearing the gospel and being lost."[8]

I am more than bewildered by this mere possibility of Craig's. If God exists, then presumably God decides where people are born and when. This means God has the kind of foreknowledge whereby, before people are born, he knows whether they would believe if they heard the gospel, and he places them on the earth appropriately. But if God has that kind of foreknowledge he could foreknow who would not believe the gospel and never create them in the first place. Then Hotel Hell wouldn't have even one occupant. This possibility makes God out to be barbaric—a God who has the chance to keep people out of hell but doesn't care to do so. *The probability that the Christian God exists is inversely proportional to the amount of religious diversity that exists in the world (i.e., the more religious diversity there in the world, the less probable it is that the Christian God exists), and there is just way too much religious diversity to suppose that he does.*

But Craig isn't done yet. Along with J. P. Moreland, he opines, "We have no way of knowing that in a world of free creatures in which God's existence is as obvious as the nose on your face that more people would come to love him and know his salvation than in the actual world."[9] *No way* of knowing? Are they serious? In this mere possibility they are attributing to human beings an irrationality that I find very disturbing. *The probability that more people would believe is proportional to the amount of evidence that there is for Christianity in the world (i.e., the more evidence for Christianity there is in the world, the more people would believe).* This seems self-evident to me. Possibilities don't count. Only probabilities do. Given the amount of religious diversity in the world, there just isn't enough evidence for more people to believe in Christianity, period.

What Craig describes are mere possibilities, akin to Plantinga's possibility that Satan is the cause of all natural suffering. I wish Christian apologists would stop trying to defeat the logical argument from evil against a good God. But they are simply stuck in that mode of thinking since Plantinga appears to have used it successfully. The problem is that Plantinga was responding to an argument that claimed evil was logically incompatible with a good God. The one Craig is responding to is not that type at all. He cannot respond to a probability type of argument with a possible defense as a thinking adult. Something is clearly wrong with his brain. He is not an honest seeker of the truth. Anyone in today's world who believes there is an eternal conscious torment in hell for even the worse of "sinners" has serious mental health issues. I'm happy to report the traditional hell is on its way out. In this case, if you are an apologist you must reject what Craig is doing, and yet he's recognized as one of the best of the best apologists for Jesus.

Randal Rauser's Responses

Elsewhere I have made a sustained case regarding what I call the *Problem of Divine Miscommunication*.[10] I argue that if God exists and revealed his will through the Bible, then he is an incompetent communicator. He did not have the slightest forethought for how his words would be "misunderstood" by his followers. Because of this, his words authorized the Inquisition, the Crusades, witch hunts, slavery, and the wars after the Protestant Reformation that caused eight million Christians to slaughter each other over things most of them think are silly today. As but one example, all God would have had to say is: "Thou shall not buy or own slaves or beat them into submission." But he didn't.

Christian apologist Randal Rauser responded to my argument by saying:

> Now is [the Bible] as effective as it could be? I just don't think we could say as we are very much in the midst of history. Let's say that in two decades the church reaches a pacifistic unanimity on the texts and this ushers in a time of world peace for the next one hundred thousand years. If this happened, and I don't know why it couldn't, then the text might indeed be maximally effective in the long term for establishing and maintaining the peaceable kingdom. I just don't think we have enough data to go on either way and so the argument Loftus presents appears to me stillborn.[11]

In this case Rauser punts to future possibilities rather than relying on the probabilities of the past and present. But the future hasn't arrived yet, so he cannot rely on it to help solve this problem. Even if the future turns out the way he hopes for, then that future was built on the backs of millions of people who suffered because God did not communicate his revelation clearly to his followers. The so-called revelation we find in the Bible is indistinguishable from God not revealing anything at all. It looks like it was written exclusively by ancient prescientific people who had no clue at all about the future. This has led many people through the ages to reject the Bible as revelation who were presumably cast into hell in the meantime. And Rauser thinks this is all good, that his God could not have done better? *The probability that there is a good, omniscient God behind the revelation in the Bible is inversely proportional to the amount of divine miscommunication we find in it (i.e., the more divine miscommunication we find in it, the less probable a good, omniscient God is behind it), and there is just way too much divine miscommunication in the Bible.*

I've argued we should think exclusively in terms of probabilities. Faith has nothing to do with this reasoning process. Probabilities are all that matter. Faith is superfluous, utterly irrelevant, completely unnecessary, and even irrational. The probabilities are best described in Bayesian terms, something that can be done conceptually without the math. Rauser responded to what I've argued by saying I was wrong, for I left out the word "probably." I should instead say "we should 'probably' think in terms of probabilities," leaving room for the possibility of faith. Others ask me to prove what I say, or ask that I provide irrefutable conclusive scientific evidence for it. Still others say it's practically impossible to think exclusively in terms of probabilities. All of these responses basically prove my point. Why would any rational person argue that we should not think exclusively in terms of probabilities? If the probabilities were on the side of Christianity then apologists would be the first ones touting this and crowing about it.

Rauser is correct though. Whenever I make an argument the reader must almost always inset words like "probable" or improbable" into it. This is a given. But there are more specific words to be inserted, stretching from "virtually impossible" to "virtually certain." In between these two extremes there are a lot of different words that could describe the odds, stretching from "extremely improbable," to "very improbable," to "improbable," to "even odds," to "slightly probable," to "probable," to "very probable," and to "extremely probable." We don't have a word to differentiate between the odds on that continuum stretching from virtually impossible to virtually certain. But does anyone really want to suggest the word "faith" applies to all of these different probabilities, that there is the same amount of faith required to accept any one of them? If so, that is being irrational.

Since Rauser is playing that game then let me say instead that "it is virtually certain (or extremely probable) that we should think exclusively in terms of probabilities." There is no better alternative since this is how to think like a scientist. Science operates on the varying levels of probabilities. It's how we reasonably judge things in every other area of life except religion. Yes, it's possible that we should not think exclusively in terms of probabilities, but that conclusion is such a remote possibility it's a virtually impossible (or extremely improbable) one. No, we don't always do this, so the fact that we don't think exclusively in terms of probabilities is not a criticism at all. We should.

Every Bayesian statistical model has three components: the prior, the consequent (or likelihood) on a particular hypothesis, and the consequent (or likelihood) on that hypothesis being false. So for apologists who keep saying that life doesn't arise from nonlife, and that consciousness is hard to explain without reference to God, or that design implies a designer, the two hypotheses to be compared and contrasted would be (1) the nonsupernatual viewpoint, with the hypothesis that (2) one particular religious sect among the myriads that have existed, presently exist, and will exist in the future is true.

When it comes to providing scientific evidence we must think in Bayesian terms as well. The two hypotheses to be compared are: (1) science helps us arrive at the truth, versus (2) faith helps us arrive at the truth. Since faith has no method and solves no problems the probability that science helps us arrive at the truth is a virtually certain conclusion whereas faith remains a virtually impossible conclusion. You see, we do not have to prove science leads us to think exclusively in terms of probabilities. We only need to show that it is, at the very minimum, extremely probable. But it is more than that.

Probability is all that matters. Faith is irrational. I want to drive this point into the ground once and for all. The problem is that practically nothing is certain. So the word "faith" is used to describe any conclusion of ours that leaves room for doubt. Is it possible I'm dreaming right now? I suppose that's an extremely remote possibility. Is it possible a material world does not exist? I suppose that's an extremely remote possibility too. Is it possible a good omnipotent God exists given the worldwide massive and ubiquitous suffering in it? Again, I suppose that's an extremely remote possibility. So what? Probability is all that matters when it comes to matters of fact about the world we live in. Accepting a conclusion because it's merely possible is irrational. We should never ever do that.

In fact, faith adds nothing to the actual probabilities at all. Having more of it or less of it does not change anything. If we have a "virtually certain" conclusion we don't need faith at all. The *only* sense I can make of the way believers use the word "faith" is that it's an irrational leap over the probabilities. They fill in what the actual probabilities are with faith to stretch an "improbable" conclusion to reach an "extremely probable" one, and that is quite simply irrational. Faith cannot go "beyond reason" because that means it's going beyond the reasonable probabilities. There is no rational way faith can trump reason, or go beyond it, or even be based on it. A probability is a probability is a probability. There are nothing but probabilities in matters of fact about the world.

It could still be the case that God cannot be known by use of the probabilities of reason, that a mere private personal subjective experience of God himself could circumvent all arguments and objective evidence to the contrary. Or, maybe, God values people willing to take an irrational leap of faith more than reasonable people who can only accept what the objective evidence leads them to accept in these matters. Maybe God simply chooses who to reveal himself to, without any rhyme or reason, such that they are rational to believe even though God provides no solid objective evidence for others to believe, and even thwarts our reasoning processes by providing contradictory evidence.

If believers have to resort to any of these kinds of defenses in order to believe, then there is probably little I can say to convince them otherwise. All we can do is look for solid objective evidence and, upon not finding it, reasonable people should not believe. If God wanted us to believe despite this lack of evidence, then for all I know, he could snap his hypothetical fingers and take away my critical thinking capabilities so that I would believe too. Or, he could convert me in a Damascus Road experience like Saul was, who converted without having his free will abrogated. Until such time as that happens, I cannot do differently, nor can I argue differently either. All I can do is focus on the probability of the arguments and the evidence. We need to think exclusively in terms of the probabilities when it comes to matters of fact like the nature of nature and which religion is true, if one is. If God exists and if he created us as reasonable people, then he created us to think this way. He created us to require that which he withholds from us. Strange, that God!

Anomalies or Possibilities?
My claim is that in order to maintain and defend Christianity the Christian must resort to offering possible scenarios at almost every turn. My claim is that the more Christians are forced to resort to these possible scenarios then the less likely their background knowledge is true that forms the backdrop to legitimately use these possible scenarios in the first place.

There are always some anomalies, or unsolved mysteries, that have not yet been solved when we hold certain things to be true. When it comes to these anomalies we place them on the back burner and hope future discoveries or evidence will surface to help us solve them. And we can legitimately try to offer possible answers for how we think these anomalies can be solved. These anomalies are not considered probably true, but only possibly true. In the meantime we interpret them in light of a greater set of background ideas we hold to be probably true. But at almost every turn the Christian faith is based on possibilities. So Christianity can only at best be shown to be possibly true. There is no probability to their background knowledge at all, so resorting to possible scenarios is all they have. Since that is clear to demonstration the Christian faith is only possibly true, not probably true.

Time after time Christians retreat to the merely possible when trying to defend their faith.

- Christians claim it's possible that an eternal 3-in-1 Omni-God has always existed without ever learning anything, or growing incrementally.

- Christians claim it's possible that an immaterial Supreme Being can act in the material universe even though they cannot show how this can be done.

- Christians claim it's possible there is divine intervention in the evolutionary process even though there is no room for it.

- Christians claim it's possible there is an answer to why God allows such massive and ubiquitous suffering in the world.

- Christians claim it's possible there is an explanation for how Jesus is 100 percent God and 100 percent man with nothing left over.

- Christians claim it's possible to gain sure knowledge about the historical past, which is enough to base an ultimate commitment to God upon.

- Christians claim it's possible that Jesus was resurrected even though the tools and methods of the historian don't lead us to think he was.

- Christians claim it's possible to reasonably accept second-hand testimony (at best) of a resurrection found in ancient written sources that cannot be interrogated, but it's not reasonable to accept someone's testimony who claims he levitated without seeing such a thing personally, or without some personal interrogation.

- Christians claim it's possible that miracles occurred in the superstitious past, even though there is no credible evidence they take place in today's world.

- Christians claim God may have possibly done a plethora of miracles in the past and will do so again in the future.

- Christians claim it's possible God can foreknow every human action and yet those same human actions are truly free ones.

- Christians claim it's possible that the billions of people who have never heard the gospel of salvation wouldn't have accepted it even if they had heard it.

- Christians claim it's possible that the Christian faith is true even though evolution has enormous negative implications for religion.

- Christians claim it's possible that petitionary prayers are efficacious even though scientific studies have shown they work just about as well as chance.

- Christians claim it's possible the Christian faith is true and the others are of Satan even though believers in different religious faiths adopt, defend, and believe with near certainty the religion of their culture.

- It's possible Christians are right after all. But then it's possible the Loch Ness Monster exists and is evading our attempts to detect her too!

- Christians must be convinced that their faith is nearly impossible before they will ever consider it to be improbable, which is an utterly unreasonable standard.

The Omniscience Escape Clause
It doesn't matter what the particular problem is for a person's faith. Having an omniscient God concept solves it. It could be the intractable and unanswerable problem of ubiquitous suffering; or how a man could be 100 percent God and 100 percent man without anything leftover, or left out; or how the death of a man on a cross saves us from sins; or why God's failure to better communicate led to massive bloodshed between Christians themselves. It just doesn't matter. God is omniscient. He knows why. He knows best. Therefore punting to God's omniscience makes faith pretty much unfalsifiable, which allows believers to disregard what reason tells them by ignoring the probabilities.

There is only one way to convince believers in an omniscient God that their faith is false. They must be convinced their faith is impossible before they will consider it to be improbable, and that's an utterly unreasonable standard since the arguments to the contrary cannot hope to overcome the *Omniscience Escape Clause*. So think on this: Given that there are so many different faiths with the same escape clause, let believers seriously entertain that their own God might equally be false. Sure, an omniscient God might exist (granted for the sake of argument), but how we judge whether or not he exists cannot rely over and over on his omniscience since that's exactly how other believers defend their own culturally inherited faith. Reasonable people must **not** have an unfalsifiable faith, and yet an omniscient concept of God makes one's faith pretty much unfalsifiable.

Believers must be forced to acknowledge that other believers in different religions (or sects within their own) who have the same concepts have the same exact problems when it comes to reasonably evaluating their own faith.

And they too must be convinced their faith is nearly impossible before they will consider it to be improbable, which is an utterly unreasonable standard of proof, making their faith pretty much unfalsifiable as well. This is something believers reject when it comes to evaluating the probability of other faiths. Why is it they don't reject this when it comes to their own?

My goal is to force believers to see this. They must approach their faith with open eyes given the nature of religious faith concepts. They must have a *gestalt shift* in the way they see their faith. Seeing things differently demands such a paradigm change in the fundamental way people view something. It can be facilitated with more knowledge and evidence of course, but as with any enculturated or indoctrinated mind, it might not produce a change. It demands a willingness to see the Christian faith differently. Nothing less than that will do the trick.

9

You Must Gerrymander for God

I have used the term "logical gerrymandering" to describe what Christian apologists do in unfairly "redistricting" what people like me say out of context, in order to gain an unfair intellectual advantage, or to ridicule us. I also use this phrase to describe what Christians do when caught in an inconsistency. Calvinists, for instance, claim God decrees (or ordains) everything we desire to do and everything we do, yet they want to describe God as good, and blame us alone for everything bad we do. Using a flood of words they *logically gerrymander* around this inconsistency.

The first person I know of to use this term outside of political spheres is Walter Kaufmann, in his 1958 book, *Critique of Religion and Philosophy*, although he merely calls it "gerrymandering." He claimed

> many theologians are masters of this art. Theologians do not just do this incidentally: this is theology. Doing theology is like doing a jigsaw puzzle in which the verses of Scripture are the pieces: the finished picture is prescribed by each denomination, with a certain latitude allowed. What makes the game so pointless is that you do not have to use all the pieces, and that pieces which do not fit may be reshaped after pronouncing the words 'this means.' That is called exegesis.[1]

Kaufmann knew in advance there would be theologians who would *gerrymander* the words in his book. He said: "This *Critique* is exceptionally vulnerable to slander by quotation and critics cursed with short breath, structure blindness, and myopia will be all but bound to gerrymander it." So Kaufmann quipped:

Quotations can slander
if you gerrymander.[2]

Of course, the principle of charity is the exact opposite of gerrymandering and is the way to deal with intellectual opponents. It is also akin to how Christians believe they should deal with people in general (1 Corinthians 13). If we followed this principle when dealing with opponents we'll be less likely to commit the informal fallacy of attacking a strawman, and thereby less likely to make fools of ourselves. However, that being said, if you want to be an apologist you must gerrymander for God since so many of the best apologists do. If you want to be a *good* apologist, you shouldn't do this at all. But then if you didn't do it at all, you wouldn't be an apologist at all.

What follows are five different ways Christian apologists gerrymander for God. It's sort of a potpourri of cases showing the same phenomenon.

1. You Must Depend on the *Tu Quoque* "You Too" Fallacy

When encountering the many difficult problems of your faith, you must do as other recognized apologists do by repeatedly depending on the *tu quoque* or "you too" informal fallacy. This fallacy is committed when someone skirts the impact of an argument by claiming the person making it speaks or acts in a way hypocritical to it. It's the fallacy of hypocrisy by which someone cannot make an argument if he or she maintains a position that undercuts it.

The Example of C. S. Lewis

My first example comes from C. S. Lewis, who offered what I consider one of the most asinine arguments I've heard, attempting to exonerate his God from the problem of suffering. It concerns whether an atheist can make that argument without an objective standard to know evil. Now I don't usually call Christian arguments asinine, so hear me out.

In *Mere Christianity*, C. S. Lewis argues from the start that there can be no evil without absolute goodness (God) to measure it against. "A man does not call a line crooked unless he has some idea of a straight line" (*Mere Christianity*, II, 1). In other words, I need some sort of objective moral in order to say something is morally evil. But the word "evil" here is used both as a term describing the fact that there is suffering, and at the same time it's used as a moral term to describe whether or not such suffering makes the belief in a good God improbable, and that's an equivocation in the word's usage. The fact that there is suffering is undeniable. Whether it makes the belief in a good God improbable is the subject for debate.

Let's talk about pain—the kind that turns our stomachs. Why is there so much of it when there is supposedly a perfectly good omnipotent God? The amount of intense suffering in this world makes the belief in a good God improbable from a theistic perspective, and I may be a relativist, a pantheist, or a witchdoctor and still ask about the internal consistency of what a theist believes.

The dilemma for the theist is to reconcile senseless suffering in the world with his own beliefs (not mine) that all suffering is for a greater good. It's an internal problem for the theist and the atheist is merely using the logical tool for assessing arguments called the *reductio ad absurdum*, which attempts to reduce to absurdity the claims of a person. The technique is to force a claimant to choose between accepting the consequences of what he or she believes, no matter how absurd it seems, or to reject one or more premises in his argument. The person making this argument does not believe the claimant and is trying to show why his or her beliefs are misguided and false to some degree, depending on the force of the counterargument. It's that simple. If atheists cannot use this argument here on this issue then we should disallow all *reductio ad absurdum*-type arguments. Just ask yourself whether, in order to show George Berkeley's *idealism* argument implausible, you must first abandon your view that there is a material world, and you'll see what I mean.

Christian theists argue that in the natural world nothing can count as evil for the atheist, since everything that happens is part of nature. So, they claim atheists have no objective basis for arguing there is any evil in the natural world that can count against the existence of the Christian God. But this is fallacious reasoning. What counts as evil in my atheist worldview is a separate problem from the Christian problem of evil. They are distinctly separate issues. Christians cannot seek to answer their internal problem by claiming atheists also have a problem with evil. Yet, that's exactly what they do here. Christians must deal with their internal problem. Atheists must do likewise. I will not skirt my specific problem by claiming Christians have one. They shouldn't do it either.

The fact that many professional philosophers agree with me on this can be seen in reading through the book, *The Evidential Argument from Evil*, edited by Daniel Howard-Snyder.[3] Not one scholarly Christian theist attempted to make this argument in that book—not Richard Swinburne, not Alvin Plantinga, not William Alston, not Stephen Wykstra, not Peter Van Inwagen, and not Daniel Howard-Snyder. I suggest it's because they know it is not dealing with the problem at all. They recognize it as a bogus argument, and obviously so.

That this is a theistic problem can be settled once and for all by merely reminding Christians that they would still have to deal with this problem even if no atheist ever raised it. It would still be a serious problem for the Christian view of God. The Christian would still have to satisfactorily answer the problem. So to turn around and argue that as an atheist I need to have an objective moral standard to make this argument is nonsense. It's an internal problem that would still demand an answer if no atheist ever argued for it. The problem of suffering is one of the reasons why Process Theologians have conceded that God is not omnipotent. It didn't take atheists to persuade them to abandon God's omnipotence at all. The problem speaks for itself.

The Example of Victor Reppert
My second example comes from Christian apologist Victor Reppert, who claims scientists too have the same cognitive biases that he has as a Christian apologist. Well that's true of course. The results of the social sciences have confirmed several biases we have as human beings and have conclusively shown us we believe what we prefer to believe. In fact, when faced with contrary evidence we actually dig our feet in deeper into what we believe, depending on our vested interests. Okay so far? Wait, let's start from the beginning. He says,

> Science is not a monolithic "method" that can be applied across the board to deal with questions all the way from whether there are four bonds on a carbon atom to the question of whether your wife is faithful, or when abortion is justified, or whether it is wrong to inflict pain on little children for your own amusement. There's no magic pill that will make us stop this tendency, except being aware that wishful thinking is possible and considering that when you think.

Reppert merely offers some examples to show that science cannot tell us about everything. I think it can tell us a great deal though. Trust me. Science can indeed tell us if a spouse has been unfaithful, unless Reppert hasn't a clue what science is or what a private investigator can do with a hidden camera. Science looks at the evidence. If there is evidence for an unfaithful spouse then we know he or she has been unfaithful. Ask criminal detectives and they look at the evidence for crimes just as private investigators look for the evidence of an unfaithful spouse. How did Reppert miss this?

Reppert continues, saying, "Some subjects are experimentable, and some are not." This is a mere assertion. How do we know this for sure? Science is based on the empirical evidence that we gather with our five senses and any scientific instruments that augment them, like the microscope or the telescope. If empirical evidence plus sound reasoning based on that evidence cannot settle something then what can? Even if there are areas where science cannot investigate, like the intersubjectivity of our private experiences, how does this apply to what Reppert is really getting at, the existence of his God? If science cannot help settle whether his God exists, what makes him think there is a better method? Faith? If his God exists then he should be detectable. Science operates on that which is detectable. That which is not detectable cannot be known by any reliable method at all. So if God cannot be detectable and if science is the only sure way we can know God then it's wrongheaded to blame science for this. God is to be blamed for creating a world where science works so well, who subsequently doesn't allow himself to be detectable by science. Get. Point. The.

Science has a built-in corrective in that it only deals with objective facts. To answer that Reppert knows his God exists subjectively leaves so many questions left unanswered it's hard to know where to start, especially since people all over the world claim the exact same thing for their particular god-beliefs that contradict his particular god-belief. Next Reppert turns to scientists themselves:

> Even when they are experimentable, scientists who hold the theory that "loses" the experiment don't just give up on their theories. They adjust their theories to deal with the negative experimental results, using auxiliary hypotheses. In fact, they can go on doing this forever if they feel the need to. They usually quit when they die off. It's a myth that Michelson-Morley caused a complete and immediate abandonment of ether theory. So there is no such thing as a "crucial experiment" in science. That's just basic philosophy of science going back to Pierre Duhem.[4]

In my opinion Reppert is not that far off the mark here (except the "forever" part, really Vic, "forever"?). After all, if nothing else this is exactly what cognitive bias theory predicts. Science is a human enterprise and as such some scientists have maintained their pet theories for a long time after they had been shown false by others. This usually takes place on the cutting edges of science though, not on the overwhelming consensus that takes place after science moves on to other fruitful questions.

Let me make three observations here: First, if cognitive biases inhibit the scientist when facing hard cold evidence counter to what was expected, then how much more will cognitive biases operate in the mind of a believer when there are no mutually agreed-upon scientific experiments that can disconfirm one's faith! Second, Reppert paints a picture of a mad scientist that is utterly divorced from reality even given cognitive bias theory ("forever"?). He has never been a scientist and hasn't a clue what it means to write a peer-reviewed article in a scientific journal. I don't think any scientist is determined to undermine religious faith by skewing any results. For there is always a peer-reviewed process based on the evidence presented. No scientist wants to be branded by his or her peers as skewing the evidence in favor of anything. With important discoveries backed by the evidence and accepted by peers, scientists can make names for themselves and have a place in the history of science. Why is it that whenever a scientist discovers something that goes against religious faith the believer thinks he or she had an agenda to do so? Oh, that's right, this is what Christians say about anyone who rejects their particular faith! Third and finally, science has progressed despite the personal biases of a few stubborn scientists. It has literally changed our world because of the evidence. Where, by contrast, is the progress among religionists?

2. You Must Depend on Definitional Apologetics

Another way to gerrymander for God is to become an expert in obfuscation by playing semantic games with words, what I call "definitional apologetics." You must twist their meaning beyond recognition in many cases. If done effectively the nonbeliever will be forced to chase you down that never-ending rabbit's hole of definitions so you won't have to deal in concrete examples like an incarnate God who was born of a virgin, who healed a man born blind from birth, who calmed a storm and walked on water, who raised a man up from the dead, and who was himself resurrected and then ascended into the sky from where he presumably came, and from where he will come again (if he hasn't already). You won't have to deal with axe heads that could float, snakes and donkeys that could talk, long hair that could give a man superhuman strength, and a great fish that could swallow a man who lived to tell about it, along with the healing powers of handkerchiefs, shadows, skirts, and pools in the ancient superstitious prescientific past.

Take for instance Randal Rauser's definition of faith, that it "consists of assent to a proposition that is conceivably false," something I've analyzed in detail.[5] How is this definition remotely what Jesus describes in Matthew 17:20:

> I tell you the truth, if you have faith as small as a mustard seed, you can say to this mountain, 'Move from here to there' and it will move. Nothing will be impossible for you.

How legitimate can it be to define faith in such a way that the original Christian did not? Rauser's definition is foreign to the views of Jesus. It is intended to obfuscate that faith consists of a leap beyond (or over) the actual probabilities. He uses this definition to say atheists have faith too. The goal is to obfuscate the fact that believing the sun stood still, or that it backed up a stairway, is the same thing atheists do when arriving at scientific conclusions based on solid sufficient evidence, because we could all conceivably be wrong.

From this apologists like Rauser go on the claim atheism is a religion, or that atheists have religious faith.[6] If we do, then please define religion in such a way that it equally applies to people who disbelieve in supernatural forces/

beings and to people who believe in them. Hint, it cannot be done. Rauser goes on to claim that atheists worship science in our cowritten book *God or Godless?*[7] What can worship mean unless it means ascribing ultimate worth to an ultimate being, something no atheist does?[8]

Christian apologists play other semantic word games with the same obfuscatory goals in mind. The goal is to bring down real knowledge based on sufficient scientific evidence into the realm of faith. This is nothing but a word game that only believers will accept. And accept it they do, because they need to believe. Christian philosopher Matt Flannagan has misused the argument of philosopher of science Larry Laudan, that there is no clear demarcation between science and nonscience.[9] Flannagan argues this undercuts the method of science in an attempt to bring science down to the level of faith. But the problem of defining the precise demarcation point between science and nonscience is not a problem for science at all. It's like trying to specify which whisker, when plucked, no longer leaves us with a beard, an informal fallacy. Just because we may not be able to define the exact point between science and nonscience doesn't mean there isn't a difference. There is most emphatically a difference between science and nonscience. It does nothing to show there is a small point at which they may converge.

But wait! There is more.

What is skepticism? Evangelical apologist Thomas Talbott claims he is a true skeptic because he is skeptical of skepticism.[10] What can that possibly mean? Skepticism is a filter we subject claims to. We cannot doubt that filter without letting in all kinds of unsupported claims. But yes, I'll grant he's skeptical, but it's merely a faith-based skepticism as opposed to a science-based skepticism. Ed Babinski lists several things Christians have been skeptical about, including: Satan, cats, forks, Christmas and other holidays, plays, the use of musical instruments in church, the abolition of slavery, the right of women to vote, child labor laws, educational information about Sex and birth control, condoms, anesthesia and anesthetics, cures for malaria and syphilis, inoculations and vaccinations, striped clothes, split-breeches, short dresses, long hair (on men), short hair (on women), drinking, dancing, rock-and-roll music, playing cards (or billiards or pool), going to the movies, watching TV, masturbating, dishwashers, democracy, working or playing on Sunday, and, touching women. By contrast, a true skepticism is science-based.[11]

What is naturalism? Randal Rauser claims we cannot define it unless we contrast it with supernaturalism, thus bringing supernaturalism in the back door with our attempts to define it.[12] I could reverse this strategy easily enough by saying he cannot define supernaturalism without contrasting it with naturalism. In any case, here is a good enough definition of naturalism: All that exists is matter in motion.

What is an extraordinary event? It's an "out of the ordinary" one, I reply. The more "out of the ordinary" it is then the more extraordinary it is, and the more evidence needed to substantiate it. If someone claimed to levitate then we would need more than his testimony to accept it. "But," says a Christian apologist, "you still have not precisely defined what you mean." "I know," I reply. I give concrete examples. Words can be very difficult to define and this is an important goal, but I'm not playing your obfuscatory language game. So I prefer to talk in terms of concrete examples.

I find all of these attempts to be semantic obfuscatory games, plain and simple. This is the kind of intellectual gerrymandering we expect from believers. When pressed against the wall they will say anything to defend their faith. Stephen Law, as quoted earlier, is right: "Anything based on faith, no matter how ludicrous, can be made to be consistent with the available evidence, given a little patience and ingenuity."[13] It reminds me of a story:

Consider the oft repeated story of the man who thought he was dead. He went to his doctor, who tried to reason with the man that he was really still alive. Finally the doctor asked the man, "Do dead men bleed? If you cut a dead man, does he bleed?" The man replied, "No. The heart is not beating, there is no blood pressure, so if you cut a dead man, he does not bleed." The doctor then took a scalpel and nicked the man on his finger, and he proceeded to bleed. As the blood continued to come forth, the doctor said to the man, "See, you are bleeding. What does that tell you?" And the man answered, "Well, I guess dead men do bleed after all."

This story illustrates what skeptics see over and over again, and why faith is irrational. Believers will either deny the evidence or they will reinterpret their faith to adjust to the evidence. Only a very rare few of them will ever seriously question faith itself.

3. You Must Ignore Arguments You Cannot Answer

If you want to be a Christian apologist you must ignore objections to your faith that cannot be answered. Sweep them under the rug in hopes the faithful won't hear of them. Consider two Christian apologetics books. The first one is titled *Holy War in the Bible: Christian Morality and an Old Testament Problem*, edited by Heath A. Thomas, Jeremy Evans, and Paul Copan (InterVarsity Press, 2014). These evangelicals are dealing with the problem of holy war in the Bible. Well, Hector Avalos's book, *Fighting Words: The Origins of Religious Violence* (Prometheus Books, 2005) is not mentioned at all even though he offers some trenchant criticisms of the biblical view in his book.

Who is Dr. Avalos?

Hector is a Harvard-trained biblical scholar, that's who. Can the contributor's to this anthology do enough research to find out who offers the best critiques of their faith, or do they simply ignore the best criticisms of it in hopes no one notices? Pseudo-intellectuals do not engage the best critiques, so I can only conclude the authors in the book are pseudo-intellectuals.

Another author these scholars neglected to mention, or engage, is Dr. David Eller, a critically acclaimed author and anthropology professor who wrote the book *Cruel Creeds, Virtuous Violence: Religious Violence across Culture and History* (Prometheus Books, 2010). Until Christian scholars can do better research and engage the best of the best critiques, this evangelical book is nothing but special pleading, and here's how it works: "We know God is good so let's make the data fit our preconceived beliefs somehow, no matter how much gerrymandering it takes."

A second book that exemplars this same thing, edited by Steven B. Cowan and Terry L. Wilder, is titled, *In Defense of the Bible: A Comprehensive Apologetic for the Authority of Scripture* (Broadman and Holman, 2013). As we read through Cowan and Wilder's book we see little more than special pleading and cognitive bias running amuck. "We know the Bible is true so therefore it is." I have little hopes of convincing true believers of this, but having once lapped up this stuff it's clear as day this is what the authors are doing. It reads like something one would expect to see from Mormon scholars who put out their own defenses of their so-called inspired books.

This book purports to be "a comprehensive apologetic for the authority of scripture," but look at the books representing evangelical thinking that they ignore. There is no reference to Peter Enns's books, *Inspiration and Incarnation: Evangelicals and the Problem of the Old Testament* (Baker Academic 2005) and *The Evolution of Adam: What the Bible Does and Doesn't Say About Human Origins* (Brazos Press, 2012). There isn't any mention of Kenton L. Sparks's book, *God's Word in Human Words: An Evangelical Appropriation of Critical Biblical Scholarship* (Baker Academic 2008). Nor is there mention of Christian Smith's book, *The Bible Made Impossible: Why Biblicism Is Not a Truly Evangelical Reading of Scripture* (Brazos Press, 2012). Each of these books more than adequately destroy the thesis of Cowan and Wilder's book.

I consider a pseudo-intellectual someone who does not take on the strongest criticisms of the thesis being proposed, and the authors in Cowan and Wilder's book do not do this. Bart Ehrman's earlier work was addressed a bit, but now with his book, *Forgery and Counter Forgery: the Use of Literary Deceit in Early Christian Polemics* (Oxford University Press, 2012), I think all critics have been effectively silenced. When it comes to higher criticism of the Old Testament, I was amazed that Richard Elliot Friedman's book, *Who Wrote the Bible* (HarperOne, 1987) wasn't mentioned or dealt with. Even if there has been some further reflection about Friedman's book since 1987, it is still considered to be one of the best in recent years. When it comes to higher criticism of the New Testament, G. A. Wells's book, *Cutting Jesus Down to Size: What Higher Criticism Has Achieved and Where it Leaves Christianity* (Open Court, 2009) is a tour de force. Yet it isn't dealt with at all. Neither was Thom Stark's book, *The Human Faces of God: What Scripture Reveals When It Gets God Wrong* (And *Why Inerrancy Tries To Hide It)* (Wipf & Stock Pub., 2011) It's also a tour de force when it comes to genocide, and it's even recommended by evangelical-leaning thinkers.

This, my friends, is not scholarship. When it comes to slavery in the Bible, Hector Avalos's book, *Slavery, Abolitionism, and the Ethics of Biblical Scholarship* (Sheffield Phoenix Press, 2013) absolutely destroys any attempt to argue the Bible does not condone slavery. And *The Women's Bible Commentary: Expanded Edition*, edited by Carol A. Newsom and Sharon H. Ringe (Westminster John Knox Press, 1998), destroys any hope of arguing the Bible is not sexist.

It's so sad to see this, but that's what I see. Most evangelical Christians will never pick up and read any of the books I mentioned. They don't even know they exist because the authors in Cowan and Wilder's book don't mention them or deal at length with any of their substantive arguments. What most evangelical Christians are looking for is a confirmation of what they already believe. They are not looking for arguments to the contrary because they would prefer to believe what they do. It's confirmation bias running amuck. If you are an honest Christian, then after reading this book by Cowan and Wilder, read just one of the books I mentioned above, just one. Try it. Become informed. What are you afraid of if you really want to know the truth? Just one. If you depend on Cowan and Wilder's book it will mistakenly lead you to think the Bible is inerrantly true without telling the reader they are not dealing with the best objections to the contrary, some of which come from other evangelicals. Of that I am sure, and I have been on both sides of the fence.

Some people have commented that from time to time I've been too hard on these poor pitiful apologists. But seriously, given the track record of the best of the best of them how can I think otherwise? The ball is in their court. They could change my mind. Deal with the best arguments out there. Convince me you are honestly searching for the truth. Convince me your brain has not deadened your desire to know.

4. You Must Demand What Nonbelievers Are Not Obliged to Produce

Nonbelievers don't have the burden of proof, as I successfully argued in my book *The Outsider Test for Faith*. We don't have to prove theistic claims are false either, nor must we offer objective evidence that nonbelief is more rational or probable. Christian apologists for their specific Christian theisms must do that, if for no other reason because nonbelief is the position of nonbelief. Get it? Most believers won't get it, but it is as I say. Nonbelievers aren't affirming anything. We may deny something but we don't have to. All we need to do is remain unpersuaded by any specific case presented on behalf of any given deity's existence.

Take Dr. David Marshall, please! He wrote a rambling, lackluster, wide-of-the-mark review on Amazon of my anthology *Christianity Is Not Great: How Faith Fails*. First off, he complained the book was a lopsided presentation of the harms of Christianity, neglecting the good that Christianity has done in the past and is doing today. Marshall demanded we tell the whole story, not just the bad but also the good. Get that? Based on his objection readers shouldn't trust what we have to say because, well, it's clear we have an axe to grind against Christianity. The book is an unbalanced one, he argues. It's not a fair representation of the case. It represents that of the prosecution, which as we all know, can be a skewed one that takes the guilt of the defendant as a given.

Ladies and gentlemen of the jury, I most emphatically object.

Even if Christianity has been overall good for the world, the harms it has done need to be explained rather than explained away. Since so many Christians are beating the drum day and night about how great Christianity is, we focused on the harms it causes. The book is big enough without having to make it bigger by telling of the good that Christians have done. Consider that anthology a book that tells the rest of the story. It really hasn't been told before, not by Christian apologists like Marshall. It represents the corrective to their nonobjective telling of Christian history. So they shouldn't complain about this to us. If they had told the whole story of the church, we wouldn't have had to do so. We're under no obligation to tell the other side of the story when they refuse to tell the side we're telling.

5. You Must Fail to Ask the Right Questions, the Key Ones

David Marshall again. In that same book review of his we learn another thing apologists worthy of the name must do. *If you want to be an apologist fail to ask the right questions, the key ones.* Marshall wrote: "If you want to claim Christianity had a bad impact on society, you must first ask, and answer honestly, what was the state of society before Christians showed up. That, the authors of this book seldom do." This is the fatal flaw of Marshall's whole review. He failed to ask the right question—the prior question—the key question—and answer it honestly. *Why were previous societies in such a poor state before Christianity showed up?* This question grants his view that they were in poor shape for the sake of argument. Granting it, where was his God before the time Christianity showed up? Did his God not have the means or power to keep those societies from going bad in the first place?

Take slavery for instance. Why did Marshall's God not do something about it prior to the rise of Christianity? Did he not care for slave girls before that time? If Christianity cleaned up the mess that societies were in, then what accounts for the mess they were in? If Christianity can be credited with the abolition of slavery (which it cannot), why didn't his God care for enslaved people prior to the rise of Christianity? Furthermore, why did it also take his God so long to do something about slavery after Christianity arose?

What Marshall is doing is using a misguided view that Christianity has been overall good for the world as an apologetic, without ever consciously considering that there were real people who lived prior to the rise of Christianity who suffered because his God didn't care for them. They too were supposedly created by a perfectly loving God. They too needed God's love, help, compassion, and guidance. But according to Marshall's view God waited for the rise of Christianity before helping these societies. God apparently waited to help them in order to show the world afterward the benefits of Christianity. So given the need to defend Christianity Marshall shows no concern, no empathy for the people prior to Christianity. They only serve as an apologetic. Marshall cannot allow himself to step inside their skins and feel the lash of the slave owner before Christianity showed up. These people are mere fodder for defending the goodness of Christianity, that's all. They are nonpeople, nonpersons. They are to be thought of just as their masters thought of them.

The lack of empathy toward other people is a very dangerous thing. It also keeps believers from accepting the truth about their faith. If you were a slave, standing with your family on the auction block under the threat of the blood-soaked cowskin, and you watched as your family members were bought by different masters never to be seen again, wouldn't you wish the Christian God had helped eradicate slavery much earlier or consistently condemned it from the very beginning? God's defenders simply lack empathy for these people. They refuse to feel their pain. They need to feel it if they honestly want to know the truth. But they can't allow it, since they must defend the faith no matter what the cost. Their faith acts like an anesthetic, deadening the pain they might have for these slaves. Faith is the opiate of the masses in this sense, too, following Karl Marx. People on opium don't have clear heads when it comes to the truth.

10

You Must Master
the Art of Mischaracterization

It surprises me the lengths Christians will go to mischaracterize an argument. It takes madness. I have argued they should not trust their brain. It's lying to them. It didn't evolve to search for truth. The first step is to know this. The second step is to train it to think like a scientist. The brain seems to find truths inadvertently through trial and error. Science augments the truth finding capabilities already in our brain. The person who does not think like a scientist will be the person who, more likely than not, mischaracterizes arguments.

If you want to be an apologist you must master the art of mischaracterization, since so many of the best apologists do. If you want to be a *good* apologist, you shouldn't do this at all. But then if you didn't do it at all, you wouldn't be an apologist at all. Two such examples of mastering the art of mischaracterization are Christian apologists Drs. John Dickson and David Marshall. In my 2013 book, *The Outsider Test for Faith*, I dealt decisively with every major objection to that test. In what follows I'll comment on Dickson and then more extensively on Marshall, since what they wrote has to do with the OTF and requires my attention too.

The Mischaracterizations of John Dickson
John Dickson is a senior research fellow of the Department of Ancient History, Macquarie University, Australia, codirector of the Centre for Public Christianity, and the author of more than a dozen books. In March 2015 he wrote about hearing an atheist repeat the following "atheist joke," as he calls it—"There have been 10,000 gods through history. You reject 9,999 of them. I just go one god further!"—which he described as both silly and laughable.

> For one thing, believers in any particular religion do not reject the other gods in toto. . . . There is, in other words, an irreducible shared core of conviction among most worshipers: we all hold that the rational order of the universe is best explained by the existence of an almighty Mind (or Minds) behind it all. [1]

Therefore, Dickson says, "Atheists are simply misguided to liken a Christian's rejection of particular versions of divinity with the atheist's denial of divinity altogether." He then offers a marriage analogy, comparing the atheist rejection of all deities to a celibate person who might say to a married man: "When you consider why you rejected other women in favour of your wife, then you will see the good sense of rejecting marriage altogether."

Dickson is mischaracterizing the heart of this atheist aphorism, the more sophisticated version of which can be found in my book on the OTF. A bit later I'll deal more extensively with Dickson's superficial understanding of religions, when commenting on Marshall's own superficiality. Three points should be made here though. First, the only agreement between all believers is that supernatural being(s) and/or force(s) exist. That's why it's very difficult to even define the word "religion." Dickson is too steeped in Westernized religions to see this for what it is. Sure, we would expect all supernaturalists to agree about supernaturalism, you see. But that's where any agreement ends. Second, there is no such thing as a nebulous religion with a social grouping of adherents who merely worship "an almighty Mind." There are only *particular* religions with *particular* gods who are worshipped by *particular* groups of people who share *particular* beliefs preached by *particular* religious leaders. All religion is particular and localized, having specific beliefs that worshippers must adhere to if they want to be part of a given religious group. For instance, the Christianity adhered to in different locations around the world is different from each other, sometimes in huge ways.[2] So given that this is the case, particular religionists do in fact reject each other's particular religion.

I argue there is no such thing as theism, or Christian theism, or "Mere Christianity."[3] First, there are many varieties of theism. Islam is a theism, as is Judaism. Polytheism is theism. So is pantheism and panentheism. Deism is one too, at least earlier versions of it. There are many varieties of Christian theism, as we know all too well, which includes existential Christian theism, mystical Christian theism, Process theism, and Open theism (the evangelical sect from Process theism). Historically there have been many varieties of Christian theism like the various "heretical" ones that were condemned and killed off, some of which can be seen in Bart Ehrman's book, *Lost Christianities: The Battles for Scripture and the Faiths We Never Knew.*[4] Most other Christian theisms are represented by the various Christian denominations and so-called cults. These various sects all began as cults anyway, and I'm not about to get involved telling churches who claim to be Christians they are not Christians.

Finally, what about Dickson's analogy? I swear I could fill up a small book with the number of times Christian apologists have offered up something disanalogous to the actual point. They'll take something we all agree on, something undeniable in the real world, and act as if that real world example applies to God. We know there are married people and we know there are celibates, okay. What we don't know is if there is a God and that God is the one Dickson worships. So ignoring the question of the lack of evidence for the existence of God, Dickson substitutes the question of whom to marry, if anyone, when we know that eligible partners for marriages exist. The point of the atheist aphorism is that believers in different particularized religions reject other particularized gods because of the lack of sufficient evidence and the abundance of incoherent concepts. So believers themselves should be consistent and reject their own religions for the same reasons. Now someone like Dickson can argue there is sufficient evidence to believe in one particularized deity out of the others. But I don't see anything silly or laughable about the aphorism itself, when grasped for what it is.

In fact, the requirement for sufficient evidence applies to the existence of other beings that are believed to exist. The same things could be said about the existence of unicorns, hobbits, trolls, devils, angels, fairies, and all sorts of mythical beasts. If some people were to argue for the existence of trolls but deny the existence of the others, I could reasonably say I go one mythical being further, by rejecting them all for the same reason they reject all but one, the lack of sufficient evidence. That which is common here is faith. The Irish people in Ireland still have the power to derail a road project because the townsfolk think leprechauns live in the rocks that the road crews want to dynamite. What objective evidence do these folks have for such a belief? None. Now Christians think there is evidence for God just like the Irish locals think they have evidence for leprechauns. I reject both beliefs for the same reason, the lack of sufficient evidence.

Dickson replied to my unicorn and mythical beast comparison by saying these beasts could be observed if they existed, whereas "God by definition is not part of the universe. He can no sooner be observed in the universe than an architect can be found in a room of the house—even if you search long and hard!"[5] Seriously? If God is placed beyond the reach of our five senses and the scientific instruments that augment our senses (like microscopes, telescopes, and so forth), then he has been placed beyond detection at all. How convenient! This does not get Dickson off the hook though, for he believes

God acted in history and still does today. If we don't have sufficient evidence to conclude God acted in history or in today's world, we don't have sufficient evidence to believe he has acted at all. And a nondetectable or nonacting God is indistinguishable from no god at all.

The Mischaracterizations of David Marshall

I must admit I like David Marshall. He's highly educated, knowledgeable about a wide range of issues, pretty damn smart, very passionate, and kinda funny, like me. He's written and edited a number of books and maintains a blog, like me. If you search the web you'll find him almost everywhere there's a serious debate between Christianity and atheism, sort of like me. He reviews books on Amazon and comments there, like me. He's polite until he meets up with what he considers sheer ignorance or is personally maligned, like me. He's indefatigable, like me. I gotta love a guy like that!

But Marshall also dogs my steps every step along the way. He has monitored my blog and my writings to argue with me. Seems he thinks I'm important or something. He's not interested in an honest search for truth, as I wrote about in chapter 3. Instead he has the truth and seeks to disabuse me of my arguments, and with them any influence I might have. He's written reviews for each of my books and those reviews are all about as good as his book, the one I'll be discussing in this chapter. More than anything else coming from Christian apologists, Marshall majors in mischaracterization as an art form. At his level of education and understanding he exemplifies it more than anyone else.

First of all I am thankful that at a very minimum Marshall claims in his book to embrace the OTF,[6] unlike other Christian scholars who disagree with it, which is good as far as that goes. (I included an introduction to the OTF in chapter 6 of this present book.) Even though Marshall says he embraces the core point or overall aim of the OTF, none of his criticisms of it make any reasonable sense. He first wrote a chapter on the OTF,[7] then he later expanded it into a book titled, *How Jesus Passes the Outsider Test: The Inside Story*.[8] Marshall must be very happy at the reviews that first came in on this book. He's been likened to G. K. Chesterton and C. S. Lewis, who represent the best of the best Christian apologists of the last century. Whether this is true of him or not (surely not), I don't think much of Chesterton or Lewis. My overall opinion of Marshall's book is the exact opposite. Marshall offers nothing in rebuttal to the OTF. He provides nothing as an alternative to the OTF. And his four reformulated tests offered in defense of his particular brand of Christianity are extremely lame. His book as a whole is completely irrelevant to the truth of Christianity and he doesn't even realize it. That's because he badly mischaracterized it.

Marshall's first mischaracterization is that he claims I'm presenting the OTF "as an argument against Christianity."[9] Now I do think the OTF ends up being a good argument against the Christian faith, but in my book I go out of my way to make clear it's merely a test for faith. My conclusion is that Christianity fails the test, that's all. There are three stages in OTF argumentation: (1) we must acknowledge the problem of religious diversity and dependency; (2) we should accept the test as the best and only alternative to know which religion is true, if one is; and (3) then and only then can we debate faith based on the test. In the second stage I argue the test is neither unfair nor faulty. It allows for a faith to pass the test, as well as for all faiths to fail the test. In the third stage I argue the test shows Christianity fails the test, but that's not actually part of accepting the test itself.

Another mischaracterization of Marshall's is that he dismisses my understanding of religious diversity as "superficial," much like Dickson said the atheist aphorism above was laughable. Marshall opines that this is the "most essential problem with Loftus' version of the OTF."[10] He tries to inform the uninformed that the diversity of faiths is, "genuine, but in some ways superficial. As Chesterton noted, religions around the world commonly included four beliefs: in God, the gods, philosophy, and demons." Agreeing, Marshall says, "Peel away labels, and many beliefs seem to be universal or at least widespread."[11] Now I must strongly object to this mischaracterization. His view of religious diversity is the superficial one, as is Dickson's analogy laughable.

Marshall should first of all know there are major disagreements about these four minimal beliefs. Religionists accept the existence of one supernatural being (i.e., one God), or many supernatural beings (gods, goddesses, angels, spirits, ghosts, demons), or they accept one supernatural force (Process theology, deism), or many supernatural forces (i.e., karma, fate, reincarnation, prayers, incantations, spells, omens, voodoo dolls)—or some combination of them. Religionists also disagree with each other over who these beings or forces are, how they operate, and for whom they operate. Everything else is up for grabs. When it comes to the Devil, for instance, only some versions of Christianity accept his existence. And philosophy? Define it and we all do it, all of us. The root meaning of the word is to "love wisdom." What we should look for is whether or not we agree when we think about the nature of nature. And it's crystal clear that we don't.

To really understand the problem of religious diversity Marshall should have paid more attention to what I said in my book. Professor of anthropology David Eller tells us about the precise nature of religious diversity, as I quoted on pages 34–36 of my book, that "there are many religions in the world, and they are different from each other in multiple and profound ways. Not all religions refer to gods, nor do all make morality a central issue, etc. No religion is 'normal' or 'typical' of all religions; the truth is in the diversity." When it comes to belief in god(s), I quoted Eller as saying,

> Many or most religions have functioned quite well without any notions of god(s) at all, and others have mixed god(s) with other beliefs such that god-beliefs are not the critical parts of the religion. . . . Some religions that refer to or focus on gods believe them to be all-powerful, but others do not. Some consider them to be moral agents, and some do not; more than a few gods are downright immoral. Some think they are remote, while others think they are close (or both simultaneously). Some believe that the gods are immortal and eternal, but others include stories of gods dying and being born . . . not all gods are creators, nor is creation a central feature or concern of all religions. . . . Finally, there is not even always a firm boundary between humans and gods; humans can become gods, and the gods may be former humans.

I also quoted Eller as saying:

> Ordinarily we think of a religion as a single homogeneous set of beliefs and practices. The reality is quite otherwise: Within any religion there is a variety of beliefs and practices—and interpretations of those beliefs and practices—distributed throughout space and time. Within the so-called world religions this variety can be extensive and contentious, one or more variations regarded as "orthodox."

I concluded with this final quote from Eller, that

> religion is much more diverse than most people conceive. . . . "Religion" does not equal "theism" and certainly not "Christianity," let alone any particular sect of Christianity. Indeed, there is no specific religion or type of religion that is really religion, the very essence or nature of religion. . . . Not only that, there is no central or essential or uniquely authentic theism but rather an array of theisms. . . . "Christianity" consists of a collection of Christianities including Catholic, Orthodox, and Protestant. And there is no central or essential Protestantism: it is a type of Christianity/monotheism/theism/religion with many branches. No one Protestant sect is more Protestant or more religious than any other. . . . In fact, there is no "real" Christianity at all, only a range of Christianities.

I do understand the nature of religious diversity. Marshall does not. For instance, there is nothing when reading Marshall's book where he shows us he understands there are various Christianities, nothing. As far as the reader is concerned he's defending the one and only Christianity, his, without so much as telling us which one that is. If anyone has a superficial understanding of religious diversity it is Marshall. The only thing religionists all agree on is that there are supernatural beings or forces with everything else up for grabs, and that's it.

The problem of religious diversity is so bad that Robert McKim tells us, as I quote on page 40 of my book,

> There is not a single claim that is distinctive of any religious group that is not rejected by other such groups, with the exception of vague claims to the effect that there is something important and worthwhile about religion, or to the effect that there is a religious dimension to reality and that however the sciences proceed certain matters will be beyond their scope. Obviously even claims as vague as these are rejected by nonreligious groups.

More Mischaracterizations by Marshall
Having taken a few unsuccessful and superficial pot shots at my level of understanding regarding the problem to be solved, which is widespread worldwide religious diversity down through the centuries as well as in different cultures today, Marshall turns to the question of religious dependency. I argue that the best explanation for this religious diversity is that adopting and justifying one's religious faith is not a matter of independent rational judgment. Rather, to an overwhelming degree, one's religious faith is causally dependent on brain processes, cultural conditions, and irrational thinking patterns. About this Marshall takes issue with me saying, "cultural dependency in our 'Christian' culture may be real, but is by no stretch of the imagination 'overwhelming.'"[12]

Marshall seems to be objecting to what I said by claiming that while we're living in largely Christian cultures we're not living in *overwhelmingly* Christian cultures. However, I wasn't just talking about Christian cultures, but cultures in general, and it is as demonstrable of a fact as one can get that one's religion is dependent to an overwhelming degree on one's culture. That is, was, and will always be the main point. Nothing Marshall said can dispute that fact. It is overwhelming that children of Muslim sects in Muslim countries will adopt the religion of their parents. Overwhelming. That is the most extreme example of course, but it sets the rule for other cultures as well. Even without the demand that apostates be killed inside many Muslim theocracies, what we find in non-Muslim countries is that Islam is still growing very fast without force.

The rule is that people within a given culture will overwhelmingly adopt the religion of their culture, so it depends on the degree they are immersed in that culture. Christian theists respond by asking me to explain the exceptions. I am asking them to explain the rule. Marshall seems to be objecting to the rule by arguing that we're not living in an overwhelmingly Christian culture. But this objection of his mischaracterizes my main point, and therefore does nothing at all to undercut it. Marshall ends up denying the rule that people adopt the religion of their culture by irrelevantly claiming that Western culture does not provide an overwhelming cultural influence to adopt evangelical Christianity. So what if it doesn't? That still doesn't undercut the rule, even if so. It just means religious cultural dependency may be headed in another direction after 1500 hundred years of Christianity or more.

In any case, I do think many Western societies still provide overwhelming cultural support for Christianity in general. Stretching back for centuries and into the present, Christianity still shows up in our language, critical life events, everyday habits, bodily habits, institutions, and even understandings of time and space, as David Eller writes in the first chapter of my book *The Christian Delusion*.[13]

But with a sleight of hand that Houdini would be proud of Marshall's mischaracterizations continue. He says, "by all means, let's explain the rule before the exceptions! Are boys and girls raised by snake-handlers and bigots in white sheets the exception even in American society, or the rule?" The rule, he says, is that "snake-handling KKK home-schooled kids are rare as falling stars."[14] He completely missed the point. The rule, once again, is that people adopt the religion of their cultures. While snake handlers and the KKK are weird countercultural groups within our larger culture as a whole, the children in those families, if kept away from the larger culture, will indeed adopt their parent's beliefs. This represents the rule. No exception here.

The fact is that most all of our beliefs are culturally dependent as any others. We're all raised as believers. Whatever our parents taught us we believed. We didn't know not to do so. This is my point. It's not something Marshall can tell me about with regard to atheism, or secular humanism either, since I know this much better than he could ever admit. He cannot remind me of this. I already knew it. Our brains lie to, deceive, and fool us. Our thinking is irrational much of the time. I know this all too well. It's the reason I proposed the OTF in the first place. We need an objective standard, a non–double standard based on objective scientific evidence and reasoning about the evidence, for determining which religion is true, if one is. Since we are all in the same drifting rudderless epistemological boat, as I have said, we need a test that allows for all options to be on the table, including the nonreligious option in which all faiths fail the test.

Marshall even goes so far as to ask if his belief "that the earth circles the sun is 'culturally dependent.'"[15] Of course not. Not in today's world of modern science with space explorations and moon landings. Is he really serious? He cannot tell the difference between objective science and cultural opinions? Here's a hint, Marshall, you can do the experiments yourself, and barring doing them, you can learn to appreciate how the scientific method works and listen to the overwhelming consensus of scientists who all agree. If you refuse to do this you are a science denier. That's what it takes for you to believe, in my opinion. You must deny science in at least a few areas to believe. I can even agree with you when you say believing the earth circles the sun is culturally dependent, if that's what it takes to convince someone like you, and it doesn't change a thing. It's true, not all cultures have accepted the heliocentric view of the solar system. However, it is a fact that the earth circles the sun. A fact! So some cultures have got it right, and the reason we've gotten it right is because of science.

Lastly Marshall accuses me of committing the genetic fallacy: "If we adopt certain beliefs because we have been taught them, does that really mean they are probably false? Obviously not. The general form of Loftus' argument is: 1) Ideas about X vary among cultures; 2) The beliefs one adopts about X originate in one's culture, and in that sense depend on it; 3) Therefore one's beliefs are probably wrong. This seems to commit the genetic fallacy."[16] But because he mischaracterizes what I said he responds with nothing relevant. The genetic fallacy is committed whenever it's argued that an idea is false because of its origination or source rather than based on its merits. Even unreliable sources can produce ideas that are true. So just showing that an idea originates from an unreliable source does not necessarily make the idea false.

But this accusation of his is false. I allow that a religion could still pass the OTF even despite its unreliable origins in our respective diverse cultures, so I'm committing no fallacy by arguing correctly that those origins are demonstrably unreliable. At best there can be only one true religion in what we observe to be a sea of hundreds of false ones, which entails a very high rate of error for how believers first adopt a religion. Hence, believers need some further test to be sure their faith is the correct one. That conclusion is not fallacious, nor is the skepticism that it entails. I'm not arguing that religious faiths are necessarily false because of how believers originally adopt them. I'm merely arguing that believers should be skeptical of their culturally adopted religious faith because of it.

I have probably never met anyone who has committed the genetic fallacy. Instead, people use their background knowledge about the general reliability of an idea's source to determine the likelihood that an idea originating from that source is true. Almost no one says, for instance, that we can never trust a particular tabloid news story because of the tabloid's past reputation for dishonesty. What people might say instead, or intend to say, is that we *probably* cannot trust a particular tabloid news story because of the tabloid's past reputation for dishonesty. People can reasonably judge the odds of an idea being true based on their background knowledge about the general reliability of the source of that idea. If an idea originates from a known unreliable source then it's entirely reasonable to doubt any idea coming from that same source, even though we have not yet shown that idea to be false in any other way.

Take for example a person who has the paranoid belief that the CIA is spying on him, and let's say we find that it originated from his taking a hallucinogenic drug like LSD. Since we have linked his belief to a drug that creates many other false beliefs, we have some really good evidence to be skeptical of it, even though we have not actually shown it to be false in any other way. Likewise, when many false beliefs like these are produced at a very high rate by the same source we have a good reason to doubt any beliefs arising out of that same source.

The Four Theses and Tests of Marshall

On page 29 of Marshall's book he attempts to reformulate the OTF with four different theses: (1) "Universal beliefs that agree are more likely to reflect universal realties in some fashion than those that are solely created by individual cultures"; (2) "It is wise to pay particular attention when the wisest men and women in diverse cultures disagree"; (3) "One interesting result . . . may therefore cast a little doubt on atheism itself, since awareness of divine realities is almost universal, and is generally recognized by the wisest within most great civilizations"; and (4) "One should therefore test great faiths not with blind skepticism, but looking for areas of common agreement."

In every single thesis of his, wait for it, agreement and disagreement do almost all the heavy lifting, all of it. If a religion has a consensus to it then it passes the OTF. Whoa! Who is really superficial? Where can we find any worldwide consensus? It doesn't exist. Agreement means something, I'll admit, but people who all agree with each other who also denigrate or deny observable data aren't being reasonable at all. The OTF leads us to a reasonable skepticism that demands sufficient evidence before accepting a claim about the nature of nature as true. People who reject the need for sufficient evidence when it comes to the nature of nature don't get any traction at all with me. Reasonable skepticism becomes the default adult attitude, the one the OTF forces upon us all.

Given Marshall's four theses there would never have been a time in the past when atheism would be embraced based on cultural agreement or consensus. So Marshall's four theses exclude atheism as an option. Since any real test should allow for all options to be on the table, Marshall is not offering a way to find out which religion is true, if one is. He's stacking the deck just as surely as any thieving dealer of blackjack would. Typical Christian apologist. Additionally, I think atheism is the wave of the future, as it marches extremely slowly but inexorably over time and place. So let's say in the year 2100 the earth is almost completely inhabited by atheists. The question then becomes what a future David Marshall living in that era would think of the David Marshall of our era, who argued in his book for these four theses based almost totally on the consensus of majorities of people. My bet is that a future Marshall would sing a different tune and reject all four theses of our own Marshall, just as he would reject them if Islam were the religion of the planet in 2100.

By contrast, scientific thinking is the basis for the OTF: "(1) It assumes one's own religious faith has the burden of proof; (2) it adopts the methodological-naturalist viewpoint by which one assumes there is a natural explanation for the origins of a given religion, its holy books, and it's extraordinary claims of miracles; (3) it demands sufficient evidence before concluding a religion is true; and most importantly, (4) it disallows any faith in the religion under investigation, since the informed skeptic cannot leap over the lack of evidence by punting to faith."[17] How do Marshall's four theses represent anything at all close to the OTF I formulated? I don't see it. What reasonable basis is there for Marshall to say we should continue to look for consensus when no religious consensus has been produced in thousands and thousands of years? Majorities simply don't exist among religionists because faith is the problem. Religious diversity is a much bigger problem than Marshall realizes.

Nonetheless, based on these four theses Marshall puts forth four tests that supposedly correspond to the four theses.[18] Keep in mind the OTF is a test for faith in order to determine which religion is true, if one is. In other words, the goal of the OTF is to help us determine the truth about religion. Marshall thinks he has created four better formulations of that single, simple non–double standard test of faith. I ask any fair-minded person to tell me how these four reformulations offer us any help at all in knowing which religion is true, if one is.

Marshall's first test is that it's to be considered evidence of the truth of a particular religion if it convinces many people in many cultures throughout history. Yet, several mutually exclusive religions pass this test. Buddhism, Islam, Mormonism, Scientology, and even Hinduism pass this test, as even Marshall acknowledges. Here then is a good solid reason to reject Marshall's first test. Any test for truth that allows mutually exclusive religions to pass it cannot be a good test for truth. These religions cannot all be true. Therefore this test is faulty to the core.

What Marshall means by the second test of prophecy may stun my readers. He's not using the so-called prophecies about a virgin-born incarnated son of

God, who resided in Nazareth, and the Messianic Suffering Servant's death on the cross (there was no prediction about a resurrection). No siree bob. What Marshall is saying is that the prophecies about the reach of the gospel to the ends of the earth are evidence of the truth of Christianity, since it has reached the ends of the earth. Seriously? Any budding religious movement that has an agenda or a passion to convert others would predict that their movement would grow and grow and be a worldwide phenomenon. All of them. But until these religious groups predict when their movement will reach such and such a place, and it's global reach for a particular time period, along with the circumstances of that growth, it's merely propaganda used to gain more followers, nothing more. And what about new religious faiths who make their own predictions? Shouldn't we give them more time before we settle on the winner of these types of prophecies? A test that offers nothing conclusive while we wait on history is not a good test to know which religion is true, if one is. We want to know now.

The third test is whether or not a religion has a positive impact on the world. Marshall argues Christianity has bettered the lives of people around the world. Pffft. I have already dispensed with such ignorant and uneducated reasoning in my anthology *Christianity Is Not Great: How Faith Fails*.[19] Marshall focuses on Yahweh's promise to Abraham, that his seeds (the original Hebrew word is plural, which Paul the apostle fails to get right in Galatians 3:8 and 3:16) would bless all nations. But Jews and Muslims trace their ancestry to Abraham too, and they would certainly claim they are blessing the world and will eventually dominate it too. Listen up, even if a religion has been good for people this doesn't tell us whether that religion is true in part, or in whole. Someone argued against evolution by saying that if evolution is true there would be no basis for morals. I simply responded by asking what morality, or the lack of it, has to do with the evidence for evolution? The answer is nothing. So this third test of Marshall's doesn't help us know which religion is true, if one is.

The fourth test is whether a religion can infuse itself into a different culture and how it transforms that culture with its message. If you want a definitive answer to this so-called test of his then read David Eller's chapters in my anthologies. The bottom line is that every religion can infuse itself into a different culture. Every major religion has already done so, and by its own standards would say it brought peace and a good life to the people who live there. Many people in different cultures think the capitalistic scientific materialistic militaristic Western world is ugly. Many other religions would reject Marshall's religion and say their culture is better for it. Even the Amish people would claim their religion brings a better world than other forms of Christianity. What results when a religion and a different culture come into contact is a different culture AND a different religion. I would think, if anything, that any religion that comes into contact with a different culture and remains the same exact religion would have more going for it, but we never see that of any religion, do we? The Christianities that exist in Russia, China, Europe, America, and Africa are simply NOT the same kinds of Christianity.

The bottom line is that if first-century people had actually accepted these four tests of Marshall's then Christianity would have been rejected outright by the people in that era, since Christianity was still in its infancy and had no track record yet. Furthermore, I see no reason at all to accept tests like Marshall's when they cannot apply to nonbelief in its earliest historical stages for the same reason. Until Marshall can show how these four tests can apply to first-century Christianities along with any new religion, or the rise of nonbelief itself, there is no reason to accept them at all.

11

When All Else Fails Lie

Earlier in chapter three I referred to some solid research showing the brain lies to its host. So we can expect that the lies of a believer's brain would become the lies used to defend the Christian faith as well. After all, a brain that privately deceives its believing host is the same brain used to publicly defend the Christian faith.

I actually think I can make a good case for lying for Jesus, despite the fact that lying is considered unethical and condemned in the Bible. One of the Ten Commandments is against "bearing false witness" in Exodus 20:16 (see also Leviticus 19:11; Proverbs 12:22; Colossians 3:19; Revelation 22:15). We're told God doesn't lie in Numbers 23:19 (why did this need to said unless what was being said was questioned?). The father of lies is the Devil in John 8:44. Despite these Bible quotes others tell us most emphatically that God is in the business of lies and deception (1 Kings 22:23; 2 Chronicles 18:22; Jeremiah 4:10, 20:7; Ezekiel 14:9; Romans 1:18–25; 2 Thessalonians 2:11). So which is it? Ahhh, answering that question takes some gerrymandering, right?

In any case, if people are going to an eternal conscious torment then lying for Jesus is justifiable in the same way as lying to save our children from a kidnapper or a killer is justifiable. After all, a kidnapper/killer has lost all moral and legal rights to the truth from someone negotiating a child's release. In the Bible we're told the prostitute Rahab lied to save two Israelite spies from death (Joshua 6:3–5). So given an eternal conscious torment I would think every Christian should be a liar for Jesus.

I am not suggesting would-be apologists should lie to defend the Christian faith. But historically this is what Christians have done from the very beginning, so why not? In fact, without lies Christianity would never have gotten started, much less grown to be the world religion it is today. So if you as a would-be apologist desire to follow the examples of other apologists you must lie to defend you faith. Or perhaps more precisely, you should be willing to defend the lies that have been told to defend your Christian faith. However, if you want to be a *good* Christian apologist then you should not lie for Jesus, nor should you defend the lies told in support of your faith. But if you refuse to lie, or to defend those who have lied, you wouldn't be an apologist at all. Of course, it may turn out that your whole faith is built on too many lies to begin with. Then what should all honest seekers of the truth do? You should abandon your faith.

A few lies for Jesus at the beginning of church history may have helped convert people away from an eternal conscious torment in hell. No harm, no foul, as they say. Okay, maybe. But Christians have lied so much in defense of their faith that even if Christianity is true there just isn't a good reason to believe it. Scholars have noticed so many lies that we can even wonder whether there is much truth to it at all. We wouldn't believe a known liar who tells us something strange but true, would we? Why? Because he's already established himself as a liar. Like the shepherd boy in Aesop's Fables who repeatedly lied to villagers about a wolf attacking his flock of sheep, the villagers did not believe him when it finally turned out he was telling the truth, so the wolf eats the boy and his sheep.

"'You are my witnesses,' says Yahweh" (Isaiah 43:10). Jesus even prayed that based on the Christian witness the world would know God sent him (John 17:20–23). I think it's demonstrably the case that his prayer has never been fulfilled. It's exceedingly probable it will never be fulfilled in the future either. Even if it will be answered in the future it doesn't change the fact that people all over the world have been sent to hell (however conceived) because it hasn't been answered yet. Christians are not credible witnesses. You'd think if the credibility of what they believe is on the line then their God would do something about this. But he doesn't do anything discernible at all. So let's rehearse some of the facts to see what you as an impartial judge, an outsider, would say.

Let the Lies Begin
Lying for Jesus started at least as far back as the time of King Josiah, who ruled over Judah in the South from about 640–609 BCE. We find that Josiah alone was rated as the best king who ever reigned: "Now before him there was no king like him, who turned to Yahweh with all his heart, with all his soul, and with all his might, according to all the Law of Moses; nor after him did any arise like him" (2 Kings 23:25). In fact Josiah was not just a good and important king; he was someone to be compared with Moses himself.

In one instance the biblical text "prophetically" names Josiah three hundred years before he was born. His life was prophesied to Jeroboam, the very first king of the northern tribes (probably 922 to 901 BCE): "By the word of Yahweh a man of God came from Judah to Bethel, as Jeroboam was standing by the altar to make an offering. By the word of Yahweh he cried out against the altar: "Altar, altar! This is what Yahweh says: 'A son named Josiah will be born to the house of David. On you he will sacrifice the priests of the high places who make offerings here, and human bones will be burned on you'" (1 Kings 13:1–2). And surprise of surprises, at the end of that history Josiah is born and is given that name and does exactly what had been prophesied earlier (2 Kings 23:15–20). No other explicit prediction of a person by name three hundred years in advance can be found in the Bible.[1] It is clearly a lie for political propaganda, something the writer(s) inserted into the text. And why not? The writer(s) told the story to please King Josiah. Why is this not hard to understand? Scribes under the power and authority of a despot were instructed to highly praise their king or they would die. In fact, scribes were probably under the control of a king in most cases.

The prophetic ministry of Jeremiah took place under the reign of Josiah, where we see quite a bit of conflict between him and the old guard of prophets and scribes. God even told Jeremiah this: "My people do not know the requirements of Yahweh. How can you say, 'We are wise, for we have the law of Yahweh,' when actually the lying pen of the scribes has handled it falsely? The wise will be put to shame; they will be dismayed and trapped" (Jeremiah 8:7–9). Wait! What did God just "say" to Jeremiah? He said lying scribes have falsely altered the law—that there are lies in it! What lies? For one, Jeremiah denied God instituted the priestly sacrificial system. God says through him: "I spoke not unto your fathers, nor commanded them in the day that I brought them out of the land of Egypt, concerning burnt offerings or sacrifices: But this thing commanded I them, saying, 'Obey my voice, and I will be your God, and ye shall be my people: and walk ye in all the ways that I have commanded you, that it may be well unto you'" (Jeremiah 7:22–23). What Jeremiah seems to say is that God did not do what we find in the book of Leviticus, that he did not command the Hebrews to offer up burnt offerings and sacrifices.

There is surely something going on here, and the clue can be found in 2 Kings 22:8–13, which contains a very interesting story. We read that Josiah had just come to be king of Judah in the South. He wanted to repair the temple and told the High Priest, Hilkiah, to go through all the stuff and see how much money they had. While Hilkiah was looking around, we're supposed to believe he found the "Book of the Law" and gave it to a secretary who read it to Josiah. When Josiah heard it, he tore his clothes because he realized they had not been obeying God. Given the fact that King Josiah is treated with a favoritism that betrays reality, scholars think that instead of "finding" this book, whatever it was, it was actually compiled, edited, and/or written at this time. It was a time in the kingdom of Judah when Josiah needed greater control over the people he was ruling over. It was written to support a reform that centralized all religion and political authority within Jerusalem, in order to keep a crumbling kingdom together in light of internal and external pressures. In order to legitimate these novel reforms, they were to be found in a lost "Book of the Law" that Josiah's regime claimed was written by Moses himself. This kind of forgery was common among regimes in the ancient Near East. Since Jeremiah's prophetic ministry took place during Josiah's reign, Jeremiah may have been the author of a large part of this history.[2]

This helps explain why we're told the Passover Meal was not celebrated for about eight hundred years before King Josiah's time (if we're to believe biblical chronology). In 2 Kings 23:21–23 we find Josiah commanding his people to celebrate the Passover, and the text says: "Not since the days of the judges who led Israel, nor throughout the days of the kings of Israel and the kings of Judah, had any such Passover been observed. But in the eighteenth year of King Josiah, this Passover was celebrated to Yahweh in Jerusalem." If it's possible to know what happened, the Passover Meal may have been first celebrated during King Josiah's reign. The unthinkable alternative is that the Israelites stopped celebrating their origins within a generation of being freed from Egyptian slavery. For the Passover Meal would remind them that when the tenth plague hit Egypt their first born sons were saved, and the Egyptian Pharaoh was forced to release them from slavery. Forgetting to celebrate that event would be like Americans forgetting to celebrate Independence Day when the Declaration of Independence was adopted by the Continental Congress on July 4, 1776.

That there is truth to this is supported by the utter lack of archaeological evidence for the tales of the Israelite Exodus from Egypt, their wilderness wanderings for forty years, and their conquest of Canaan. They too were lies, or at least they were borrowed lies from other tales and compiled with a particular agenda.[3] In fact, the reigns of David and Solomon before the reign of Josiah, at the minimum, did not cover as much territory as was claimed in the biblical texts. They too were lies.[4] David killing Goliath the Philistine giant was pure government propaganda.[5] This explains why there were so many borrowed myths and tales from other Mesopotamian cultures in the Old Testament, which were specifically tailored to suit the Hebrews. To get a look at them read Gary Greenberg's book, *101 Myths of the Bible: How Ancient Scribes Invented Biblical History*,[6] or Tim Callahan's book, *Secret Origins of the Bible*.[7] The creation story, the Adam and Eve story, the Flood story of Noah, the tale of Exodus from Egypt, the conquest of Canaan, and many other tales including Samson, who's long hair gave him superhuman strength, were tall tales, plagiarized myths, legends, and lies. They did not take place in history. The Israelite scribes plagiarized and rewrote older stories they inherited from other Mesopotamian cultures like the Enuma Elish (Creation story), *The Story of Gilgamesh* (Flood story), *The Decent of Ishtar to the Nether World* (Jewish view of the grave), and *The Legend of Sargon* (the story of the birth of Moses).

This means Moses didn't write the first five books in the Bible, even though lies are told that he did (Deuteronomy 31:9, 24–26). There are clear indicators Moses didn't write those books, if he even existed in the first place: (1) In Deuteronomy 34:6 we read about the burial of Moses. It says that "no one knows his burial place to this day." This indicates that it was written some time far removed from his death; (2) In Deuteronomy 34:10 we even read, "There never again arose a prophet in Israel like Moses." Such a statement could not have been made at the time of Moses, much less by a man who tells us he was the humblest man on earth (Numbers 12:3); (3) In Deuteronomy 34:1 Moses is said to have seen the "land of Gilead, unto Dan" from the eastern side of the Jordon River. The problem is that Dan was not the name of that city until the time of Samson, three centuries after Moses died. In Moses' day the city was named Laish, not Dan. The Danites named it after their forefather Dan (see Judges 18:27–31); (4) The Edomite kings listed in Genesis 36 lived well after Moses died. Edom didn't even achieve statehood until the seventh century BCE, so there couldn't be any Edomite kings until then; (5) Deuteronomy 3:11 says that the iron bed of King Og of Bashan "can still be seen in Rabbah of the Amorites." In this passage his bed is already an ancient relic in the city of Rabbah, which was not even conquered until King David ruled over Israel (2 Sam. 12:27–30).

Forged Texts
Not only does the biblical history start off with lies, but there are many examples of forged texts. The facts are in with regard to the book of Isaiah. Two and probably three different authors wrote it. Professor James D. G. Dunn states it forthrightly:

> We can speak of an overwhelming consensus of biblical scholarship that the present Isaiah is not the work of a single author. . . . It is not simply a question of whether predictive prophecy is possible or not. It is rather that the message of Second Isaiah would have been largely meaningless to an 8th century Jerusalem audience. It is so clearly directed to the situation of exile. Consequently, had it been delivered a century and a half before the exile, it would be unlike the rest of Jewish prophecy.[8]

Likewise, this is the case with the prophetic book of Daniel. That Daniel was not written entirely during Babylonian king Nebuchadnezzar's reign (605–562 BCE) is admitted even by evangelical scholar Kenton Sparks. He argues that when we consider the prophecies in the book of Daniel it becomes clear that they are "amazingly accurate and precise" up until a certain point where they "fail." He wrote:

> Scholars believe that this evidence makes it very easy to date Daniel's apocalypses. One merely follows the amazingly accurate prophecies until they fail. Because the predictions of the Jewish persecutions in 167 BCE are correct, and because the final destiny of Antiochus in 164 BCE is not, it follows that the visions and their interpretations can be dated sometime between 167 and 164 BCE.[9]

There are forged insertions into biblical texts and there are forged texts themselves. These forgeries are known by the disingenuous term pseudepigrapha ("pseudo" = false, plus "epigraphein" = inscribe). The books known as pseudepigraphical are considered by scholars to be works that are lies, by today's standards. They are either purported to be authored by a famous person of the past or to contain material claimed to have been from a famous person of the past. Bart Ehrman simply calls them what they truly are, "forgeries."[10]

And there are many such Old Testament examples: 1 Enoch, Questions of Ezra, 2 Enoch, Revelation of Ezra, 3 Enoch, 2 Baruch, Treatise of Shem, 3 Baruch, Apocryphon of Ezekiel, Apocalypse of Abraham, Apocalypse of Zephaniah, Apocalypse of Adam, the Fourth Book of Ezra, Apocalypse of Elijah, Greek Apocalypse of Ezra, Apocalypse of Daniel, Vision of Ezra, Testaments of the Twelve Patriarchs, Testament of Moses, Testament of Job, Testament of Solomon, Testaments of the Three Patriarchs (Abraham, Isaac, and Jacob), Testament of Adam, More Psalms of David, Prayer of Joseph, Prayer of Manasseh, Prayer of Jacob, Psalms of Solomon, Odes of Solomon, Wisdom of Solomon, and so on.

Some of the New Testament examples include *documents falsely attributed to Paul*, such as 3 Corinthians, the Epistle to the Alexandrians, the Epistle to the Laodiceans, the Epistles of Paul and Seneca, the Apocalypse of Paul, the Vision of Paul, the Acts of Paul, the Martyrdom of Paul, and the Martyrdom of Peter and Paul; *documents falsely attributed to Peter*, such as the Apocalypse of Peter, the Gospel of Peter, the Preaching of Peter, the Acts of Peter, the Acts of Andrew and Peter, and the Martyrdom of Peter; and *documents of Mary the mother of Jesus*, such as the Birth of Mary, the Gospel of the Birth of Mary, the Passing of Mary, the Questions of Mary, the Apocalypse of the Virgin, the Assumption of the Virgin, and the Coptic Lives of the Virgin.

There are clear and obvious instances of forged texts that made it into the New Testament. The most obvious cases are Mark 16:9–20; John 5:3–4; Acts 8:37; John 7:53–8:11; and 1 John 5:7–8. Just compare these passages in the King James Version (KJV) and later translations. Notice them missing in the later ones? How did they get in the text in the first place? Who wrote them? Why were they accepted as scripture for way too long? In Revelation 1:11 the phrase "I am Alpha and Omega, the first and the last" (KJV) was not in the original Greek texts. Just look at Jude 14, which reads: "Enoch, the seventh from Adam, prophesied about these men: 'See, the Lord is coming with thousands upon thousands of his holy ones.'" Enoch, the "seventh from Adam," did not say this, because the book of Enoch was written in the second century BCE and couldn't have come from Enoch himself. The book of Jude is quoting as authoritative into scripture a forged text!

There are whole books in the New Testament purported to be written by someone other than who wrote them. The science of philology showed us that biblical texts could be dated based on grammar, vocabulary, and dialect. The four canonical gospels have names attached to them who did not write them. Almost certainly the apostles Matthew and John did not write the gospels Matthew and John. There are books we simply don't know who wrote them, like Hebrews, the epistles of John, 2 Peter, the apocalyptic book of Revelation, and the Pastoral letters purportedly coming from the apostle Paul, 1 & 2 Timothy and Titus. But none of the apostles wrote them.

The stories in the gospel texts that exist contain lies, as seen in Randel Helms' book, *Gospel Fictions*.[11] This is best illustrated by the infancy narratives that biblical scholars overwhelmingly agree could not be true.[12] Modern Christian translators even lie when translating from the original languages of these texts, as Hector Avalos argues in chapter one of his book, *The End of Biblical Studies*.[13]

There is even a widely recognized forged interpolation in Josephus' work by a later Christian author, which claims that Jesus was the Christ and that he arose from the dead. Found in the *Antiquities of the Jews* (18:63–64), the *Testimonium Flavianum* reads:

> Now there was about this time Jesus, a wise man, if it be lawful to call him a man, for he was a doer of wonderful works, a teacher of such men as receive the truth with pleasure. He drew over to him both many of the Jews, and many of the Gentiles. He was the Christ; and when Pilate, at the suggestion of the principal men amongst us, had condemned him to the cross, those that loved him at the first did not forsake him, for he appeared to them alive again the third day, as the divine prophets had foretold these and ten thousand other wonderful things concerning him; and the tribe of Christians, so named from him, are not extinct to this day.

Not even conservative scholars think Josephus made these claims, because he was a Jew not a Christian.[14] Christian scribe(s) inserted it, or parts of it.

Lorenzo Valla (c.1406–1457) showed that the *Donation of Constantine* decree was a forgery. In this forged decree the Emperor Constantine transferred authority over Rome and the western part of the Roman Empire to the pope. That document was a lie. Catholics in particular have lied in saying not only that the land St. Peter's Basilica sits on was donated to them by Emperor Constantine, but also that Peter was the first pope. In fact, I'll betcha the Vatican records themselves show this and priests who have access to them already know Peter was not the first pope—that there was no such office. So the Catholic Church is lying to us this very day. They have lied about their mafia-style banking practices and covered up with lies many child molestation cases.[15]

The church spread other lies. Let me quote another one from the inside flap of the cover of Candida Moss's book, *The Myth of Persecution: How Early Christians Invented a Story of Martyrdom*:

> According to cherished church tradition and popular belief, before the Emperor Constantine made Christianity legal in the fourth century, early Christians were systematically persecuted by a brutal Roman Empire intent on their destruction. As the story goes, vast numbers of believers were thrown to the lions, tortured, or burned alive because they refused to renounce Christ. These saints, Christianity's inspirational heroes, are still venerated today.

Surely you've heard these stories and the ones about the martyrdom of the apostles, right? Well those lies have been exposed as lies by Candida Moss, professor of New Testament and early Christianity at the University of Notre Dame. She exposes the so-called Age of Martyrs as a fiction: "There was no sustained 300-year-long effort by the Romans to persecute Christians. Instead, these stories were pious exaggerations; highly stylized rewritings of Jewish, Greek, and Roman noble death traditions; and even forgeries designed to marginalize heretics, inspire the faithful, and fund churches."[16]

Fake Relics

The Christianized medieval world was filled with sacred relics. Bones, heads, bodies, skin, and fingernails were produced, faked, bought, and stolen because they were highly revered. Producing, preserving, promoting, and presenting sacred relics to the populace was a cottage industry for the medieval church. To climb up high on the religious prestige ladder was to have a relic—the more important the relic, the more important the church that had it. Crowds came from around the known world to venerate these relics. They brought with them their donations. You could build a cathedral with one of them! So you had to have one. A sacred relic meant a lot of power, prestige, and paychecks.

Sacred relics included St. Peter's bones, Mark's body, John the Baptist's head, along with other bones, bodies, heads, fingers, and tongues. There was Mary's holy belt, the tunic of the virgin Mary, the chains of Peter, the veil of Veronica, which was used to wipe the sweat from Jesus' brow as he carried the cross and supposedly bears the likeness of the face of Jesus, and many more.[17] The relics of Jesus that were considered sacred were thorns from his crown, the nails that hung him on the cross, pieces of his cross, the lance that pierced Jesus' side as he hung on the cross, his robe, his sandals, and the Holy Grail he drank from the night of his betrayal.[18]

My all time favorite sacred relic is the Holy Foreskin, the only piece of the circumcised Jesus believed to be with us today! I can imagine the priest or bishop who displayed it having a very hard time holding back his laughter during mass, knowing he's duping the people of his city and surrounding areas. Austin Cline tells us:

> In France, Charroux claimed they inherited their foreskin from Charlemagne. In the early twelfth century they took it to Rome and paraded it through the streets alongside one of those pieces of the True Cross and Jesus sandals, bringing them before Pope Innocent III (1161–1216). At the same time, however, the parish of Calcata north of Rome also claimed to possess Jesus' foreskin. Then there was the abbey of Coulombos in the diocese of Chartres claiming that they were the owners of the True Foreskin. Other claimants included Puy, Metz, Anvers, the church of Notre-Dame-en-Vaux, and Hildersheim.... In the end, it was Charroux who won the battle of the foreskins when Pope Clement VII (1523–1534) issued a bull granting indulgences to any and all who made a pilgrimage to the Charroux foreskin.[19]

Oh, and let's not forget the Shroud of Turin, the piece of cloth supposed to be an image of Jesus as he resurrected from the dead. It's a lie too. Are we really to believe the Shroud of Turin is real when the many other sacred relics are clearly fakes? No, no way, not a chance. End of story, although I'll footnote everything an intelligent person needs to know about it for further research.[20] Let's have done with this nonsense, shall we? The Shroud of Turin is a fake, okay? It's a fake.

Fabricated Discoveries
Who hasn't heard of the many failed attempts at finding Noah's Ark, from people who offer a wide assortment of excuses for why they didn't actually find it? The reason why they cannot find the ark is because the story itself is a lie. To

defend why the ark wasn't found requires more lies, for explorers must defend why the ark wasn't found.

But Christians have lied about finding the ark.[21] The latest fabricated discovery was claimed in 2008 and announced by "We report, You decide" Fox News in 2010:

> A group of Chinese and Turkish evangelical explorers say wooden remains they have discovered on Mount Ararat in eastern Turkey are the remains of Noah's Ark.
>
> The group claims that carbon dating proves the relics are 4,800 years old, meaning they date to around the same time the ark was said to be afloat. Mt. Ararat has long been suspected as the final resting place of the craft by evangelicals and literalists hoping to validate biblical stories.
>
> Yeung Wing-Cheung, from the *Noah's Ark Ministries International* research team that made the discovery, said: "It's not 100 percent that it is Noah's Ark, but we think it is 99.9 percent that this is it."[22]

However, the find was exposed as a fraud. Randall Price, a professor at Liberty University, was involved to some degree with this expedition and its funding. He explained that the "discovery" was a carefully orchestrated hoax. He said: "I was the archaeologist with the Chinese expedition in the summer of 2008 and was given photos of what they now are reporting to be the inside of the Ark. . . . To make a long story short: this is all reported to be a fake."[23]

Another fabricated discovery was the James Ossuary announced to the world in 2002. An ossuary is a container for bones of dead people. This ossuary had an inscription on it that said, "James, son of Joseph, brother of Jesus." The inscription made the ossuary seem significant since it might be related to the Jesus in the New Testament. Well, turns out, Oded Golan and Robert Deutsch, well-known dealers in antiquities, tried to foster this fabricated ossuary with the forged word "Jesus" on it. After investigation the Israel Antiquities Authority declared it to be a fraud.[24]

A Few More Lies Then I Must Stop
There is a fascinating and well-researched book called, what else, *Liars for Jesus*.[25] I've read through parts of it and it is quite enlightening. The book description on Amazon.com says:

> *Liars for Jesus* debunks many of the historical lies invented and used by the Christian nationalist history revisionists in their efforts to further their far right political agenda and destroy the wall of separation between church and state in America. *Liars for Jesus* is not a book about religion. It is a history

book, presenting and fully documenting the true stories and historical facts that are distorted in the "Christian nation" pseudo-history promoted by the religious right.

Christians also lie about their church attendance and what they believe, says a few studies cited by *Slate* in a piece titled, "Why Do Americans Claim to Be More Religious Than They Are?":

> Two in five Americans say they regularly attend religious services. Upward of 90 percent of all Americans believe in God, pollsters report, and more than 70 percent have absolutely no doubt that God exists. There is only one conclusion to draw from these numbers: Americans are significantly more religious than the citizens of other industrialized nations.
>
> Except they are not.
>
> Beyond the polls, social scientists have conducted more rigorous analyses of religious behavior. Rather than ask people how often they attend church, the better studies measure what people actually do. The results are surprising. Americans are hardly more religious than people living in other industrialized countries. Yet they consistently—and more or less uniquely—want others to believe they are more religious than they really are.
>
> Even as pundits theorized about why Americans were so much more religious than Europeans, quiet voices on the ground asked how, if so many Americans were attending services, the pews of so many churches could be deserted.[26]

Bill Wiese is a liar for Jesus. His story told in the book, *23 Minutes in Hell: One Man's Story About What He Saw, Heard, and Felt in that Place of Torment,*[27] is a lie intended to scare people into becoming Christians (and for him to become rich!) since he was never there. Who believes this crap? Really? Bill claims that in 1998, at 3:00 in the morning he was swiftly transported to hell. That place was at least 2,000 degrees, toxic smelling, and pitch-black. He was tortured by two enormous demons before he got away and found Jesus, who tells Wiese to tell the world he's returning to earth again soon.

Alex and Kevin Malarkey are liars for Jesus. Alex told his story, not of going to hell but of going to heaven, in the book he cowrote with his father, *The Boy Who Came Back from Heaven: A Remarkable Account of Miracles, Angels, and Life beyond This World.*[28] It goes like this (it's the same old song, you know the tune, so sing along):

> In 2004, Kevin Malarkey and his six-year-old son, Alex, suffered an horrific car accident. The impact from the crash paralyzed Alex—and medically speaking,

it was unlikely that he could survive. 'I think Alex has gone to be with Jesus,' a friend told the stricken dad. But two months later, Alex awoke from a coma with an incredible story to share. Of events at the accident scene and in the hospital while he was unconscious. Of the angels that took him through the gates of heaven itself. Of the unearthly music that sounded just 'terrible' to a six-year-old. And, most amazing of all . . . Of meeting and talking to Jesus.

Alex retracted his story but Kevin reportedly got rich before the publisher pulled the book.[29]

Roy Varghese and Pastor Bob Hostetler are liars for Jesus. Probably the most important atheist philosopher of the last century was Antony Flew.[30] But toward the end of his life he fell into the hands of theologians, so to speak. Psychologist Valerie Tarico tells us the story:

British philosopher Antony Flew, a life-long atheist now in his eighties announced that he believed in some sort of god. Possibly this god was simply a prime mover, possibly it was a person-god. Flew's public statements were sometimes contradictory. Nevertheless, Flew made a published appeal in support of intelligent design, among other things, and over the course of several years he became the darling of evangelicals in search of a credentialed ally. Flew was a "catch," courted hard and won. Recently, two public defenders of literalist Christianity, self-funding apologist Roy Varghese and evangelical pastor Bob Hostetler even helped the aging philosopher write a book *There is a God*,[31] which tells the story of how and why he converted from atheism to a fuzzy deism with theistic overtones that are fuzzier yet.

There is a catch. Antony Flew, possibly for several years, has been showing signs of dementia. . . . When he first announced his reversal, fellow atheists were dismayed and believers thrilled. But it is only in hindsight, in a context of unambiguous dementia that Flew's recent years can be understood.

Is it not incredible, given this state of affairs, that people who claim to serve the God of Goodness and Truth would put Flew's name to their own cherished arguments about what is right and real? If Flew showed symptoms of dementia . . . and then someone convinced him to donate his financial assets rather than his good name to their cause, criminal charges could apply!

For me, the real curiosity in the Flew story is not whether a once-brilliant philosopher caught in the throes of cognitive decline dies professing atheism or some form of faith-based belief. Rather it is the fascinating psychological question the story raises: Why would men who earnestly care about god concepts and goodness engage in the shameful behavior of manipulating and then speaking on behalf of an elder with diminished capacity?[32]

Pastor Timothy Keller is a liar for Jesus. Keller wrote a *New York Times* best-selling book in defense of Christianity titled, *The Reason for God: Belief in an Age of Skepticism.*[33] In chapter 2 he cavalierly treats the problem of a perfectly good God and suffering in just thirteen pages. Listen, no one can do that effectively. Inside that chapter on suffering Keller quotes from William P. Alston on suffering, who was a distinguished philosopher. Keller said "the effort to demonstrate that evil disproves the existence of God 'is now acknowledged on (almost) all sides to be completely bankrupt.'"[34] That part between single quotation marks is supposed to be what Alston said, since Keller footnotes him.[35] Keller is quoting Alston as saying that the problem of suffering in general is considered bankrupt by (almost) all sides, that is, "completely" bankrupt in their eyes. What Alston really said had to do with the *Logical Problem of Evil*, something we'll discuss in chapter 12 later. What Alston actually said was, "It is now acknowledged on (almost) all sides that the logical argument is bankrupt . . ."[36] Absent is the word "completely" that Keller deceptively inserts. And also absent is any context. Deceptive? Yes! A lie? It doesn't seem to be anything else. Philosopher Bryan Frances brought this to my attention so I'll share his three options with regard to Keller. He may be (1) "completely" uniformed, (2) intentionally deceiving his readers, or (3) deceiving himself. Frances says, "Regardless of which characterization is right—clueless, fraudulent, or self-decieved—Keller is 'completely' untrustworthy when it comes to the Problem of Evil."[37]

William Lane Craig is a liar for Jesus. Dr. Craig claimed in a debate with Dr. Stephen Law on the existence of God that all animals except higher primates lack a prefrontal cortex.[38] This would mean these animals are unaware they are in any pain. Dr. Law responded on his blog later, saying,

> that's a load of pseudo-scientific rubbish. . . . Indeed, Joaquin Fuster, the author of a classic textbook on the pre-frontal cortex, says about Craig's statement that it is "wrong on several counts", and explains that all mammals and some birds have a pre-frontal cortex. . . . Hopefully Craig is a straight enough guy to issue an unqualified *mea culpa* on this one. He's just got the science very wrong.

So Dr. Law thinks Dr. Craig should admit he made a mistake. It's the honest thing to do. Ahhhh, but intellectual honesty isn't a trademark of the believing brain. What Craig said was just plainly false, so false it's hard to think such an excellent researcher in other areas didn't just do a Google search about it and find the case otherwise. He lied to win the debate. Maybe most of the people who watch it won't notice, right?

See a pattern here? I sure do. So no wonder sir_russ on my blog is hard on Christians when rightly saying:

> Christians cannot be trusted concerning miracles, but that's to be expected since they lie about everything else associated with their religion. Christians lie about church attendance. Christians lie about reading the Bible. Christians lie about how much money they give to their churches. Christians lie about so much that every Christian miracle claim should be dismissed out of hand.
>
> Realize that the Christians who tell so many lies concerning their religion today live in the information age when empircism and data analysis techniques can reveal their lies. Those who wrote the Bible lived at a time when no one could check up on their lies. We have no reason to believe in Christian miracles today, and we sure as hell have no reason to believe the drivel in the Bible. When one fucks up the simple stuff like the Earth orbiting the Sun and the make believe of Adam and Eve, and then continues to teach it to children as fact for centuries, they get no additional opportunities to bamboozle and defraud us. Credibility is shot.[39]

I would think if Christianity is true then Christians wouldn't have to lie for Jesus. But they have a long, long history of it. In fact, to the degree they lie to defend their faith is the same degree their faith is false, and we've discovered too many lies to think it has any credibility at all.

"'You are my witnesses,' says Yahweh" (Isaiah 43:10). Yep, and this witness falsifies any attempt for Christianity to be considered credible.

Christians can claim the free will thingy all they want to, and that sometimes people lie, which isn't God's fault. This does nothing, however, to sidetrack the evidence that Christianity and the story of the church is told with lies. If God cannot do anything to counter the effect of these lies then that makes no difference at all. Even if it's not God's fault it still falsifies Christianity. Even if it's not the fault of good honest Christians who would never tell a lie, it still falsifies Christianity. And since that's the case a reasonable God should know that reasonable people cannot believe. He would know the credibility of his demand to believe has been shot through and through with no hopes of being revived short of a set of miracles for the whole world to see.

Part 3

HOW TO DEFEND GOD
IN A WORLD OF PAIN

12

Skirt the Strength of Three Challenges

In this third and final part of the book I want budding apologists to reflect on what most everyone considers to be the biggest problem for Christian theists, intensive ubiquitous suffering in the world. The overarching problem is this one:

> If God is perfectly good, all-powerful, and all-knowing, then the issue of why there is so much suffering in the world requires an explanation. The reason is that a perfectly good God would be opposed to it, an all-powerful God would be capable of eliminating it, and an all-knowing God would know what to do about it. So for the theist the extent of intense suffering in the world means that either God does not care enough to eliminate it, or God is not powerful enough to eliminate it, or God is just not smart enough to know what to do about it. The stubborn fact of intense suffering in the world means that something is wrong with God's goodness, his ability or his knowledge.[1]

There are two categories of suffering that must be explained by Christian theists: (1) *moral suffering caused to sentient beings due to the choices of moral agents*, and (2) *natural suffering caused to sentient beings due to nature's tragedies*. Examples of the former include the Holocaust, terrorist killings, gang rape, molestation, slavery, torture, beatings, kidnappings, and so on, and so on. Examples of the latter include tsunamis, hurricanes, tornados, volcanic eruptions, droughts, earthquakes, and so on, and so on, including the massive and ubiquitous suffering caused by the kill or be killed law of predation in the animal kingdom, which is red with blood in tooth and claw.[2]

The overall force of this problem has been stated by James Sennett, who said:

By far the most important objection to the faith is the so-called problem of evil—the alleged incompatibility between the existence or extent of evil in the world and the existence of God. I tell my philosophy of religion students that, if they are Christians and the problem of evil does not keep them up at night, then they don't understand it.[3]

Christian apologist William Lane Craig agreed with the force of the problem:

The problem of evil is certainly the greatest obstacle to belief in the existence of God. When I ponder both the extent and depth of suffering in the world, whether due to man's inhumanity to man or to natural disasters, then I must confess that I find it hard to believe that God exists.[4]

The force of this problem depends on one's religious or nonreligious views. It's much greater for evangelicals, who believe in an all-powerful God who allows people to go into an eternal conscious torment in hell, as opposed to liberal panentheist Christians who don't. It has much more force for Calvinists, who don't believe in free will, as opposed to non-Calvinists who do. The problem of suffering is even a different one for pantheists, who believe everything is an illusion (or *maya*) but still personally experience suffering, and for polytheists, whose gods aren't big enough to overcome suffering. For atheists the existence of suffering is what we would expect to find in a world that evolved by natural selection.

My focus will be on how non-Calvinist evangelical Christians attempt to answer or mitigate this problem. Some of the top evangelicals collaborated together to do this for us in just one book, *God and Evil: The Case for God in a World Filled with Pain*, edited by Chad Meister and James K. Dew Jr.[5] In this part of the book, I'll evaluate their answers and show how recognized apologists answer this problem. Would-be apologists should do better, if possible. If you cannot find a way to do better, you should not bother being a career apologist at all.

The Logical Challenge from Suffering

In what follows I'll examine how noteworthy evangelical scholars deal with three types of challenges for God from the existence of suffering, all found in the book, *God and Evil: The Case for God in a World Filled with Pain*. The challenges are the logical challenge, the evidential challenge, and the emotional challenge.

First up is the logical challenge, or the logical problem of evil, as it's usually called, discussed by James K. Dew Jr.[6] The logical challenge is one that claims there is a logical (or deductive) inconsistency with the existence of suffering and God's omnipotence, omnibenevolence, and omniscience. The late atheist philosopher J. L. Mackie presented the most formidable defense of this problem. Alvin Plantinga presented the most formidable objections to it with his *Free Will Defense*.[7] Mackie's argument was that God is either not good, not omnipotent, or evil doesn't exist. He argued that a good being always eliminates evil as far as it can; and there are no limits to what an omnipotent being can do. So he asks: "Why couldn't God have made people such that they always freely choose the good?" And, "Why should God refrain from controlling evil wills?"[8] Without a possible answer such a God cannot exist—it is a logical impossibility.

Plantinga's free will defense seeks to answer this problem.[9] He denies offering a theodicy, or solution to the problem, since he's not attempting to show why God is justified in allowing so much suffering in the world. No, rather he's offering what he calls a "defense," which only purports to show that it is "possible" that suffering is compatible with the theistic God. He argues that God cannot bring about just any possible world he wishes containing free agents with significant choice-making capabilities who always do what is right. Plantinga introduces the concept of transworld depravity: it is logically possible that every free agent makes a wrong choice and that everyone suffers from it. If this is even a remote possibility then the logical problem of evil fails, for it is not impossible that free-willed creatures make at least one wrong choice. Upon considering Plantinga's total objections, Mackie conceded defeat by saying, "the problem of evil does not, after all, show that the central doctrines of theism are logically inconsistent with one another."[10] So Dew triumphantly declares, "The logical problem of evil fails to disprove God's existence."[11]

Done deal, right? Not so fast. At best, even if we grant this, it's a Pyrrhic victory similar to the Romans who won a war against Pyrrhus even though they suffered greater casualties. All that Plantinga has done is to show that at best it's possible a perfectly good omniscient omnipotent God exists. Is that anything to crow about? Even if there is no logical disproof of the existence of God here, that doesn't say much at all. The reason is that there are very few, if any, logical disproofs of anything.

Noticeably absent from this chapter by Dew are the arguments presented by atheist philosopher Graham Oppy in his book, *Arguing about Gods*.[12] In fact, not only does Dew not mention Oppy's book, *it is not mentioned in any other chapter of Dew's book either*. Oppy doesn't exist you see, even though he presents some cogent arguments from the existence of suffering for "an orthodoxly conceived monotheistic god." Oppy argues "there is still plenty of life left in the kinds of considerations that are appealed to in Mackie."[13] Oppy argues "there is a lot of heavy metaphysical machinery that is built into Plantinga's free-will defense, and that the use of this machinery has consequences for what one can consistently say and do in other contexts," most notably the principle of sufficient reason, and with it cosmological and fine-tuning arguments.[14]

Oppy shows that theists have a serious lack of imagination too, for if an omniscient God really exists then he knows of an infinitely number of possible worlds. Surely it's reasonable to suppose that in one of these possible worlds God could create people who never do a morally wrong action. I can easily imagine such a world if there is free will in heaven. For in such a world with no fleshly bodies attached to us that would lead us into fleshly—presumably sinful—pursuits, people would always love and obey God. So this is where God's omniscience ends you see, where the apologist needs it to end to solve a problem for faith. Go figure. Typically Christian. Furthermore, Oppy argues that, even if there is no logical contradiction with suffering and "an orthodoxly conceived monotheistic god,"

> if there is a perfect being, then it is as close to certain as you please that that being *was* able to choose to make a universe in which everyone always freely chooses the good; and if [otherwise] . . . then it is as close to certain as you please that if not everyone always freely chose the good, then these departures from optimal choice would be minimal.[15]

If such a God could not make a universe like the two he suggested then Oppy argues "the perfect goodness of that being ensures that it will make no universe at all."[16]

The worst part of Plantinga's defense, one that Dew never mentions, is that in order for there to be no logical inconsistency when it comes to naturally caused suffering, Plantinga says it's possible Satan and his demons are behind all natural disasters.[17] I don't have the words to express how imbecilic such a mere possibility is, but it is. This has a virtually zero possibility to it, and if I'm right, then Plantinga's defense fails. Christian philosopher Richard Swinburne said that it is an "ad hoc hypothesis."[18] As such, according to J. L. Mackie, it "tends to disconfirm the hypothesis that there is a god."[19]

The Evidential Challenge from Suffering

Dr. Gregory Ganssle and Yena Lee (presumably his student at Yale University) tackle the evidential challenge from the problem of suffering in *God and Evil*.[20] I want to first focus just on William Rowe's argument. It goes like this:

1. There exist instances of intense suffering that an omnipotent, omniscient being could have prevented without thereby losing some greater good or permitting some evil equally bad or worse.

2. An omniscient, wholly good being would prevent the occurrence of any intense suffering it could, unless it could not do so without thereby losing some greater good or permitting some evil equally bad or worse.

3. (Therefore) There does not exist an omnipotent, omniscient, wholly good being.

Rowe offers two specific instances of suffering that support his argument, one involving morally caused suffering, and the other involving naturally caused suffering. The moral suffering case came from a *Detroit Free Press* story on January 3, 1986, that reported on a little girl from Flint Michigan who was severely beaten, raped, and then strangled on New Year's Day. About the death of this girl Rowe argues: "No good state of affairs we know of is such that an omnipotent, omniscient being's obtaining it would morally justify that being's permitting it." The natural suffering case he describes is of a fawn badly burned in a forest fire that slowly dies, without any human observer. Rowe argues that an omnipotent, omniscient being could have "prevented the fawn's apparently pointless suffering."[21] A wholly good omnipotent being could have stopped the lightning, diverted it, kept the tree from starting a fire, or kept the fawn from being burned, or, if burned, spared the fawn its intense suffering by quickly ending its life. But since God didn't do any of these things to help, such a wholly good omnipotent God doesn't exist, for he would not have allowed this fawn to suffer if it did not serve some outweighing attainable good.[22]

Ganssle and Lee respond to Rowe with Stephen Wykstra's *Noseeum Argument*.[23] Wykstra argued that just because we cannot "see" a God justifying reason for suffering doesn't mean there isn't one. Said differently, just because we "no-see-um" doesn't mean there isn't a God justifying reason for suffering just beyond our view. For example, if we walked into a "dog park" and didn't see any hippopotami then we are justified in concluding there are no hippopotami in that park. Okay so far. But if we don't hear any dog whistles being blown then we are not justified in concluding no dog whistles are being blown. Why? Because human beings are not in the position to hear dog whistles.

Ganssle and Lee claim that Rowe's argument against God's existence is analogous to the dog whistle example, where human beings are not in a position to reliably judge if any dog whistles are being blown in the park. And since Rowe's case depends on the probability that we are in a position to reliably judge whether there is a God justifying reason for suffering, Rowe's argument fails for the same reason as someone who claims there are no dog whistles being blown. We are just not in a position to judge, they argue. It's not that it's impossible to discern some God justifying reasons for some kinds of suffering. No. According to Ganssle and Lee it's rather that, given the gulf between God's knowledge and our knowledge, it seems unreasonable to expect that we could know the God-justifying reason *for every case of evil*, even if such a reason were to exist. . . . In fact, if theism were true, we would *expect* there to be situations for which we cannot give a full explanation. The existence of some evil that cannot be fully explained is just what we would expect if theism were true [emphasis mine].[24]

There are a great many things I could say in response, but I cannot take up the space. Notice that they claim "it seems unreasonable to expect that we could know the God-justifying reason *for every case of evil* [emphasis mine]." Now I have read a great deal from Rowe on this matter and not once can I find him requiring that theists should explain "every case of evil." He always refers to the two cases I mentioned above. He wants theists to explain those two cases, one involving morally caused suffering and the other involving naturally caused suffering. So I find this phrase to be a mischaracterization of Rowe. As we've seen if you want to be an apologist you should do this too. They say this is because most reasonable people would agree that if there is such a God it would be unreasonable to expect apologists to explain "every case of evil" in the world. True dat!

The question Rowe poses is whether or not intense suffering of these two specific cases can have a God-justifying reason. He is not asking apologists to explain all cases, just these two. Although, I'll grant that it's also a challenge to explain two *categories* of suffering, not just two instances of suffering—specifically, intense moral and natural suffering. If, for instance, no God-justifying reason for these two categories of suffering can be found then it's probable such a God doesn't exist. That's Rowe's argument by extension. So if Ganssle and Lee admit they cannot explain these two cases within these two categories, then what specific cases can they explain? Surely even though they cannot explain them all they can explain a few, right? How about just these two specific cases for starters? I could offer tons of other examples if these two don't suffice. Just read your daily newspaper. The problem is that this kind of horrendous suffering takes place around our world in one form or another almost every minute of every day. What Ganssle and Lee are admitting is not just that they cannot explain these two cases but that they cannot explain any similar kinds of suffering given their God-hypothesis.

Now to the heart of their objection. Are we in a position to see a God-justifying reason for this kind of intense suffering? Remember, we're not just talking about an omniscient being, but one who is also omnipotent and wholly good too. I wish theists would make up their minds about which God concept they are trying to defend.

When theists want to talk about an omnipotent God they will point to a serpent or ass that could talk, an axe head that could float on water, fire that was called down from the sky, or a sea that parted allowing six million Israelites to pass on dry ground who subsequently lived for forty years in the desert where their sandals never wore out and were fed by miraculous manna from heaven. Or they'll point to a virgin who had a baby, the supposed resurrection of Jesus, or a blind man from birth who was made to see again. With an omnipotent God anything is possible they'll argue. Such a God concept allows for these kinds of miracles and more, you see. He can do anything like this. He is a miracle-working God. But when the issue is why there is so much intensive suffering in the world they will switch gears, saying we cannot understand why God fails to intervene. I call this the *Omniscience Escape Clause*, a get-out-of-jail-free card that is repeatedly used to escape from any number of problems for Christian theism, or theism in general. They selectively choose one of these attributes of God depending on the problem to be solved.

The fact is when it comes to intensive massive ubiquitous suffering in the world, we should know enough about God to conclude he is good from what he's doing (or not doing). It's that simple. It seems very likely we should be able to see God's reasons for allowing suffering since theists also claim God wants us to believe in him and will condemn us to hell if we don't. If we don't have a clue about such matters then we cannot know enough to know God is good either, much less wholly good. Ganssle and Lee admit as much. They are skeptical theists, which by their lights is that "there are cases in which we cannot recognize a reason God might have to allow something evil no matter how hard we search," even while maintaining this doesn't imply "there are no such reasons."[25]

So let's compare what we have on this issue. On the one hand, Ganssle and Lee admit they don't have a clue with regard to intense suffering highlighted in Rowe's two examples. They admit they are also clueless to explain any number of other examples in the same category that I could mention. On the other hand, we know of plenty of ways an omnipotent God could intervene to help alleviate all cases of intensive suffering. That's right, all of them. Name me one and I can show how an omnipotent God-concept worthy of the name could intervene to help. David Hume suggested several possible scenarios. Here are some other ways God could have shown he cares but didn't:[26]

A heart attack could have killed Hitler and prevented World War II. Timothy McVeigh could have had a flat tire or engine failure while driving to Oklahoma City with that truck bomb to blow up the Murrah Federal Building and the people in it, including babies and children. Several of the militants who were going to fly planes into the Twin Towers on 9/11 could've been robbed and beaten by criminals on the way to the airport (there's utilitarianism at its best). A poisonous snakebite could've sent Saddam Hussein to an early grave, averting the Iraq War before it happened. The Zyklon B pellets dropped down into the Auschwitz gas chambers could have simply "malfunctioned" by being miraculously neutralized (just as Jesus supposedly turned water into wine).

The one I use the most concerns the 2004 Indian Ocean tsunami that killed a quarter of a million people. It was caused by an earthquake. An omnipotent God could have averted that earthquake such that no one would suffer or die, and no one would be the wiser that he did it. If it would take a *perpetual miracle*, as I've called it, then what's the problem? Is God lazy or something? So while skeptical theists don't have a clue, reasonable people can come up with a multifaceted number of ways an omnipotent, wholly good, omniscient God could alleviate cases of intense suffering.

The bottom line is that Wykstra's *noseeum* argument cuts both ways. We're told that we can't understand God's purposes, and this is true: we can't begin to grasp why there is so much suffering in our world if a good omnipotent God exists. But if God is omniscient, as claimed, then he should know how to create a better world, especially since we do have a good idea how God could've created differently. So which is more likely, that we cannot even begin to understand God's omniscient ways, or that we can have some kind of idea about them? If we accept the Christian idea that we're created in God's image the answer seems obvious. We should indeed have some kind of idea about God's omniscient ways. Since this is so, and since we do not have a clue as to why there is so much senseless suffering if God exists, and since we do have some good ideas about how God might have done things differently, the most reasonable conclusion by far is that such an omniscient omnipotent wholly good God does not exist.

The Emotional Challenge from Suffering
The emotional challenge of evil is about solving the emotional dislike people have for a God who permits suffering. William Lane Craig believes

> that most people who reject God because of the evil in the world don't really do so because of intellectual difficulties; rather it's an emotional problem. They just don't like a God who would permit them or others to suffer and therefore they want nothing to do with Him.[27]

Charles Taliaferro and Gary Habermas in two chapters for the book *God and Evil* attempt to deal with this challenge.[28] Let's first look at what Taliaferro could have done with his chapter on prayer but chose not to do. He could have focused on why reasonable people conclude his God doesn't answer petitionary prayers. With the massive number of prayers being offered to his God, reasonable people can conclude it only appears prayers are answered due to chance alone. What does Taliaferro say in response to this? Nothing. Christians merely count the hits and discount the misses. This is a known cognitive bias to be avoided if one desires to know the truth, called *Selective Observation*.

Taliaferro could have tried to show that Christian prayers work more often than non-Christian prayers, or, if not, why the anecdotal evidence is the same for them all. If Taliaferro's Christian God is answering the prayers of all believers, then by answering them Taliaferro's Christian God is providing confirming evidence against the truth of Christianity to other believers in false religions who will be condemned to hell. Why would a good God do that? It doesn't seem compassionate at all, and would mean his God is the cause of all kinds of violence between opposing religious believers who consider answered prayers as evidence their religion is true.

Taliaferro could also have told his readers why his God requires petitionary prayers before alleviating suffering in the first place. Does a father require a stubborn teenage daughter to ask for his help before he'll rescue her from a burning house?

Let's picture this:

Father: The house is burning! Come with me, hurry. I know the way out.

Daughter: Leave me alone. I can get out by myself without you.

Father: You're going the wrong way. Don't open that door.

Daughter: I know what I'm doing.

Father: Okay, since this is what you want. Have it your way.

Father leaves her and escapes a different way from the burning house. Daughter opens the door and the backdraft instantly burns her alive. Mother and father stand outside in the yard:

Mother: Where's our daughter?

Father: She wouldn't ask me for help. She even refused.

Mother: What a shame. I'm sure you tried.

Father: I did all I could.

Along the way Taliaferro could have pointed to the many scientific clinical studies conclusively establishing that prayers are efficacious (that is, they produce results). But there are none. In fact it's the complete opposite.

Petitionary prayers tested in clinical trials have more than confirmed that, statistically speaking, they are answered no better than chance.

What does Taliaferro do with most of his chapter? He offers an overview of prayer, saying at the end that "probably one of the greatest uses of prayer involves praise." He identifies ways that prayer helps the person praying, and argues for the virtue of "set traditional prayers" over spontaneous ones. Taliaferro finally gets around to questions that might be of real help to believers in pain on just one page. So let's look at what he says on page 159. He suggests that offering petitionary prayers is good because, if nothing else, the petitioner will be motivated to alleviate suffering (or should, if sincere). When prayers are not answered it's still sometimes good since "simply aligning oneself with the good aims of God can itself be good." Okay. Nothing really much to disagree with here (depending on which aims someone thinks God has, of course). The question is, however, whether his particular God does anything upon hearing a particular prayer.

When it comes to providing evidence that his particular God answers petitionary prayers, which would be comforting to believers in pain, Taliaferro asserts that "the question of evidence is very difficult" since "everyone and everything is prayed for." There are many prayers that ask God to help everyone in the world, you see. The good news though is this means "there is no one who is in a hospital who is not being prayed for, even if they aren't being prayed for by name." He says with optimism, "I doubt an omniscient being would have trouble identifying who is in trouble." In this way Taliaferro discounts all evidence making his faith unfalsifiable by using the aforementioned *Omniscience Escape Clause.* Typical Christian. This is special pleading. Only people of faith would ever accept such an answer given the massive and ubiquitous amount of suffering in this world. Can you hear the son of Dr. Pangloss here from Voltaire's satirical novel *Candide*?

When it comes to why some petitionary prayers are answered and some are not, Taliaferro offers the typical answer that God chooses not to be overwhelmingly obvious, or evident, so that people can refuse to believe if they want to do so. Again this is special pleading. Other religionists say the same thing. Then he offers an either/or false disjunction: "If every petitionary prayer were answered on the time specified by the petitioner, God might even be thought of as an instrument or tool for earthly benefits." Such a mischaracterization is typical among Christian apologists. Would-be apologists should take note. No one argues that God should answer every prayer, only that he should answer prayers to alleviate the most horrendous types of suffering. If a perfectly good omnipotent God existed, there would not be so much massive suffering in the world. *In fact, the probability that such a God exists is inversely proportional to the amount of suffering there is in the world (i.e., the more suffering there is, then the less probable it is that God exists), and there is way too much suffering to suppose that he does.*

Turning next to the chapter by Habermas, let me say it is unapologetically emotional in nature. He understands pain and doubt. In it he tells about the pain of watching his wife dying of cancer. Here's how he put it in an article that was probably the springboard for his chapter:

> In 1995 my wife Debbie had the flu. When it didn't go away as quickly as it should have, we were sent to the hospital for tests. The first sentence I remember the doctor uttering was, "You've got some serious problems here." My heart sunk into my stomach and both turned instantly to water. I had to sit down. Little did I know that my belief in Jesus' resurrection was about to be severely tested by the sting of pain and grief. Debbie was diagnosed with stomach cancer. Four months later she passed away at the age of 43 years, after just celebrating our 23rd anniversary. I had lost my best friend. Companionship became my most noticeable lack, sometimes seeming unbearable. Further, all four children lived at home. Witnessing their pain was another huge hurt. Did they have to suffer like this? Would watching their mom die leave extended scars? Would they blame God? I was suffering a double dose of grief. I often thought that I could not have experienced any worse pain.
>
> During Debbie's suffering, I regularly took refuge in the truth of Jesus' resurrection. It had been my major research area for 25 years. So I appreciated the student who asked, "What would you do now if Jesus hadn't been raised from the dead?" I knew this event had a historical, theoretical side, but I wasn't fully aware of its practical power. I had much to learn about applying the resurrection to life.[29]

Doesn't your heart just break for him as does mine, even though this happened twenty years ago? He knows pain. That's why he can offer pastoral advice.

But is it any good? Does his faith cause more emotional pain than if he didn't have it? Is his answer reasonable based on evidence from within his own religious faith? He does not argue for the truth of the Bible nor for the resurrection of Jesus in this chapter. He assumes both. Undercutting his faith, as I do, would show that he has a false hope, even if it helps him overcome the difficulties of life. So even if his faith helps him, I would rather have my feet planted firmly on solid ground. I think that's the difference, the dividing line, between people of faith and nonbelievers like me. People of faith don't have the inner strength or mental fortitude to accept the facts of life apart from a false hope. Faith is an unnecessary crutch believers use to walk with, while others of us don't need it.

Let me offer some emotional advice for my atheist friends in pain before proceeding. The most blunt way it has been put is this: "Shit happens and then you die." Not too comforting is it? Sounds pretty bleak, even sort of depressing when put like this. But nonbelievers do not reject the evidence for a conclusion simply because they dislike the conclusion. It takes a special sort of person to do this. This makes all the difference between us and why we are nonbelievers. We can handle the truth. We can face the facts. And we can live good, loving, productive, meaningful, hopeful, and happy lives knowing the truth. It makes no difference to us now that in a billion years nothing we do will matter. However, what we do matters to the ones we love and who love us.

The emotional and physical pain we experience in our lives is the same as believers. What we don't have to struggle with, as Habermas does, is the intellectual pain of God's silence when we suffer. That kind of pain adds to the pain of suffering. We don't have it. We are better off without it. Death and suffering are what we expect in life. We take the good with the bad. We can only hope that we have more happiness in our lives than pain.

I'm reminded here of M. Scott Peck's famous opening to his book, *The Road Less Traveled*:

> Life is difficult. This is a great truth, one of the greatest truths. It is a great truth because once we truly see this truth, we transcend it. Once we truly know that life is difficult—once we truly understand and accept it—then life is no longer difficult. Because once it is accepted, the fact that life is difficult no longer matters.[30]

Like Habermas and other believers, everyone experiences suffering and pain, some of us more than others. Nonbelievers just don't have to struggle with why life is difficult, and that makes all the difference. For if we truly accept it, life is no longer as difficult.

Nonetheless, Habermas offers the best advice I have read to Christians who experience pain, based on Christian assumptions. First off he admits that for all of the Christian responses to divine hiddenness arguments (which I'll address in chapter 15), Christians are still quite bothered by God's silence. Habermas even knows of the Christian responses to these arguments and yet he has still struggled with the pain of losing his wife. He says, "probably the most common issue I hear today has to do broadly with believers who are bothered by the subject of God's silence."[31] Sounds about right to me. If God cares for people then at the very least he could tell us why we suffer so much so often. If he had done so it would help alleviate the pain somewhat.

Habermas argues, correctly in my opinion, that "the primary cause of our emotional suffering is internal, emanating from our own false beliefs. Whereas rational, true or good beliefs about reality promote positive results, irrational or bad beliefs often have painful consequences."[32] Okay so far. But which beliefs serve as a corrective to help Christians in their pain and suffering? The first one is that "suffering is at the heart of the gospel." God never promised a life without suffering, he notes. In fact, Jesus suffered as did the early disciples. So "believers should actually expect to suffer" as well. He says, "Scripture does not teach that believers will be exempted from suffering, even from the worst sorts. Neither do the lives of the saints bear this out." And he argues that, "Somehow we need to drive home these points, and forcefully so."[33] A second belief, only briefly mentioned, is that God knows why Christians suffer and is by their side. The third belief is that Christians should focus on their heavenly reward, saying, "This is a truth that we should always concentrate on, for it both changes our perspective on this life as well as providing motivation in the present."[34]

What can we say in response? First, his advice almost completely ignores God's many promises. Let's look at them:

God will provide for our daily needs: "Do not be worried about your life, as to what you will eat or what you will drink; nor for your body, as to what you will put on. Is not life more than food, and the body more than clothing? . . . For the Gentiles eagerly seek all these things; for your heavenly Father knows that you need all these things" (Matthew 6:25–32).

God answers prayers: "This is the confidence which we have before Him, that, if we ask anything according to His will, He hears us. And if we know that He hears us in whatever we ask, we know that we have the requests which we have asked from Him" (1 John 5:14–15).

God gives us the desires of our hearts: "Delight yourself in the Lord; and He will give you the desires of your heart" (Psalm 37:4).

God heals our diseases: "Bless the Lord, O my soul, and forget none of His benefits; who pardons all your iniquities, who heals all your diseases" (Psalm 103:1–3).

God promises long life: "For through me your days will be many, and years will be added to your life" (Proverbs 9:11).

God promises protection: "The Lord will keep you from all harm—he will watch over your life; the Lord will watch over your coming and going both now and forevermore" (Psalm 121:7, 8).

God Promises deliverance: "For God will deliver the needy when he cries, the poor also, and him who has no helper" (Psalms 72:12).

There are a lots of these kinds of promises in the Bible. Promises. Promises. If God does fulfill his promises, even partially, then where is the evidence of this in the lives of so many Christian people? No wonder Christians struggle so much when they suffer! If Habermas is correct then why did his God make these promises? That doesn't make any sense to me. Either Habermas is correct or God is, you see. It seems clear to me Habermas is haphazardly eisegeting the Bible based on the facts of experience, not properly exegeting it. He needs to have an emotional answer so badly that he denies the Bible, even though he is a card-carrying inerrantist. Typical Christian. *Do or say anything that can to be said in order to save one's faith.* The problem is that the faith he saves is not the faith handed down to him. For now he doesn't have any real hope in God's promises.

What Habermas says is probably the best pastoral answer I've read. But it falls on deaf ears. I dare say it will fall on his own deaf ears should some other painful experience come his way, something I do not wish upon him. As I have said before, it's better over here. Only people with a certain disposition, people who can handle the truth, people who can be brutally honest with the evidence wherever it leads, people who are not afraid of letting go of that crutch to see whether they can walk without it, will ever find this out.

13

Honestly Admit
There Are No Solutions

There have been several historical attempts to fully justify a perfectly good omnipotent omniscient God in light of the suffering we experience in this world. There have been three major solutions offered, also known as theodicies. None of them work so would-be apologists should just honestly admit there are no solutions.

The Solution of Augustine

The traditional answer usually associated with Augustine in the fourth century CE is that natural and morally caused suffering entered the world as the result of an angelic and then a human fall into sin. All suffering is either due to our sin or the consequences of our sin, explaining why there is both natural and moral suffering in our world. God allows us to reap the full individual, societal, and global consequences of our own sins. But God sent Christ to ransom us on the cross from Satan's power and thereby overcame that which brought evil into the world—sin. Sin that is justly punished in Christ is thereby canceled out and no longer mars the universe. God will eventually be victorious over evil in the end on Judgment Day.

There's more to it and R. Douglas Geivett is a good guide, who finds merit in Augustine's approach.[1] Geivett claims Augustine's deductive proof for God's existence "plays a crucial role" in his theodicy. Augustine reasoned like this in three steps: (1) God exists based on the need to ground eternal truth (a Platonic argument); (2) God is necessarily good whereas all other things by virtue of being created are contingent goods; (3) Therefore, a necessarily good God couldn't create evil. By definition God cannot be responsible for it. (I'll confess this is a rather simple account for brevity's sake.) As I indicated this is a deductive argument, one based on definitions. If we define things in the way Augustine did then we'll get the same result. That is, if it is in fact deductively true beyond doubt that God is necessarily good, then he couldn't create the massive amount of suffering in this world (i.e., evil). The question is how Augustine gets from A to Z.

Geivett says Augustine's argument to a necessarily good God is not just a deductive one. For Augustine offered inductive support for it as well, in the feelings of guilt we all have from time to time. However, I can conceive of no reasonable argument that would lead us to think God is necessarily good given the nature of the world we see around us, especially given other God-hypotheses. Consider the world we see around us. There is no way we can conclude there is a perfectly good God if we inductively look at the world and try to determine whether such a God, if he exists, is necessarily good. At best we could only inductively conclude God has a mixture of both good and evil in him (Paul Draper's *Hypothesis of Indifference*). Perhaps God is a glorified human being? After all, human beings contain a mixture of both good and bad, which is what we would inductively conclude about God from the world. So Augustine's so-called inductive support for his deductive argument to God's goodness is merely used in defense of something he already determined from his deductive argument, devoid of any inductive reasoning at all. Augustine is defining God as necessarily good without any noncontroversial inductive support (the experience of guilt is no indication there is a perfectly good God given naturalistic explanations that locate it in the conscience regions of our brains). With his definitions and the deductive nature of his argument he doesn't need any inductive evidence at all. In fact, such evidence is irrelevant.

Now consider other more probable God-hypotheses. One such God-hypotheses is that a trickster (or deceiver) God exists, rather than a good one.[2] Based on this conception alone the best any believer can claim is agnosticism. For any evidence suggesting God is good is placed there by a trickster God who seeks to deceive us. Another one is the God of Process theology whereby God is not omnipotent. God cannot intervene to help us. He only has the power to persuade moral agents like us to do good deeds. He cares. It's just that he cannot directly intervene because he cannot control his creatures. He can only influence them. With such a theodicy God does not need to be justified for permitting evil, since it is not within his power to prevent it. Basically, Process theology concedes the whole argument.

Augustine also argued that evil is a privation, that it doesn't exist except as a privation of goodness. It is a corruption of the good. Plato's allegory of the cave is illustrative here (although Geivett doesn't mention it). Augustine essentially borrowed some of Plato's insights (with Christian deviations). In Plato the real is the "Good" (i.e., the highest of the forms) to be found when prisoners escape the cave, while that which is unreal are the "shadows" on the cave wall that the prisoners saw. When we substitute the word "God" for Plato's "Good" and substitute the word "evil" for Plato's "shadows" we basically get Augustine. Evil is unreal like the shadows on the cave. It doesn't exist except as a parasite on the good. So evil has no actual substance (or existence) in and of itself. It's a privation of the good.

Augustine argued that evil is a privation, but could he argue that suffering is a privation? Just substitute the word "suffering" in place of the word "evil" as is my preference, and see what we get. You see, that's what we're talking about, suffering, a massive amount of intense suffering that is caused naturally and morally. It exists. No Platonic deductive argument nor any alternative definitions can deny this fact. How does suffering not exist? Sentient creatures all experience it as real. To say evil is the absence of goodness puzzles me to no end, for all I can think of when reading this are the individual people who have suffered, especially children. What exactly does it mean to say children are born addicted to cocaine, or with cystic fibrosis, Down's syndrome, congenital heart disease, or leukemia? Do we really want to say they're experiencing the absence of goodness? Does this language make any sense at all?

What we have here, ladies and gentlemen, is a language reversal game with the privation theory. For rather than "the problem of evil," we have "the problem of less good." Why didn't God create a world with more good in it? Andrea Weisberger explains: "'Less good' simply functions as a euphemism for evil, and the problem reduces to a matter of semantics. No matter what we wish to call the particular phenomenon in question, the pain feels the same. . . . Certainly the problem of evil disappears, it is true, but the problem of less good which takes its place is equally vexing."[3] Weisberger continues in her book, *Suffering Belief*: "There is clearly a major problem with the privation theory: it does not seem to satisfactorily account for our experience of evil."[4] She also argues the solution of Augustine (and Aquinas) is a concessionary one, for it concedes that the problem of evil as traditionally formulated is a sound argument; it just denies one of the premises (i.e., that evil exists). Geivett admits that Augustine's view of evil as "a privation" is "often met with incredulity (or something worse)."[5] These are some of the reasons why.

Geivett ends his chapter with some lessons for today.[6] Let me mention the first and the last lessons, the only ones worthy of comment. The first lesson is, "Every worldview and philosophy of life must reckon with the reality of evil, including the evil of human moral failure." Again, let's substitute the word "suffering" for the word "evil," and this now reads: "Every worldview and philosophy of life must reckon with the reality of suffering, including the suffering of human moral failure." He opines that atheists cannot answer this problem, that we "loath to say what evil is." Really? I just did. It's called suffering, meritless blind undeserved suffering. Surely a child who suffers and dies from leukemia doesn't merit it. And what accounts for such suffering? In a word, evolution.

The fourth and final lesson is, "Christianity is attractive, in part, for its solution to both the existential and the intellectual problems of evil." My response, given all that I'm saying in this section, is what I do every time I get a physical at the doctor's office—*cough*. Such a statement is little more than masturbatory madness. It's circle-jerk time folks. For people who want to believe, all it takes is a little patience and some ingenuity. To see this for what it is, look at Scientology's solution to the problem of "evil." Look at Christian Scientist's solution. Look at the pantheist's solution. Look at the Calvinist's solution. They all claim to have the best solution, so take your pick. Just try to argue them out of their solution and you will see the same resistance coming from evangelicals. Hint: They will disagree. That's why faith needs no evidence. That's the nature of faith. Objective evidence doesn't count, and when it does, it's forced into the service of faith.

The Best of All Possible Worlds Solution of Leibniz

G. W. Leibniz (1646–1716) coined the word "theodicy" and argued that this is the best of all possible worlds. His reasoning went like this: A perfect God has the power to create any possible world. Being perfect, God would create the best possible world. No creaturely reality can be totally perfect, but must contain some evil. So God created a world possessing the optimum balance of good and evil—this is the best of all possible worlds. In Jill Graper Hernandez's chapter on Leibniz for the book *God and Evil* she tells us his theodicy:

> Our actual world is the result of the convergence of God's perfection and freedom, even though the actual world contains imperfections that arise out of metaphysical limits (like my imperfect rationality) or out of choice (like my propensity to sin). But even though this created world is not perfect, it is the best possible, and so it would be impossible for God to create a better world or to intervene in the world to prevent or limit suffering within the created order. A perfect God would create only the best out of any world that could be conceived; since this is the world God created, this is the best possible of all worlds that could be conceived—the best of all possible worlds.[7]

Leibniz's view was ridiculed by Voltaire in his satirical novel *Candide* (French for "optimism") published in 1759, a satire that Hernandez fails to mention. In the novel we watch Candide's slow and painful disillusionment with Leibniz's theodicy as he witnesses and experiences great hardships in the world.

Since Voltaire's day Christian philosophers tried to escape from these criticisms by arguing God does not need to create the best of all possible worlds. Most philosophers think the notion of a best possible world is incoherent, including Robert Adams, Alvin Plantinga, and Richard Swinburne. But as atheist philosopher William Rowe argued there is a distinction to be made between a *best world* and a *best possible world*. So if there is a best world (not a best *possible* world) God would have had no other choice than to create it. For, as he tells us, "to do less good than one could is to be lacking in wisdom or in goodness."[8] So even if this present world is not the best possible world, it should still be a best world.[9] In fact, if a perfect God created a world it would have to be a perfect one, otherwise God created imperfection into existence.[10]

In partial defense of Leibniz, and recognizing his theodicy has a lot to answer for, Norman Geisler claimed this present world is the best possible way to get to the best possible world, in heaven.[11] But this is clearly not the best possible way to get to the best possible world. For with just one fewer murder or drought or rape this would be a better world leading up to the best possible world.

Hernandez tells us the Leibnizian theodicy is based on the fact that God acts for good reasons and is consistent with Leibniz's principle of preestablished harmony (which is laughed at by almost everyone who studies the brain-mind problem) and human free will, which is a "crucial" requirement. Hernandez tells us, God "sees the entire sequence of events in the world as a whole, and when he chooses, he chooses the entire series, which is the best."[12] Since God is perfect he "will always be obligated to limit the amount of evil in the world, unless his intervention would result in more (or qualitatively worse) evil obtaining."[13] Hernandez says Leibniz's solution "has remained philosophically compelling for many reasons" yet mentions a telling criticism that it is "divorced from the lived suffering of people." She admits it "might be too abstract" since Leibniz "doesn't engage in significant discourse over pernicious harms."[14]

On both counts and for many reasons she's right about these two criticisms. That's because Leibniz's theodicy is pure philosophical speculation based on an idea, perhaps based in the *Ontological Argument* to the existence of a perfectly good God. Grant it and this has to be the best possible world for such a being to create (or at least a perfect world among other perfect worlds he could have created). However, no matter what world we could have experienced, no matter what world God could have created, apologists in those other worlds could still say the same thing as Leibniz did. The world could be much, much worse and apologists could still deduce from the undemonstrable first principles of their philosophy that such a world would be a perfectly good one based on the idea of a perfectly good God. That's why pure deduction as a theodicy does not work. We must begin by looking at the world we experience and inductively conclude from it what kind of God must exist, if one does. Otherwise, what apologists are doing is nothing less than special pleading. *A solution to the problem of suffering based in Leibniz's deductive form of special pleading is no solution at all.* Potential apologists should take note.

The Soul-Making Solution of John Hick
John Hick has argued for a *Soul-Making Theodicy*, something far removed from traditional Christianity.[15] For him, two stages of creation are involved. In the first place, humans were brought into existence as intelligent animals, and then secondly, through their own free choices, human beings are gradually being transformed into God's children. Perfection lies in the future of our existence through successive reincarnations, or more properly, the successive creation of exact "replicas" of us. This theodicy requires an "epistemic distance" from God where the world was created so it appears as if he doesn't exist at all. This makes it possible for us "to freely accept God's gracious invitation and to come to Him in uncompelled faith and love."[16] This theodicy also requires that we reject a historical fall from innocence and accept a universal salvation of all people. In Hick's world the sufferings we experience and overcome are necessary for our character building.

I find it very interesting, of course, to see liberal Christians like Hick trying to remodel their faith in light of the advancement of the sciences. He accepts that science has seriously damaged the house of Christianity, yet he tries to rebuild the Christian faith out of the discarded timber using other religious beliefs like reincarnation.

As an evangelical James Spiegel is not defending this soul-making solution or theodicy in his chapter in *God and Evil* on the subject.[17] He doesn't even mention Hick's two stages of creation, Adam and Eve's fall into sin, "epistemic distance," or reincarnation.

In his chapter Spiegel is arguing that some suffering is necessary for our character building. That's his thesis. It only has a tangential relationship to the soul-making theodicy that "receives its most extensive treatment" by John Hick.[18] But if this is his thesis, and if some suffering is necessary, then he should comment on just how much suffering is necessary. He needed to defend more than that "some" suffering is necessary and tell us just how much suffering is represented by that little word "some." Sometimes people are absolutely devastated by their sufferings to the point of suicide or debilitating depression. How does that create good moral character in them? Do these people suffer for the express utilitarian purpose of helping the rest of us learn moral traits when we help them? Does the amount of intense suffering in this world help us better than working with people on a project like building a house, or being a member of a sports team (that's sometimes a struggle, even a battle of egos)? Does a mother not learn to love her children until they suffer and die from leukemia? How do suffering children teach a mother to love them more than if her children didn't suffer at all?

Spiegel also needs to tell us what he thinks of the fall into sin by Adam and Eve. Was that necessary too? It has to be if he wants to defend his thesis. Otherwise, without any suffering there would be no character building. Spiegel should also comment on how human beings can achieve enough character development through suffering on earth to be perfect when they reach heaven. If there is no suffering in heaven then character building stops upon entrance to it. If the saved have not been perfected by that time then they will forever remain in the moral stage they were in when they died. That's why Hick also proposed successive reincarnations, so that exact replicas of us could somehow attain perfection. Spiegel needs to tell us if his God instantaneously makes people perfect upon arrival in heaven. If so, wouldn't this abrogate their free will? And if God does this in heaven then why couldn't he do so for people before reaching heaven? If God is prepared to violate free will in heaven then why not on earth? Furthermore, Spiegel writes as if compassion, patience, and generosity are all important moral traits to learn from suffering, but he never answers the question as to why we should need these traits in heaven if there is no suffering. Without suffering in heaven there is no need for those moral traits at all. There would be no reason for compassion since no one suffers, nor patience since there is nothing to be impatient about, and no need for generosity when there is no want.

Lacking an answer to these types of questions Spiegel isn't defending a theodicy at all. At best he's offering a partial solution, something he admits. He asserts the other part of his solution is the free will theodicy of Augustine. When the soul-making theodicy is taken together with Augustine's theodicy Spiegel thinks they "provide a powerful response to the problem."[19] But until he answers the type of questions I have asked we don't know if these two theodicies are complementary at all. Are they? He cannot just assert that they are complementary. Hick's theodicy stands opposed to the theodicy of Augustine. If Spiegel wants to pick and choose between them he needs to compare and contrast them. He did not do that. Until he does it's hard to know how to criticize arguments that are left unstated.

Spiegel's thesis is a very small one, almost irrelevant to the real issue. It gets him nowhere toward the larger issue of the immense and ubiquitous amount of intensive suffering in this present world. He doesn't come close to defending the thesis that "most" suffering is necessary at all. And for him to defend a real theodicy he needs to argue that all suffering is probably necessary.

Process theologian David R. Griffin criticized Hick in these words:

> Hick provides no reason why God should have wasted over four billion years setting the stage for the only thing thought to be intrinsically valuable, the moral and spiritual development of human beings. And the high probability that hundreds of millions of years of that preparation involved unnecessary and unuseful pain counts against Hick's defense of the omnipotent God's total goodness. . . . Surely an all-wise, omnipotent being could have found some happier middle ground between our present, all-too-destructive world, and the "hedonistic paradise" Hick fears would make us morally and spiritually flabby. . . . Is a creator who has the power to create a completely different type of world and yet who deliberately builds earthquakes, tornadoes, and cancer into the structure of the world, who creates us so that moral evil is necessary—moral evil that can produce Hiroshimas and Auschwitzes—is a deity who would do all this, solely for the sake of knowing that some of its creatures came to love their creator freely, "limitlessly good?"[20]

So not only does Hick's God not care for animals, which is an argument I've made before, it seems like a complete waste of successive human lives along with our sufferings to perfect our souls like this, when other means to the same end could work just as effectively. David Hume argued that it's quite possible we could be motivated by pleasure alone rather than pain. Hume argues,

> pleasure alone, in its various degrees, seems to human understanding sufficient for this purpose. All animals might be constantly in a state of enjoyment: but when urged by any of the necessities of nature, such as thirst, hunger, weariness; instead of pain, they might feel a diminution of pleasure, by which they might be prompted to seek that object which is necessary to their subsistence. Men pursue pleasure as eagerly as they avoid pain; at least they might have been so constituted. It seems, therefore, plainly possible to carry on the business of life without any pain. Why then is any animal ever rendered susceptible of such a sensation? If animals can be free from it an hour, they might enjoy a perpetual exemption from it; and it required as particular a contrivance of their organs to produce that feeling, as to endow them with sight, hearing, or any of the senses. Shall we conjecture, that such a contrivance was necessary, without any appearance of reason? and shall we build on that conjecture as on the most certain truth?[21]

As illustrations of Hume's pleasure principle in action, neither children nor pets need to be hit, spanked, or beat in order for them to learn how to behave well. Rewards and praises can do this very effectively. If they misbehave then a stern look of displeasure or a time out in the corner can be effective. We can even ground our children or cage our pets. These kinds of things do the training trick quite nicely, and humanely. And even if we think some kind of pain is necessary for embodied people to have, like hunger pains that can motivate us to work for a living, or to help us avoid touching a hot plate, the pain we experience does not need to be as intense as it presently is. God could give us a greater pain threshold, or he could deaden our senses by degrees.[22]

Special Pleading God's Attributes

Before ending this chapter I want to briefly indicate how special pleading is used as a substitute for apologetics when it comes to the problem of suffering and an omni-God. If you want to be a Christian apologist then you must master this art. If you want to be a *good* Christian apologist you must avoid doing so entirely—although, if you avoided doing so you wouldn't be an apologist at all.

I have found Christian apologists to be experts at picking and choosing between God's attributes of omnipotence, omniscience, and omnibenevolence (or perfect goodness), depending on the problem to be solved. When it comes to God's omnipotence in the face of so much intense suffering, apologists conveniently negate it by focusing instead on God's omniscience, saying we cannot understand his ways. God, like a father, knows best, they'll say when it comes to explaining why an omnipotent God allows so much suffering. So in order to save their faith from refutation they must allow God's omnipotence to go only so far, and no farther. This is where his power arbitrarily ends, where the apologist needs it to end to solve a problem for faith. Process theologians like John B. Cobb Jr. and David Ray Griffin have even been forced to deny God's omnipotence in order to solve the problem of suffering. According to them God merely has the power to persuade. He doesn't have coercive power.

When it comes to God's omniscience in the face of so much intense suffering, apologists conveniently negate it by focusing instead on God's omnibenevolence—that God created a perfectly good world despite the fact that doing so meant there was the probability (or real possibility) free creatures would disobey.[23] They will claim God didn't know how to create free-willed creatures who never disobey, or at the minimum don't disobey very often, or in such inhumane ways. So in order to save their faith from refutation they must allow God's omniscience to go only so far, and no farther. This is where his knowledge arbitrarily ends, where the apologist needs it to end to solve a problem for faith. Evangelicals such as the late Clark Pinnock, along with John

E. Sanders, Richard Rice, and Gregory Boyd, are even embracing Open theism, which denies God can foreknow future free-willed human actions.

Christian apologists will even negate God's omnibenevolence if that is what's required to believe. Since there is clear evidence for a great amount of gratuitous suffering in the lives of so many people—suffering that has no ultimate explanation for the individuals who are suffering—evangelicals such as Michael Peterson, the late William Hasker, and Bruce Little deny what is called *Meticulous Providence*. In their view some of our suffering is because God is not directly involved in our daily lives.[24] According to them, God does not care to be involved in our daily lives, so we suffer as a result. If this isn't their point, then what is? Certainly an omniscient God knows how to intervene. Certainly an omnipotent God has the ability to do so. Shouldn't an omnibenevolent God have the motivation to do so?

It should be easy for God to eliminate the horrendous suffering in our lives. That's not too much to ask of a truly omnipotent, omniscient, omnibenevolent deity, is it? If you name any specific example of horrendous suffering in this world I can easily show how such a God could have eliminated it without adversely affecting anything else, since such a deity would be able to perform what I have previously called *Perpetual Miracles*. If we accept that God is omnipotent for instance, and that he created the universe from nothing, then he should be able to perform perpetual miracles. So God could miraculously intervene without us ever knowing that he had done so. As I've said, he could have stopped the underwater earthquake that caused the Indonesian tsunami of 2004 with the snap of his omnipotent fingers, and a quarter of a million people would not have died. Then, with a perpetual miracle, he could have prevented it from ever occurring in the future. We would never be the wiser if he wanted to remain hidden for some unknown reason, for, from our perspective, it would never have taken place!

The fact is that the more knowledgeable and powerful a person is, the greater that person's moral responsibility to help others who are experiencing horrendous suffering. Just think of a helpless slave girl who was being whipped by a Southern plantation owner. A person who didn't know that this was taking place could not have been held morally responsible for not doing anything to stop it. A person who knew it was taking place but had no power to stop it could not have been held morally responsible for not doing anything to stop it. Since God is believed to be both omniscient and omnipotent, he bears the highest possible degree of responsibility to stop it. The best explanation for God not helping that girl, or any of us who intensely suffer, is that God isn't omnibenevolent. So in order to save their faith from refutation, Christian apologists must allow God's omnibenevolence to go only so far, and no farther.

This is where his perfect love ends, where the apologist needs it to end to solve a problem for faith.

Apologists look at the world and force their conceptions of God to fit what they see. It is emphatically not the case that they first define their God based on the perfect-being theology derived from Anselm's *Ontological Argument* to God's existence. The greatest conceivable being than which no greater being can be conceived ends up being the same one that best suits their need for faith. For when it comes to their conceptions of God they conclude he didn't have the power to create a world without naturally caused suffering, that he didn't know how to create a world where there are free creatures who never disobey, and that he doesn't care enough to intervene in our lives on a daily basis. Either their ontological conceptions of the perfect being really mean something, or they don't. Christian apologists cannot arbitrarily negate them when it suits their faith. What they should do instead is take their ontological conceptions of God and ask what kind of world *should* exist if such a God created it, rather than look at the world that presently exists and force their conceptions of God to fit it. Doing what they do is little more than special pleading. They cannot continue this type of intellectual gerrymandering if they want to be taken seriously. To paraphrase John F. Kennedy, ask not what kind of God should exist given this present world. Ask what kind of world should exist if God exists. But then, if you do this you wouldn't be an apologist at all. Seriously!

Conclusion

If Christian theists want to produce a theodicy they need to do at least five things. First, they must produce coherent notions of what they are talking about. What does it mean when they use the word "God," "good," "perfect, or best possible world," "free will," and so on. What does it mean to have "omnipotence," omniscience," or "omnibenelovence"? On these types of questions I found chapter 4 of James Lindsay's book, *God Doesn't; We Do: Only Humans Can Solve Human Challenges*, to be excellent. Especially damning on these concepts are parts 4 and 5 of Michael Martin and Ricki Monnier's anthology, *The Impossibility of God*.

Take for instance the word "good." If God is not good in the same sense we think of the word good, and if he is not held to the same moral standards we hold others to whom we call good, then God cannot be an object of worship or be viewed as morally good. For him to be worthy of worship and morally good his behavior has to be in accord with our notions of what we would consider to be worship worthy and good.

Second, they must argue to the existence of the God of their specific definitions, as opposed to other notions of God. A lot of ink is wasted between them on just how to properly conceive of the God within the Christian tradition, much less of the many other god-concepts people believe in. Third, they must consistently apply these notions. I have argued previously that they will pick and choose between God's omniscience, omnibenevolence, and omnipotence whenever it suits them depending on the issue to be solved. When pressed against the wall they will say anything to get out of any problem that calls into question their faith. Let's recall again Stephen Law's insightful observation: "Anything based on faith, no matter how ludicrous, can be made to be consistent with the available evidence, given a little patience and ingenuity."[25]

Fourth, they must show that the God they are defending is biblically based. We do not find such a God as they are defending in the Bible. All they would have to do is read Jaco Gericke's chapter, "Can God Exist If Yahweh Doesn't?" in The *End of Christianity*. Fifth, they must honestly deal with the empirical evidence we see around us. I consider the empirical evidence to be as close to a refutation of their God as we find, as I'll argue in the last chapter of this book.

What should we conclude? Michael Martin writes about a hypothetical guy named Jones who is dead, with some of his friends suspecting a cover-up by the police. It's possible there is a police cover-up of the evidence of course, but they can produce no evidence this is the case. "In the context of religion," he writes,

> the idea that God's reasons for evil are comprehensible has been widely accepted by theologians from St. Augustine to Hick, who have attempted to specify what those reasons are. Every attempt to formulate a systematic theodicy confirms the view that is commonly accepted that it is possible to understand why, if God exists, there is evil. Naturally, the failure of all such attempts might have driven theists to claim that the reasons are beyond comprehension. But without independent support, such a claim rings hollow. For example, Jones's friends could claim that despite their repeated failures to expose a police cover-up, there is one nonetheless. They could say the police are so clever and cunning that exposing such a cover-up is all but impossible. But without independent evidence this charge is ad hoc and arbitrary. The same is true in the context of the problem of evil.[26]

14

Blame Anything but the Creator God

The problem I wish to examine here is how sin and suffering originated and the final consequences for it all. In a chapter for the book, *God and Evil*, Paul Copan, the president of the Evangelical Philosophical Society, addressed how sin and suffering originated.[1] The possible suspects are Adam, Eve, Satan, the environment, or God himself. Copan argues that he has the answer, Adam and Eve dunnit. He says this even though Adam and Eve are two separate potential sources for the origination of sin and suffering. Many sexist and misogynistic theologians have simply blamed Eve. Others who blame only Adam deny that Eve could actually make such a choice on her own since she didn't have the authority to do so. If Adam had not made the same choice as Eve there wouldn't have been a fall into sin, they'll say. This is a male religion plain and simple folks. Why any woman would embrace the religion of their oppressors baffles me. Copan ignores this problem, saying instead they are both to blame. Okay.

Who Dunnit?
Those of us who don't have a problem with the origination of suffering (or "evil") are reasonable people who accept the fact of evolution. Suffering is part of the process whereby life evolves. The tales of an Adam and Eve are pure myth and science backs this up, as I have said. But it's a problem for believers given their belief in a good omnipotent omniscient God who created the world.

Copan first takes aim against R. C. Sproul Jr. (yes, the Sr.'s son) whom Copan describes as a hyper-Calvinist. Sproul argues that God himself "introduced evil into the world."[2] Now get this, Sproul argues the reason God wanted Adam and Eve to sin is because of God's eternal attribute of wrath: "God is as delighted with his wrath as he is with all of his attributes." So with this attribute God must create objects of wrath, or as God would say, "something on which I can exhibit the glory of my wrath." Without these objects of wrath God would not be able to display his glory in the fullest way. Sproul says, "It was God's desire to make his wrath known. He needed, then, something on which to be wrathful. He needed to have sinful creatures."[3] Sproul's case can be found in several biblical passages:

Isaiah 45:7:
I form the light and create darkness,
I bring prosperity and create disaster;
I, the Lord, do all these things.

Lamentations 3:37–38:
Who can speak and have it happen
if the Lord has not decreed it?
Is it not from the mouth of the Most High
that both disasters and good things come?

Amos 3:6:
When a trumpet sounds in a city,
do not the people tremble?
When disaster comes to a city,
has not the Lord caused it?

Proverbs 16:4:
The Lord works out everything to its proper end—
even the wicked for a day of disaster.

The Hebrew word for "disaster" as translated in these texts indicates war, famine, drought, floods, and so on. Copan argues these passages don't describe God doing "evil" presumably because God works all "evil" out for the good (Genesis 50:20; Acts 2:22–14; and Romans 8:28), or he's punishing people for their sins. So is God causing suffering here or not? That is what we're talking about, right? And don't children suffer when God strikes a city with a disaster? Should they also suffer along with the adults who sinned? And what about any adults who didn't sin? Were they whisked away from trouble like Lot and his family supposedly were in his day? Or were the innocents to suffer too? Would-be apologists should study what Copan says so they know how to do apologetics correctly.

Maybe Copan and Sproul should both just listen to biblical theology professor Walter Wink, who informs us about the God of the Old Testament in his book, *Unmasking the Powers*:

The original faith of Israel actually had no place for Satan. God alone was Lord, and thus whatever happened, for good or ill, was ascribed to God. "I kill and I make alive," says the Lord, "I wound and I heal" (Deut. 32:39; Isa. 45:6–7; 1 Sam. 2:6–7). It was not inconsistent, on the one hand, to believe that God might call Moses to deliver Israel from Egypt, and on the other hand, for God to want to murder him on the way (Exod. 4:24–26). When Pharaoh resisted Moses it was not ascribed to his free will, but to God's hardening of his heart (Exod. 4:21; 7:3; 9:12; 10:1, 20, 27; 11:10; 14:4, 8, 17; Josh. 11:20, etc). Likewise, it is God who sent an evil spirit on Saul (1 Sam. 16:14–16, 23), and it was God who sent a lying spirit to enter the mouths of the four hundred prophets of Ahab (1 Kings 22:22; see 2 Sam. 17:14). . . . One possible translation of "Yahweh," God's name, is "He causes to happen what happens." If, then, God has caused everything that happens, God must also cause evil. But God was also the God of justice (Gen. 18:25). So how could God be just and still be the one to cause evil? This was the terrible price Israel had been forced to pay for its belief that God was the primary cause of all that happens. Gradually God became differentiated into a "light" and a "dark" side, both integral to the Godhead. The bright side came to be represented by the angels, the dark side by Satan and his demons. This process of differentiation took a long time to complete.[4]

I think both Sproul and Copan are right, and they are both wrong. They both fail to understand the evolutionary trajectory of the texts they're dealing with. Sproul is right that given some earlier texts God does cause disasters and suffering. He is wrong, however, not to see that such a view was eventually ascribed to Satan because an evil-doing God was thought to be irreconcilable with a loving sovereign God. Given the destruction put upon the Jews by Antiochus Epiphanies in the 2nd century BC, Jews just couldn't understand why a good sovereign God would do this to them. So they concluded there must be another source for that evil, and Satan was born.[5] So if later biblical writers had to create (or adopt) Satan because of the problem of suffering then Sproul is out of touch with their evolved moral intuitions, the ones I share without punting to a mythical creature like the Devil. Sproul is out of touch with reality.

Copan is right when he argues that Sproul's view denies God's goodness and espouses divine neediness and, I add, barbarism to the core. Copan is wrong, however, to argue that Adam and Eve are the culprit (singular) with their so-called free-willed choice in the garden to disobey God. Almost unbelievably all Copan can do is to quote from creeds, Augustine, and other biblical passages. It's quite obvious that's what he's doing, at least to me. Grant Copan the creeds and the Bible, then Adam and Eve's sin was culpable, avoidable, and voluntary. He's quoting myths to explain how the primeval couple was led into sin. He totally avoids questions like: Why were they created as curious people in the first place? Why was the serpent allowed to tempt them, especially if God knew they would sin? Even if God didn't know the outcome with certainty, he surely knew the probabilities were very high. Why weren't they given enough evidence to take him at his word that eating the fruit would lead to serious consequences for all subsequent life on earth? . . . and so on. So Copan too is out of touch with reality, not unlike Sproul.

What we have in this myth is nothing but etiology. These stories are told for the purpose of helping to explain why things are they way they are, not how things originated. How did we gain knowledge and wisdom? Why do men and women marry? Why do snakes crawl on the ground? Why do women fear snakes? Why do men rule over women? Why are women subservient to men? Why do women experience pain in childbirth? Why is it so very painfully hard to work the land? Why are there weeds? Why is there famine, disease, and death? Why do we clothe ourselves rather than run around naked? Why do we die? It's all here. Etiological stories used to explain why things are they way they are litter the ancient archives. There is no historical truth to such tales at all.

If you really want to know what the Jews thought was the real fall into sin, it's told in Genesis 6:1–4. It opens up with a description of the evils that had finally taken place on earth. There is a new and horrible evil. The divine "sons of god" were having sex with the "daughters of men" and producing semidivine offspring giants called Nephilim. This biblical text tells us that divine beings have genitalia and produced offspring. Yep, that's right, nothing but myth. This was viewed as a deliberate act of rebellion that Donald Gowan tells us was understood by early Jewish commenters to be "more important than the story of the sin of Adam and Eve. . . . For several authors this was the true 'Fall Story,' the account of how evil came into the world by means of the descent of certain rebellious angels."[6] The fact is that if the story of Adam and Eve in the garden was that big of a deal there are plenty of places in the Old Testament where it could be used, specifically in Proverbs for instruction, and in Job when dealing with the problem of suffering. But it's not referred to in the whole Old Testament except in a nebulous nondescript way in Ezekiel.

The truth is that the origin of sin is never traced back to Adam and Eve in the Old Testament. This concept didn't emerge until the intertestamental period between the Old and New Testaments, especially in the apocryphal and the forged literature. In these texts we first find this as the point of the story. We find such a viewpoint expressed in noncanonical writings like the *Wisdom of Solomon* (2:23ff.), where we read, "For God created man for incorruption, and made him in the image of his own eternity, but through the devil's envy death entered the world, and those who belong to his party experience it." In 2 Esdras

7:118 we read, "O Adam, what have you done? Your sin was not only your own downfall; it was also the downfall of all of us who are your descendants." Old Testament scholar Claus Westermann accurately tells us: "The teaching of the Fall and of original sin rests on the late Jewish interpretation. It has no foundation at all in the [Genesis] narrative."[7]

Original Sin?

The doctrine of original sin is an in-house debate between Christians. There is a huge divide among evangelicals themselves over this whole issue. They don't agree with each other about the nature of original sin or the consequences of it. Paul Copan is an Arminian (which is a later improved development of Pelagianism), as are the rest of the contributors to the book *God and Evil*. No other Christians need apply. Perhaps like me, they think Calvinism does not adequately solve the problem of evil, to say the least. I think that is a major agreement between us.

If God is sovereign as Calvinists claim, then he can do pretty much anything he wants to with a complete and total disregard for decency and morality. I charge this kind of God as showing partiality by revealing himself to some people but not to others (even though he forbids us to show partiality—James 2). I think this kind of God is barbaric, since he lies to us (telling us he wants us to do one thing but secretly "causing" us to do something else); he doesn't abide by his own ethical obligations laid out in the Bible (whereby he can virtually violate all ten commandments and still demand worship as a holy God); and he condemns people to hell simply because it brings him more glory (if, however, he can control our free-willed choices, then why didn't he make us all obey in the first place)? Suffice it to say that if Calvinism is true, then God cannot be a good God because he decrees all of the evil we experience in human history. All of it. No belief in "God's inscrutable ways" can absolve God of this guilt. And no alternative definition of human freedom can absolve God of this guilt either. Clark Pinnock, an evangelical and an Open theist, responded to such a theology in these words: "One need not wonder why people become atheists when faced with such a theology. A God like that has a great deal for which to answer."[8]

Paul Copan argues for several things in his chapter on the subject of original sin: (1) original sin is contingent—not inevitable or necessary, saying, "Humans are not intrinsically, essentially or fundamentally evil"; (2) original sin is universal, saying, "Humans are not divided into two camps—the good on one side and the evil on the other. Sin pervades every heart"; (3) original sin is radical, saying, sin "is persuasive and affecting us deeply"; (4) original sin is communicable, saying, "Our sinful condition has been passed from one generation to the next extending back to Adam." He claims humans are not guilty for Adam's sin but we are "damaged or corrupted by it." We have an "original corruption, a self-centered orientation that permeates all that we do," he says, for which we cannot be blamed. However, we are morally blameworthy when we personally choose to sin.[9]

Isn't our sin therefore inevitable? he asks. No, for although "we will eventually sin," we "don't sin necessarily." Eventually we will all sin, he says, but it isn't inevitable or logically necessary to say we will all sin. What can this distinction mean when it comes to human actions? I do not have the faintest clue. If we will all sin, then it is *inevitable* that we will all sin. What else can the word inevitable mean? It does not help his case to deny that we sin out of any logical necessity. But for Copan this settles it. Is this language game of his supposed to solve the problem of a good God and human suffering? Since we don't sin out of a logical necessity God is not to be blamed when we sin, even though we will all inevitably sin? Well then, may God be praised for this tiny itty-bitty escape from his own responsibility! Did he create us or not? If so, couldn't he have done better than this? Or, is God incompetent, or worse, does he not exist in the first place? Again, would-be apologists should take note on how to do apologetics correctly.

But what about Adam in the Garden? What if we were given the same test under the same initial conditions? Then what? Copan believes God has *Middle Knowledge* such that he knows all counterfactuals of each free decision that any of us would have made, which is to say God even knows the future of any world had we made choices different from the ones we did. Therefore God would know which human beings would also have sinned in the Garden and created us into this present fallen world. If we exist on earth that means we would have sinned in the Garden, you see, even if we weren't there in the Garden of Eden. "Knowing this, God allows us all to begin exactly where each of us would have ended up anyway—namely in a fallen condition." Well, well, well. If God has that kind of foreknowledge then he could just skip the trials of earth and merely create the people who would not have sinned in the Garden directly into heaven itself. He wouldn't need to create the people who would have disobeyed either, saving them from going to hell. Furthermore, Copan's God could have also foreknown who would accept Jesus for salvation and then simply create them in heaven too. Everyone who was ever created would end up in heaven! Glory be to God!

But no. Even though God has this kind foreknowledge and could alleviate so much suffering by utilizing it, he chose not to do so. So, we are back to where we started. Whence so much suffering? Neither Calvinism not Copan's Arminianism offers us a clue. We are back to square one. The puzzling thing to me, the really puzzling thing, is why any reasonable person would accept Copan's answer? It just does not make any sense at all, not a bit. Typical apologetics. Budding apologists should one again take note.

There are plenty of other things wrong with his assumptions. I can only deal with so much at a time.

Dembski's Solution

The focus of William Dembski's chapter for the book *God and Evil* is on theistic evolution. His charge is that theistic evolution "renders the problem of evil insoluble."[10] I agree. When theists legitimately criticize each other I think they are all correct. The money quote on this comes from Clive Harden, who is a contributing writer on Dembski's blog, in response to theistic evolutionist Karl Giberson:

> Why would God be off the hook for creating a mechanism (evolution) that kills and destroys the way it does? For in Giberson's theodicy, not only did God make the process of evolution, He set it in place and started it. This would be like me letting a bunch of mice, some infected with a plague, loose into a town. The mice have their own freedom to do whatever they want and go wherever they want, and do it all without a "moral dimension." This does nothing to get me "off the hook" for whoever as a result dies.[11]

Agreed, yes! What's interesting to me is that the editors of the book *God and Evil* didn't include the main thesis of Dembski's book, which seeks to offer a theodicy in the face of so much natural suffering. I've already written about it in my book, *Why I Became an Atheist*, where I discussed several failed attempts to reconcile the Genesis creation accounts with the age of the universe. Dembski's attempt makes the list. So let me reproduce what I wrote about it below.

Dembski argues in favor of the double creation theory of J. Jay Dana, that chapter 1 of Genesis describes God's initial conceptual creation, which "was good," as the Good Book says. But because God could anticipate the sin of Adam and Eve in the Garden, Dembski says he retroactively made a second creation described in the story found in Genesis 2–3. Genesis 1 describes the first creation God had planned for the world, which is a real one, for it describes "the natural divisions" of his creative handiwork. But "in Genesis 2–3, we find the 'second creation,' which starts off great but quickly ends in ruin. Thus once humanity falls into sin in Genesis 3, God must act to undo the damage." And he says, God "could make the Fall evident in creation so that these effects, though attributable to the Fall, come temporally prior to it. In other words the effects of the Fall can be retroactive." "Thus God responds to the Fall by acting not simply after it, as held by young-earth creationism, but also by acting before it." "Genesis 1 is therefore not to be interpreted as ordinary chronological time but rather as time from the vantage point of God's purposes." Genesis 1 "summarizes the order of creation" by describing "God's original plan for creation." But, given that "God responds to human sin across time (both retroactively and proactively), there never was a chronological moment when the world we inhabit was without natural evil." Dembski claims God retroactively created the universe based on the fall into sin with natural evils built into it, like the bubonic plague bacterium, the rabies virus, and the toothpick fish of the Amazon, which can swim up a penis and cannot be dislodged short of surgery or castration, to name a few.

So God initially created a perfect world but then recreated it with natural evils from the beginning because of the later sin of humans in the Garden of Eden. There is absolutely no textual support for this conjecture of his at all. It's just speculation in order to come to grips with what science has shown us about the age of the universe. That there are two creation stories in Genesis 1–2 is evident. That other creation stories, especially the ones in Job 38:38–41, 39:26–30, and 104:20–22, describe predation in the natural world is also evident. It's just that it makes much more sense to interpret them according to the times they were written in, an ancient prescientific age. That's doing exegesis. What Dembski is doing is eisegesis, or reading into the text his own biases.

What Dembski is doing with this argument is puzzle solving. He's not interested in searching for the truth. How do we know this? Because no biblical scholar embraces such a bizarre solution. Dembski isn't one, and J. Jay Dana was a geologist. Furthermore, this "solution" doesn't solve the problem of animal pain and suffering, something I've written extensively about. Even if Dembski is correct, what did animals do to deserve their sufferings? [12] Nothing. So whence then do they suffer?

William A. Dembski isn't the only one who thinks God can answer prayers retroactively. So did C. S. Lewis and recently Kevin Timpe. [13] Since Dembski believes in a God who can retroactively change the past, his proposal presents a difficulty concerning prayer. If his God can change the past then why doesn't he do so in response to prayer? [14] If God answers prayers retroactively believers should pray for the past to be changed just as they do in praying for present and future hopes to be realized. Can these apologists really have it both ways, saying God can answer these prayers but also denying that the past can be changed? So let me suggest a scientific test if God can answer these kinds of prayers. Pick an event in the past and pray that God changes it. The event could be as simple as praying that some kids who were in a car accident and died the night before, did not die because there was no accident. My prediction is that the past will never be changed *and* that every prayer to change the past will be remembered by the one who prayed it precisely because nothing will ever change, ever. What's *your* prediction?

A "Free Process" Defense?

In a chapter for *God and Evil* Garry DeWeese aims "to deploy the empirical phenomena of 'chaos systems' to help us understand why the world is such that natural evils occur."[15] Basically arguing for John Polkinghorne's "free process" defense, DeWeese claims such a line of reasoning is "quite plausible, with considerable empirical support." He argues, "God might well have good reasons to create such a world, even with the possibility of natural evil." That is, "chaos systems in our world make natural evil possible," and even "perhaps inevitable."[16] So "even God cannot make such a world where natural evil never occurs."[17] DeWeese ends his chapter arguing that at least some natural evil is actually moral evil due to both demonic and human activity.[18]

When it comes to chaos theory, also known as the "butterfly effect," DeWeese claims that such a dynamic world order (contrasted with a static one) is beneficial to life, produces novel outcomes, and allows for human creativity. Fair enough. Of course it does! That's why we are here is the first place. Without such a dynamic world we wouldn't exist. So what DeWeese is doing is as follows: the world operates according to X, therefore God had to create a world that operates according to X.

Here God's omnipotence ends where the apologist needs it to end to solve a problem for faith. Why couldn't an omnipotent creator who creates *ex nihilo* (out of nothing) just create a different world? Go figure. Typically Christian. Same thing goes for God's omniscience. Aren't his ways supposed to be infinitely beyond our understanding? That's what we hear so many times it's nauseating. But when it comes to solving the problem of massive ubiquitous naturally caused suffering in our world, the apologist argues God didn't have the omniscience necessary to create a different world than the one that presently exists. There is such a lack of imagination and ignorance here it is stunning to me. I think faith stunts one's imagination and inspires ignorance.

Look, either omnipotence means something or it does not. Either omniscience means something or it does not. No, not even a deity can do the logically impossible, nor can he know what is logically impossible to know. But limiting God's power and omniscience arbitrarily as apologists do so often is proof that faith is irrational. I'm looking at this world and asking whether or not God exists, while the apologist already believes God exists and is trying to explain why there is intense suffering in this world given that prior belief. The fact is that this world is not the one we would expect to find if there were a good God, and these two different perspectives make all the difference in the world.

David Hume first made this distinction in these words:

> What if I show you a house or palace where there was not one apartment convenient or agreeable, where the windows, doors, fires, passages, stairs, and the whole economy of the building were the source of noise, confusion, fatigue, darkness, and the extremes of heat and cold? . . . The architect would in vain display his subtilty, and prove to you that, if this door or that window were altered, greater ills would ensue. What he says may be strictly true. But still you would assert in general that, if the architect had had skill and good intentions, he might have formed such a plan of the whole, and might have adjusted the parts in such a manner as would have remedied all or most of these inconveniences. His ignorance, or even your own ignorance of such a plan, will never convince you of the impossibility of it. If you find any inconveniences and deformities in the building, you will always without entering into detail, condemn the architect.[19]

That being said, even a child could imagine a better natural world than this one. Here I'll quote a selection from my book *Why I Became an Atheist*:

> God should not have created predation in the natural world. The amount of creaturely suffering here is atrocious, as creatures prey on one another to feed themselves. All creatures should be vegetarians and/or vegans. And in order to be sure there is enough vegetation for us all, God could've reduced our mating cycles and/or made edible vegetation like apples trees, corn stalks, blueberry bushes, wheat, and tomato plants to grow as plenteous as wild weeds do today. God didn't even have to create us such that we needed to eat anything at all. If God created the laws of nature, then what's the problem? The process of photosynthesis could have fed us, something we find in the natural world.
>
> God could've created all human beings with one color of skin. There has been too much killing and slavery, and there have been too many wars, mostly because we do not all share the same racial background and language.
>
> God could've made all creatures sexually self-reproducing. Asexual reproduction would eliminate gender harassment and discrimination, since there wouldn't be any gender differences between us. Even if there are social benefits that result from two-parent sexual reproduction, societal ties could still be instilled within us by God.
>
> God could've created us with much stronger immune systems such that there would be no pandemics that decimate whole populations. God could've created us with self-regenerating bodies. When we receive a cut, it heals itself over time, as does a sprained ankle or even a broken bone. But why can't an injured spinal cord be made to heal itself? Why can't an amputated leg grow back in a few weeks? If that were all we experienced in this world, we wouldn't know any different.

We find a lot of things in nature that God could've done for us. God could've created us with a much higher threshold of pain. He could've given us wings on our backs so we could fly to safety if we were to fall off a cliff. He could've given us gills to keep us from drowning.

Only if the theist expects very little from such a being can he defend what God has done. Either God isn't smart enough to figure out how to create a good world, or he doesn't have the power to do it, or he just doesn't care. You pick. These are the logical options given this world.

Let me comment briefly on DeWeese's claim that at least some naturally caused suffering is moral evil due to both demonic and human activity. For this argument to work there has to be evidence that Satan and his demons exist, as well as evidence there was a fall into sin by Adam and Eve in the Garden of Eden (yes, there really are pseudo-intellectuals who believe this crap!). I'll merely respond with two dilemma's.

Dilemma Regarding Adam and Eve

It's believed there was a first human pair (Adam and Eve) who so grievously sinned against God when tested that all of the rest of us are being punished for it (including animals), even though no one but the first human pair deserved to be punished. If it's argued that all of us deserve to be punished because we all would have sinned, then the test was a sham. For only if some of us would not have sinned can the test be considered a fair one. But if some of us would not have sinned under the same initial test conditions then there are people who are being punished for something they never would have done.

Dilemma Regarding Satan[20]

If Satan was the brightest creature in all of creation, and he knew of God's immediate presence, absolute goodness, and omnipotent power like no one else, then to rebel against God makes him pure evil, suicidal, and dumber than a box of rocks! How is it really possible that any creature in the direct unmediated presence of God would want to rebel against the absolute goodness and love of an infinitely all-powerful being? Even if a creature wanted to rebel, he would know that such a rebellion would be absolutely futile. But since no rational being can be that evil or stupid, he doesn't exist at all.

Furthermore, if such a God existed he would never have allowed Satan to work his evil ways upon others, unless he simply did not care about us. God should have either immediately incarcerated Satan or put him out of existence entirely. For by not doing so, God has allowed Satan something that no decent civilized society would ever allow. Once we know there is a powerful, deranged, sociopathic maniac on the loose, we put him in prison so he cannot harm anyone else in our society. We take these kinds of people out of the population. It's the decent, caring, civilized thing to do.

The Final Punishment for Sin

In Jerry L. Walls and Kyle Blanchette's chapter in *God and Evil* they try to reconcile God with hell.[21] The first thing to be noticed is that in this same book there are two chapters that disagree with each other on hell. The two authors of this chapter say of William Lane Craig's previous chapter, "Diversity, Evil and Hell: A Particularist Approach,"[22] that his "sophisticated" version of exclusivism "strikes us as implausible."[23] Craig's traditional view of hell is something I already touched on in chapter 8 of this book, when discussing the problem of religious diversity.

Why would there be two chapters on hell in the same book that disagree with each other? The answer is obvious. It's because evangelicals are presently in the process of revising their theology, that's why. So what to do? Present both sides. The traditional evangelical exclusivist view, as defended by Craig, will keep exclusivists happy. More progressively minded evangelicals will be happy that the inclusivist view has now attained such a status it can be presented on an equal footing with the traditional view. If the progressives eventually win (and I think they will), their views will be the new orthodoxy. Then amnesia will set in. Future students in evangelical seminaries will be taught this new orthodoxy as if it was always the truth.[24] I'm here to remind them that Christianity has always reinvented itself in the face of social criticisms and the advancement of learning, especially due to scientific advancement. This is just more of the same old same old gerrymandering we have come to expect from them.

When it comes to hell, the two authors of this chapter say, "there is a big difference between a claim being uncomfortable or difficult to grasp, and it being rationally untenable."[25] So far so good. Basically, they argue that the unevangelized and nonbelievers like Gandhi probably will be saved. God gives optimal grace to all sinners in which he does everything he can so people are saved—short of overriding their freedom—such that only people who make a decisive choice to reject it will end up in hell forever. In their view postmortem conversions take place in hell, since God's justice is restorative and he does all he can to save them even in hell. The language in the Bible about hell is metaphorical for the punishment that sinners will receive from God. If the damned keep on sinning forever then they will stay there forever. The nature of hell is described by the authors as a prison with some freedom and some goodness in it too, depending on the character of the prisoner.

Okay? Didn't think so.

Who would reject God's optimal grace if God does everything he can in order that people are saved? That it is crystal clear God is not doing everything in this world to save people is obvious. Listen, hell is either a painful place or it is not. If the damned prefer hell then it is pleasurable to be there, and if that's so, then heaven would hell for them. But if hell is painful then no rational person would prefer staying there, none. Only the brain dead would, the mentally challenged, the irrational.

Look, if I knew God was real and many virgins awaited me in heaven (oops, wrong religion), then I would easily and quickly confess my sins and legitimately repent from them. Who wouldn't? This would not be lip service to get a heavenly reward any more than when Christians do this for a heavenly reward. No sin would be worth staying out of paradise because that's what paradise is all about, pleasure beyond one's wildest dreams. Have they even given a minute's thought about this, or are they mindlessly quote mining the Bible and the theology they've developed based on their eisegesis of it?

Evangelicals make pathetic scholars. That's why I call them pseudo-intellectuals. They act as if the canonical Bible just fell into their laps from the sky (except when writing about how we got it). When doing theology pseudo-intellectuals ignore all of the other surrounding cultural ideas and influences on the biblical writers, even on the Jews themselves during the intertestamental period, as if they don't count. And why not? Because the biblical writers wrote down the God-breathed words to them, that's why. God, who is above culture and its influences, simply told them the truth. "We don't need no studying what other cultures taught or believed about hell, 'cause we got da truth here, baby, the whole truth. All we got ta do is eisegete, er exegete it, to fit the problems of today. Da Bible say it; we believe it (in our own way)—dat settles it."

Nowhere in their chapter nor in the footnotes is there any reference to the development of the concept of hell among ancient Mesopotamians, early and later Jewish thought, nor Roman or Greek thought on the subject. It just didn't occur to Walls or Blanchette to do any research into it, or if they did, they didn't think it necessary to alert readers to this literature. Here, try just one book on it written by Alan E. Bernstein, where you'll find other references for further reading, *The Formation of Hell: Death and Retribution in the Ancient and Early Christian Worlds*.[26] Typical evangelicals. They are pseudo-intellectuals, no question about it. Ideas develop over time and crossculturally, especially as the Jews and early Christians were located in the midway point of the Fertile Crescent trade route. What a serious study of hell would show is that the doctrine was not initially Jewish but was graphed on to the Jewish faith through these cultural influences and later became part of the early Christian tradition. It looks like a man-made religious concept, not a divine one at all.

Hell, conceived as punishment in the afterlife, is as mythical as the creation accounts in Genesis and the Adam and Eve story, period.

Walls and Blanchette's attempt to reconcile God and hell fails miserably for so many reasons I don't have the space. Their attempt reminds, once again, of what philosopher Stephen Law wrote: "Anything based on faith, no matter how ludicrous, can be made to be consistent with the available evidence, given a little patience and ingenuity."[27] This is what they do when they reinterpret key passages in the New Testament to fit their preconceived notions. They do this because they cannot give up their faith in the face of the realities of the Bible. In order to do this they must solve this puzzle. It's puzzle solving that they are doing, not trying to figure out what is the truth.

Then there's this whole notion of "genuine moral freedom." I think most evangelical "intellectuals" were born with enough of a silver spoon in their mouth that they have never experienced life on the streets of the Bronx, let alone in a place like Darfur. They need to seriously consider the nature and value of freedom.[28] I suggest reading Jonathan M. S. Pearce's book, *Free Will?: An Investigation into Whether We Have Free Will, or Whether I Was Always Going to Write This Book*,[29] as a primer. Hell is a barbaric concept created in the mythical barbaric past. Period. No modern-minded person should even bother with it, just as non-Muslims do not give a moment's thought to fearing Allah's hell. They are all empty threats from the cradle to the grave.

15

Make Illegitimate Excuses for God

In this chapter I'll examine some of the excuses offered for God's inaction in the world given the nature and intensity of suffering that exists in it. I call them excuses because when talking about a truly all-powerful, all-knowing, perfectly loving God, that's all that can be offered, excuses, illegitimate ones. If you want to be a career Christian apologist then here you'll see how to do the job right.

The Hidden God Excuse
Chad Meister deals with the hiddenness excuse in the book he coedited, *God and Evil*.[1] He begins by trying to lay out the problem, as argued by J. L. Schellenberg. I say "trying" because in some ways he gets it right while in others he doesn't. Schellenberg's argument goes like this:

1. If there is a God, he is perfectly loving.
2. If a perfectly loving God exists, reasonable nonbelief does not occur.
3. Reasonable nonbelief occurs.
4. No perfectly loving God exists (from 2 and 3).
5. Hence, there is no God (from 1 and 4).

Meister repeats this argument word for word, but on at least three occasions he mischaracterizes it. Schellenberg limits his argument to *reasonable* nonbelief. He's not dealing with nonbelief in general. He isn't arguing God's existence should be obvious to everyone either, nor does he argue there should be no room for doubt. But Meister puts words into the mouth of someone who argues on behalf of it, saying, "But if God does exist, his existence *should be obvious*. We should have clear, undeniable experiences of God, and his existence *should be so obvious that we don't have any doubts about it*."[2] Schellenberg never suggests

God's existence should be so obvious. Meister mischaracterizes his argument again: "Either God can't make his presence known to all or won't do so. If God won't make his presence known to all, God must not be omnipotent."[3] And again: "But a perfectly loving and good God, it seems, would ensure belief in God by all persons."[4] The problem is that Schellenberg isn't speaking about all nonbelief, but reasonable nonbelief.

To his credit though, in responding to Schellenberg, Meister rejects the views of Jonathan Edwards and James Spiegel, who both claim reasonable nonbelief doesn't occur at all. Instead, he thinks "there are (many?) cases of reasonable and morally nonculpable nonbelief."[5] This is a welcome agreement, since, if I don't have a reasonable and morally nonculpable nonbelief, then few others do.

In answering this problem I was oddly struck by the number of times Meister used the words, "perhaps," "maybe," "could be," "might," and "may be". He's trying to solve this problem that has the weight of probabilities to it with mere possibilities. What are the possibilities? One possibility that Meister focuses a great deal of effort on has to do with the claim that God may hide himself from people because they may not be ready to receive him yet. Here are four of his examples, with my responses:

First, if some people have suffered serious trauma they may need healing before God can reveal himself to them. No, no, no. Most people who suffer cry out to God for help in these times. They want to know God exists and cares. But God sits silently by and does nothing to show them that he exists and cares, Meister apologizes, because these sufferers need healing before God can help them. What? Isn't God supposedly the healer? "Heal thyself and then we can talk" is God's nonresponse, according to Meister.

Second, a person may not believe in God, or think the concept is meaningless, and as such would be unreceptive to faith. So for God to "force" himself on this person it "could be psychologically or emotionally damaging."[6] Why would it be emotionally damaging? Because these people might come to realize they were wrong? I guess this didn't bother God when Jesus supposedly appeared to the disciples upon resurrecting, nor to doubting Thomas, nor to James the brother of the Lord, nor to Saul of Tarsus. When will these apologists ever get their stories straight? Which is it? Is it too traumatic to appear to people and change their minds or not? Is this the same God who did so "once upon a time" (hint, hint) but doesn't do it any longer when we need him to? Apparently the trauma of being shown the truth is just too much when compared to the trauma of being cast (no, "allowed" of their own free choices) into hell. These very people may die and go to hell before the time is right. "Oh, so sorry," I can hear God say over the screams of people suffering intolerably in hell. "The time just wasn't right. You win some and you lose some, that's the way it goes sometimes. I tried, I really did. Bad timing. Damn. Maybe I'll have better luck with the next person."

Third, if God revealed himself to some people at the wrong time "it could . . . produce the wrong kind of belief or knowledge of God."[7] What Meister means is that God doesn't just want a reasonable belief in propositions about God, he wants people to have a relationship of trust with him. Listen, I do not have a personal relationship with propositions in the same way I have personal relationships with people. But there are a set of propositions I hold to about everyone I know. Propositions about God are a necessary condition to having a personal relationship with God. Given that there are so many different conceptions of the Christian God, we know God allows people to hold to a set of incorrect propositions about him, unless, of course, only people who believe exactly as Meister does have a relationship with God.

Meister later suggests that reasonable nonbelieving people just aren't listening for God, who reveals himself best in a "still small voice" (See 1 Kings 19:11–13). Or, that nonbelievers have false expectations of who God is and how he reveals himself to us. He says, "If one has flawed expectations of what belief in and experience of God should be like, then one might misconstrue the situation and falsely conclude God is absent when, in fact, he is very present."[8] So apparently God cannot reveal himself to nonbelievers and at the same time correct any important false propositions they may have about him. Really? Again folks, here's where God's omnipotence ends, where Christian apologists need it to end in order to solve a problem for their faith. Typical Christian.

Meister needs to take into consideration that this "still small voice" of his particular God is so muffled that the same religious experience Christians claim to have had is not unique to Christians at all. If religious experiences for Christians are veridical then why are they indistinguishable from all others? Is God's still small voice loud enough for anyone to hear it? Tibetan Monks who sit quietly in meditation for hours a day don't hear it. Why should anyone else?

Fourth, a person may not be ready to accept God, given that his or her present beliefs and life experiences "could cause the person to come to believe in God for the wrong reasons, perhaps out of fear or trepidation or an egoistic desire for success."[9] Come on now, really? I know of no believer who came to believe for the right reasons to begin with. They usually have an emotional experience in a tent revival meeting, were raised to believe, or had a dramatic conversion when down on their luck. Why on earth would God be so concerned about this anyway, if salvation from hell is at stake? Does a child have good reasons to believe? If not, then why does God bring so very many of them into the fold at such an early stage in life when they don't have anything more than the word of their parents to believe?

Meister opines after all of his empty rhetoric that the main reason God hides himself "is due to God's love and concern for people who are not ready to believe and have a proper relationship with him." Then he quotes a famous line from Blaise Pascal: "There is enough light for those who only desire to see, and enough obscurity for those who have a contrary disposition."[10] That is a prime example of an illegitimate excuse for God. It's based on faith, not evidence. Whenever apologists must argue based on faith not evidence, that's a clear sign their brain is lying to them. But this is how it's done right, so would-be career apologists should take note, or something.

The Gratuitous Suffering Excuse

Bruce Little offers up an illegitimate excuse concerning gratuitous suffering.[11] Gratuitous suffering is suffering that admits of no overarching purpose in God's scheme of things. In the vernacular, to admit gratuitous suffering is to admit that shit happens for no reason. Little argues the existence of gratuitous suffering would still be consistent with God's perfect goodness. His thesis is that "*if* or *when* gratuitous evil exists it would necessitate no denial or redefinition of any of the attributes of God, nor would it subvert the moral perfections of God."[12]

I have an immediate gripe with his chapter in *God and Evil*. Little often says atheists are the ones arguing that God must have a greater good purpose for everything that happens in the universe, except for one tiny parentheses where he admits "(and some theists)." Really? Who knew? In fact, I would guess that most theists have said this throughout the history of theology. Consider just two examples: Terence Penelhum said, "It is logically inconsistent for a theist to admit the existence of a pointless evil."[13] Norman L. Geisler and Winfried Corduan said, "Unnecessary evil of any kind would certainly be incongruous with an absolutely perfect God."[14] Atheists are not the ones who first made this claim. We always take our cue from what Christians are saying. If they say X is true then we respond to X. If they change X to Y then we will respond to Y. It's that simple. So would-be apologists please don't go around claiming we make this argument. It's ignorant and disingenuous. We are only responding to what Christians claim.

Little argues, along the same lines as Michael Peterson before him, against meticulous providence, which is the belief that God only allows suffering that serves a greater good. The central factor concerns human free will. Little quotes Peterson as saying: "God cannot completely prevent or eliminate gratuitous evil without severely diminishing free will. That would be logically impossible."[15] So

Little concludes, "God allows us to make real choices with real consequences because he respects his own created order. This makes gratuitous evil a real possibility without denying the moral perfections of God."[16] He does this "while affirming a traditional evangelical understanding of divine attributes of the trinitarian God of the Bible."[17]

Okay so far? I didn't think so. There is a great deal of "metaphysical machinery" needed to defend this argument.

Most of his chapter is trying to convince fellow Christians to accept the possibility of gratuitous suffering. It's an in-house debate in which Little actually concedes the point, that there might exist gratuitous suffering. It shows that atheists have a moving target here. This leads me to say something important about what's going on in his chapter. It's called apologetics, pure apologetics. Here's how it works. There is a very serious problem to be resolved, one that William Rowe forced Christians to deal with based on a greater good theodicy that most all Christians accepted prior to Rowe's arguments. Christians found it difficult to explain a greater good to come from his two cases, one involving a fawn that was roasted to death by a forest fire, and the other one about a five-year-old girl who was beaten, raped, and strangled to death. What to do? Give up their faith? Of course not. No, find a way of least resistance, some way to resolve the pain of the cognitive dissonance knocking at their door. Do whatever it takes to resolve it even if it means denying almost all theologies of the past. Change what you believe. Call it progressive revelation if needed.

Likewise, if the doctrine of hell seems too painful to a polite civilized society then argue for annihilation. If the harsh statements in the Bible toward women or slaves or animals seem abusive then reinterpret them at will. If the passages in the Bible about genocide and child sacrifice seem too repulsive then just do a revisionist reading of them. Wash. Rinse. Repeat. Repeat again. Then future generations of Christians will forget what took place and think this is what Christianity has always taught. What we're witnessing folks, in light of skeptical responses against their faith, is a reinvention of evangelical orthodoxy. It is nothing short of theological relativism, as I said in chapter 1. The whole idea of progressive revelation leads us to it, for there is no point in the history of theology where any theologian can say they have the absolute truth. God's purported revelation in the past was "true" for Christians just as God's purported revelation for this generation is "true," and just as God's purported revelation will be "true" for future generations. In the last few decades I have seen what I can only describe as a massive revisionism of evangelical theology. They are even embracing Darwinian evolution. So don't talk to me about an absolute standard for theological truth. It doesn't exist. It never did. And never say again that the Bible has withstood all the arguments of the critics. No it has not. Christians have merely changed what they believed in the face of the arguments from the critics.

Since Little did a fair enough job of arguing against the greater good theodicy, which is indeed morally bankrupt, let me just offer five criticisms of Peterson and Little's revisionist theology. First, Little finds justification for his views in the Bible and the world. In the Bible God doesn't inhibit free choices that caused harm, nor does he do so in the world. Therefore Little concludes God doesn't meticulously intervene to prevent gratuitous suffering. Little is on a problem-solving mission, trying to harmonize his faith with the facts. Yes, this takes thinking, of course, but he takes for granted his faith rather than question it in the face of this very serious problem. You see, it says so right here in the Bible. And we see it in the world too. Special pleading is what he's doing. Of course God doesn't meticulously intervene in the Bible or the world. That's because the God of the Bible is totally unlike the perfect being theology of Anselm, if he exists at all (and I don't think he does). We find biblical statements contrary to this perfect being theology. Yahweh sends disasters upon people (Isaiah 45:7), lying spirits to deceive and false prophets, and God hardens hearts and causes people to believe a lie. The omnibenelovence of God is not found in these texts. Oh, it says on occasion that he loves his subjects, but what kind of love is it for God to destroy people in floods, or genocides, or force mothers to eat their own babies, send famines, droughts, and locusts on people if they disobey, or send people into eternal suffering? This is not represented by perfect being theology at all. Such a God is modeled on the barbaric kings of the ancient times who were thought of as divine themselves. We know this.

Contrary to Little, in the Bible we even read this: "In the LORD's hand the king's heart is a stream of water that he channels toward all who please him." (Proverbs 21:1) That's what it says. And yet God isn't meticulously involved in the world's affairs? Really? There are some pretty strong biblical statements to the contrary, like the many meticulous providence Bible verses, including (Gen 50:21; Isa 45:5-7; Acts 4:27–28 Rom 8:28; 11:36; Eph. 1:11). Which is it? It doesn't matter, for with faith anything can be believed or denied.

Second, Little presents an idealized view of libertarian free will that no one has. He quotes from his guru Plantinga, who defined it like this, "if a person is free with respect to a given action, then he is free to perform that action and free to refrain from performing it; no antecedent conditions and/or causal laws determine that he will perform the action, or that he won't."[18] However, there are always antecedent conditions to all of our choices, many of them which are definitely caused. We don't have much free will, if we have it at all.

Third, let's say Peterson and Little are on to something. Then the question arises that if God is not meticulously involved in our lives, how can he help us in times of dire need? How can he answer prayers if they depend on changing the free choices of others? I know of a real case in my area where a guy drove up to the door of a good Christian mother and forced his way inside at knifepoint. Right in front of her two small children, who had just prayed for God's protection, he forced her to perform a sex act on him. He tied them all up and got away with it. I saw a program about a mother and daughter who had stopped at a highway rest stop and were abducted and repeatedly raped, before having their throats slit with a serrated knife (the guy later confessed). Read your newspapers for many, many more of these kinds of things. To admit of gratuitous suffering like this means we cannot count on God to help us at all.

Oh, but wait, Christians might ask me how I know God doesn't intervene on some occasions. Well, how do I know that there wasn't some stranger outside my window an hour ago who was seeking to rob and kill me? But perhaps God caused this bad guy to subjectively hear police sirens and see their nonexistent squad car, so he fled. The answer is clear and obvious. Since so many more worthy cases than mine go without any divine intervention, there is no evidence God did anything to help me an hour ago. With faith anything can be believed, or denied. I need evidence, and the objective evidence from daily life is that God does nothing to help. So no wonder Little is willing to embrace a nonintervening God (or it seems). That's not a faith worth sinking one's teeth into. If that's the kind of God Little needs, he can have him, for a God who doesn't meticulously help us isn't worthy of worship either.

Fourth, this brings up the issue I raised earlier with regard to the way apologists gerrymander the three divine attributes—omniscience, omnipotence, and omnibenelovence. Listen, I am a white male who is not butt-ugly (or so a few people tell me), who grew up in a middle-class family with all the privileges of my upbringing. I have had a good education. I have never spent a day in the hospital so far, and never had a broken bone. I have never gone hungry either. I have had my wits about me, most of the time anyway. ;-) By comparison to most people on the planet now and in the past I have been born with a silver spoon in my mouth, so to speak. But I am here to tell you that life is hard, really hard for me. Life is not for the weak, that's for sure. I have experienced pain, some suffering, loss, and failure. This life has tried me to the core without any horrendous suffering in it. So we do not need it if my life is any indication. All that God must do is to care enough to eliminate the horrendous kinds of suffering in our lives, the kind I have not experienced. That's not too much to ask of a perfect being, is it? There is plenty of suffering left in this life to try our souls. But according to Peterson and Little, God does not care that much to eliminate horrendous suffering. In order to save their faith from refutation they must only allow God's perfect goodness to go so far, and no farther. He is not meticulously involved in the affairs of our lives because he cannot care that much to do so. This is where God's omnibenelovence ends you see, where the apologist needs it to end to solve a problem for faith. Go figure. Typical Christian apologist.

Lastly, there is a good objection to Peterson and Little's kind of theology, but as far as I know neither Peterson nor Little have responded to it. In Little's 2010 book on this subject, *God, Why This Evil?*[19] he never mentioned Nick Trakakis's book, *The God Beyond Belief: In Defense of William Rowe's Evidential Argument from Evil*, published four years earlier in 2006.[20] And Little doesn't mention Trakakis's book in this 2013 chapter or notes either (surely at least a note is required—after all, he's dealing with Rowe's arguments and Trakakis is defending them). Just as James Dew ignored Graham Oppy's book, so also Bruce Little ignores Nick Trakakis's book. This is particularly egregious since Trakakis has a whole chapter called, "The Compatibility of Gratuitous Evil with Theism." Is this the kind of scholarship that passes muster among evangelicals? When there is an argument you either don't want to deal with, or possibly can't, then sweep it under the rug. Ignore it. Maybe no one will notice, right? ;-)

Here's one of the things Trakakis wrote in criticism of Peterson:

> To see what is wrong with Peterson's account of gratuitous evil, consider the paradoxical nature of his claim that a given moral evil may be gratuitous even though God is justified in permitting that evil for the sake of preserving human freedom. That there appears to be something incoherent about this claim has not been lost on many commentators.

So Trakakis tells:

> By proposing that the benefits accrued from free will and a law-like natural system constitute God's reasons for permitting moral and natural evil, Peterson "remains embedded in the greater good tradition," as Chrzan puts it.

On these types of considerations the Peterson and Little proposal fails, just as the greater good proposal failed before them.

The Evolutionary World Excuse

Karl Giberson and Francis Collins' chapter for the book *God and Evil*, "Evil, Creation and Evolution," was originally a chapter in their book, *The Language of Science and Faith: Straight Answers to Genuine Questions.*[21] The first thing to note is that they argue against William Dembski's attempt to make human beings retroactively responsible for all suffering before the fall, calling it a "desperate move."[22] Christians arguing against other Christians? We've never seen that before, right? The second thing to note is that Ken Ham's young earth ignorant creationism isn't given a voice in this book since Dembski, Collins, and Giberson all argue against it. But why not? Why exclude Ken Ham from this book? Sure, he's ignorant, but so also are Dembski, Collins, and Giberson, even though they are less ignorant. The ignorant thing they all share is the common belief that the Bible is in some way God's word, the divine truth.

Listen up, there is nothing we can learn about science from a supposed sacred ancient prescientific book, period. Anything the Bible might get right about science is not because we find it in the Bible, but because of science itself. Christian theology always changes in response to the advancement of science and never the other way around. If it refuses to do so, as the authors in this book recognize so obviously in the case of Ken Ham, it becomes irrelevant to modern people. So why would any person in today's world even try to harmonize modern science with the Bible in the first place? There's nothing to harmonize. Just accept that the Bible cannot tell us anything about science. Quit hamstringing science through the prescientific constraints of the Bible. Quit gerrymandering the facts to fit the Bible. Quit arguing based on the informal fallacy of appealing to ignorance. Quit trying to make your faith intellectually respectful by appealing to science. Admit science cannot point you to the God of the Bible and just say you have faith, even though faith is an irrational leap over the probabilities. Let science do its work unfettered by ancient superstitions.

When it comes to the problem of suffering Giberson and Collins claim that the "evolutionary picture of the world . . . makes the problem of widespread evil in nature less threatening to faith than the alternatives."[23] After claiming humans cause a great deal of harm due to "genuine free will," without so much as even trying to understand the nature and value of free will, the authors argue nature has been given freedom too. They write, "many processes in nature exhibit a genuine unpredictability that looks, for all the world, like freedom."[24] This sounds somewhat like the "free process" defense of Garry DeWeece examined earlier, except that they apply it to the evolutionary process itself. Suffering is the result of the freedom God gives to his creation, both human beings and the natural evolutionary processes. "Both humans and all creation have freedom,"[25] and with freedom comes the creativity to cause both good and harm. "Unless God micromanages nature so as to destroy its autonomy, such things [like the Black Death plague, which I argue in chapter 16 refutes Christianity] are going to occur. Likewise, unless God coercively micromanages human decision making, we will often abuse our freedom."[26] The reason God cannot micromanage the world, they assert, is because "God cannot constantly intervene" in human activity and the natural processes without disrupting them.

Without such an orderly and consistent world "science would be impossible . . . and the world would not be as rich with meaning and opportunity."[27] Because of this, "God is off the hook"[28] for much of the suffering we experience in the world. This is reminiscent of Bruce Little and Michael Peterson's denial of meticulous providence, as I examined earlier.

The last sentence is the key. It gives the game away. Giberson and Collins are engaged in puzzle solving. They are not interested in the truth. That's what a brain overdosing on faith does to otherwise intelligent people. The goal is clear. Try to find a way to exonerate God from causing suffering, no matter how much of a sacrifice it requires for their intellect. Do whatever it takes to maintain one's faith in the midst of the onslaught of science and so much intense ubiquitous suffering in the world. Allow your brain to deceive you.

When it comes to theistic evolution itself, professor John Shook argues in a post titled "God and Evolution Don't Mix" that:

> If God was trying to produce us through evolution, what does that tell us about a God that would use that method? Here's some suggestions:
>
> A. God prefers diversity, not heights of intelligence or self-awareness. God does not prioritize creatures that can know God and praise God.
> B. God is quite comfortable with endless horrible struggle and suffering.
> C. God is quite comfortable with death—lots of it.
> D. God likely has plans for the future evolution of life that don't involve humanity.
> E. God probably is just using us to later get whatever kind of life He really wants.
>
> What is God really up to? Maybe God is slow-breeding angels. Or cyborgs. Or the Singularity. Maybe God doesn't want worshippers—maybe God is seeing if He/She/It can eventually create another fellow God?[29]

But let's grant theistic evolution and see what we get. When it comes to Giberson and Collins, William Dembski's criticism is on target:

> We never accept such shifting of responsibility in any other important matter, so why here? What difference does it make if a mugger brutalizes someone with his own hands or employs a vicious dog on a leash to do the same? The mugger is equally responsible in both cases. The same holds for a creator God who creates directly by intervening or indirectly by evolution. Creation entails responsibility. The buck always stops with the Creator. The rage in theology these days is to diminish the power and ultimacy of God so that God is fundamentally constrained by the world and thus cannot be held responsible for the world's evil.[30]

Again, the buck always stops with the Creator! When Christians legitimately criticize each other they are all correct, leaving no basis for believing at all. They do the work for me. All I have to do is report the results. Giberson and Collins respond to Dembski that he should be consistent. Since Christian apologists "*always* do exactly what Dembski says we should *never* do" by shifting the responsibility of the Holocaust "from God to the Nazis," then Dembski should "enlarge this general concept to include the sorts of things that nature is doing on its own."[31] Who knew? Again, this is mere puzzle solving. Do and say whatever it takes to exonerate their God from being blamed. They "always" do this.

Giberson and Collins face a serious theological problem. Their God cannot create the universe directly, but neither can he intervene in the world to alleviate more suffering than exists in the world. What then becomes of God's supposed omnipotence? They have either abandoned it or seriously limited what their God can do. Once again, God's omnipotence ends where the apologist needs it to end to solve a problem for faith. Go figure. Typically Christian. Sure, maybe it's possible such a supernatural being (or force) exists, but it isn't anything like the perfect being theology of Anselm, nor is it like the tribal warlike micromanaging God of the Bible either. They're making stuff up as they go, period.

There is one thing I agree with the authors of this chapter about. They said, "God cannot constantly intervene" in human activity and the natural processes or else "science would be impossible."[32] I've argued this myself:

> Science assumes there is a natural explanation for everything it investigates precisely because this is the only way it can work. If natural explanations for events were not possible because God regularly intervened in the world, then science would not be possible at all. To be more precise, to the degree God intervenes in the universe then to that same degree science is not possible. But given the massive amount of knowledge acquired by science it's crystal clear God doesn't intervene at all. The very basis of science is predicated on a non-miraculous world order. So we must choose between God or science.[33]

However, that agreement leaves Giberson and Collins with a non-miraculous world order, where God isn't intervening in our world today and where there is no reason any person should believe the rules of nature have ever been any different than they are now. Furthermore, and more specific to their overall case, why should their God be concerned about science anyway when it comes to human suffering? I can hear God talking to himself now:

The Holy Spirit: Looks like an underwater earthquake is going to destroy Indonesia with a tsunami.

The Father: Yep, I sure hope a few more turn to me in repentance before it hits.

The Son: Hey, how about we avert that earthquake so nothing happens?

The Father: That would require a perpetual miracle since, if we averted it and then let up, it will still take place later.

The Holy Spirit: Oh, right. That would require too much work. We're omnipotent and everything, but this is asking too much.

The Father: Not only that, but if we saved the lives of a quarter of a million people in this way then the science of plate tectonics would be impossible.

The Son: Choices, choices. I love all people so much I died on the cross for them, but we must allow for science to proceed.

The Holy Spirit: Yes, the progress of science is of the utmost importance.

Michael the Archangel: But wait Your Excellencies, if I may approach your triple thrones. Aren't you omnipotent such that a perpetual miracle should not be a problem? And isn't your overwhelming love to alleviate suffering more important than the advancement of science, especially since science is presently undermining your religion and has done so ever since the times of that rascal Galileo? Besides, if you intervene, no human being will even know you did, since no one will be the wiser for your having done so?

The Father, Son, and Holy Spirit:

SILENCE! HOW DARE YOU ASK QUESTIONS OF US!

In the end Giberson and Collins admit their theistic evolutionary position doesn't resolve the problem, because "there is no resolution to the problem of evil,"[34] they note. Right that!

16

Ignore This Empirical Refutation
of Christianity

I intend to refute Christianity in this chapter, the type of Christianity largely associated with *The Evangelical Theological Society* and the *Evangelical Philosophical Society*. I'm not going to *conclusively* prove Christianity is false by showing it suffers from a logical inconsistency. Rather, I only intend to prove it falls way below the threshold of probabilities. Any Christian who believes is doing so against the overwhelming empirical evidence to the contrary. And I have little hope of convincing many devout educated Christians, but a little hope is good enough to try. It is hard to argue Christians out of their faith because they were never argued into it in the first place. They usually inherit it inside a Christian culture from their Christian parents, just as other believers inherit their respective religious faiths inside their different religious cultures by their parents.

If someone judges my case to fall short of a refutation, then so be it. That should not be a cause to dismiss it. At a minimum, the reasonable person should at least conclude from what I'll argue that Christianity is very improbable, and I will accept that, if nothing else. But I might as well shoot for the moon. The reason why I must shoot for the moon is forced upon me by Christians themselves. Their faith must be shown to be nearly impossible before they will ever consider it to be improbable, which is an unreasonable standard. So long as there is some tiny loophole for their faith in the face of an argument to the contrary, they will leap through it. Who in their right mind would demand such a high level of disproof in any other area except when it comes to religious faith? But they do, most all of them.

Would-be career apologists, are you still with me? You should be.

The Black Death Plague of 1346–1350 CE

There are plenty of undercutting defeaters to the Christian faith that come especially from evolutionary science, archaeology, psychology, neurology, anthropology, biblical criticism, and so forth. In every case, in the face of these and other defeaters, Christian apologists have resorted to possibility arguments. But the one I'll focus on in this chapter is the problem of suffering in the natural world, with specific reference to the Black Death plague of the fourteenth century. If there was ever an empirical refutation of Christianity, this is it. If a good omnipotent God exists, there would not be so much massive suffering in the natural world. *The probability that a good, omnipotent God exists is inversely proportional to the amount of suffering in the natural world (i.e., the more suffering we find in the natural world, the less probable it is that a good, omnipotent God exists). There is just way too much suffering to suppose that he does.*

The Black Death plague is thought to have started in China or Central Asia around 1346 CE. It arrived in England in June of 1348 after spreading from Sicily to Italy to Paris. Two ships arrived from Gascony, France, and docked at the town of Melcombe in Weymouth Harbour with sailors who were infected. The first inhabitants died within three days of being infected. Soon afterward more people in and around the surrounding area became ill, and many of them died. As the villagers sought refuge in other parts of the country, they spread this contagious disease with them. It didn't take long before it reached the major cities. The plague reached London in the fall of that year, and by the next summer, it had reached the entire country of England. This is documented by the fourteenth-century Franciscans at Lynn.[1] A historical marker can be found at that initial entry port, which reads:

> *The "Black Death" entered England in 1348 through this port.*
> *It killed 30–50% of the country's population.*

It was known to the people of that day as the "pestilence." It was one of the most devastating pandemics in recorded human history, killing around 100 million people in the known world, which had an estimated population of 450 million. Recent estimates show it killed nearly 50 percent of the European population. The movie *Black Death*, which hit the big screen in 2010, offers a gruesome visual glimpse at what it might have been like during this tragic, prescientific, superstitious era. It does for the Black Death what the movie *Saving Private Ryan* did for the Normandy invasion during WWII, and what the movie *Schindler's List* did to show the horrors of Jewish sufferings in concentration camps at the hands of the Nazis.

The symptoms of the Black Death were dreadful. There were painful tumors and purplish splotches that covered the body. Some tumors were as big as an egg or an apple. Pus and blood oozed from them. Then there was the fever that accompanied it that resulted in delirium. Madmen wandered through the streets acting crazily and shouting at the top of their lungs. They vomited repeatedly and coughed up blood. Once the symptoms appeared, the infected person died within days. Records show that there weren't enough healthy people to bury the dead, so the bloated bodies were left in the streets where dogs fed on them.

The people were clueless as to why this was happening to them. Most of them believed the pestilence was sent by God because of their sin. This led to the rise of the Flagellants, who went from town to town whipping themselves bloody while reciting sacred texts and praying, thus their name. They did it as an act of public repentance to God for the sins that caused him to send the plague. This only spread the disease more than before as the Flagellants moved from town to town. Many of them thought the world was ending. Some of them blamed the Jews by supposing they had contaminated their drinking water, and as a result, there was widespread killing of them. Christians burned Jews at the stake and set buildings filled with them on fire. In Germany, few Jews remained by the time the plague had ended. The Paris College of Physicians produced a report blaming the massive number of deaths on an interplanetary "fog of death." On March 20, 1345, there was a triple conjunction of the planets Saturn, Jupiter, and Mars. The report said that when this happened Jupiter soaked up evil vapors from the Earth and that the hot planet Mars ignited them. The fumes of this fire filled the air that people breathed, causing the pestilence. This was, of course, based on a pre-Copernican geocentric universe where the planets, moon, and the sun all shared the same air space with the earth's atmosphere.

They had no idea at all what to do about the disease. Most medical cures involved the use of bloodletting, by attempting to draw the "poison" out of a person's body, which actually sped up a person's death. The only effective thing they did was to quarantine travelers and merchants coming into their area or ports until it was determined they were not carrying the disease. If the travelers and sailors on ships didn't die in a week or two, they would be permitted to enter. In fact, the use of the quarantine as a medical procedure to stop the spread of contagious diseases first developed as a result of the Black Death plague. So people had to die to learn this lesson the hard way, millions of them.

How the Christian faith survived is beyond me. I know a thirty-five-year-old convenience store cashier who has serious heart problems and needs a heart transplant. He had his stomach reduced to lose body weight to alleviate the stress on his heart. I asked him how he was doing and he replied, "God is good," even though God could have done better. That's clearly what some medieval Christians concluded. Those who survived thanked God for their own health and survival. It is like a plane crash that kills everyone on board, leaving one survivor who says he is thankful to a good God who spared him. That is utterly selfish and egotistical, totally ignoring the fact that others died horrible deaths.

In general, though, many survivors of the Black Death suffered a loss of faith. The church offered no solution to it and could not offer any help. The priests themselves, since they had the most contact with the diseased people, suffered the highest rates of fatalities. If a good God cared that people believed in him and that they would not be sent to hell for nonbelief, then this is a textbook case in how not to do that.

It wasn't until a few centuries later that scientists figured out the cause and what could have cured this disease. The bacteria that caused this plague was *Yersinia pestis*, named after the bacteriologist who determined this in 1894, Alexander Yersin. *Yersinia pestis* is usually transmitted from rodents to the fleas that bite them, who in turn spread the diseased infected blood to humans by regurgitating infected blood into them. The treatment for this disease has been determined to be measured doses of streptomycin, chloramphenicol, tetracycline, and fluoroquinolones. That's science, baby. It works. Prayer does not work. Faith does not work.

When it comes to the Black Death there was literally nothing these people could do against the disease except to stay away from it. Nothing. They were utterly helpless against its attack. It took place in Christianized Europe, a place where Christianity ruled in the hearts and lives of almost everyone. And the result was catastrophic, as nearly 50 percent of the European population died and many survivors who doubted their faith were supposedly sent to hell.

Christian Responses to This Problem
In response to this problem, it is claimed God is omniscient, that his ways are higher than ours, so he knows best, using what I have called the *Omniscience Escape Clause* that seeks to overcome an improbability with a possibility. Christian apologist Stephen Wykstra best exemplifies this, as I explained before, when arguing that it is possible we cannot see a reason why an omniscient God allows so much suffering. "The disparity between God's vision and ours," he writes, "is comparable to the gap between the vision of a parent and her one-month old infant. This gives us reason to think that our discerning most of God's purposes are about as likely as the infant's discerning most of the parent's purposes."[2]

If such a response works, then the same one could justify continuing to believe in God even if most of the evidence is against God's existence, since it could be argued that an inscrutable God cannot be known to exist by means of our limited understandings. But it is duplicitous and counterproductive for such a God to have created us as reasonable people and then not given us what reasonable people need to believe. We must be able to understand enough of God's ways for us to conclude his ways are best, and there is just too much in this world we cannot understand if a good omnipotent God exists. Instead, he created us this way and withholds from us that which we need to believe, and in so doing will condemn us for how he created us. Surely an omniscient God would know the Black Death would later be seen by reasonable people after the rise of modern science to be disconfirming evidence that he exists. Yet he still did nothing to help.

In the case of the Black Death, there were a number of things a good omnipotent God could have done. At best, a good God could have created us so our bodies would be able to withstand these kinds of diseases. If not, he could have miraculously neutralized the infectious bacteria with a *perpetual miracle* if needed, which, because it would be a perpetual miracle, would not adversely affect anything else in the natural balance of things. If nothing else, God could have told us how to make the necessary vaccines and antibiotics to cure these types of diseases. At the bare minimum, he could have told us about the use of anesthesia that could help people die painlessly. But he didn't do any of this. So he knew in advance that people would have to die tragic and sudden deaths before we could figure it all out. This would be considered gross negligence on the part of any doctor, if he or she knew how to help millions and millions of people and refused to do it. For, as I said earlier, the more informed a person is about a tragedy and the more power (or authority) such a person has to alleviate that tragedy, then the more of a moral responsibility that person has to help. Therefore, God, who is supposedly maximally informed and who has maximal power, is the most culpable of them all for not helping. He sat idly by while 100 million people painfully drowned in their own blood in the fourteenth century. Sisters, daughters, mothers, brothers, and fathers all watched their loved ones die this way as God did nothing. Nothing! And this is just one pandemic. There have been several others in recorded history.

If God's "reason" for not averting this pandemic is to control over-population, a much more benevolent population-control method would be to reduce our mating cycles in the first place.

It is curious to me how most Christians just do not think about some things. It is because the brain infected with faith blinds them, that's why. Has it ever occurred to you how human beings first learned what could kill them? People, mostly children, had to die for this knowledge to be discovered. Take lead poisoning. People had to die before we could figure it out. Then think about all of the poisonous plants and venomous creatures. People had to die from eating certain plants and being bitten by certain creatures before we knew what not to do. The same thing goes for drinking polluted water. Read Steven Johnson's book, *The Ghost Map: The Story of London's Most Terrifying Epidemic—and How It Changed Science, Cities, and the Modern World*, and see for yourself.[3] People in London were dying from drinking polluted water. They didn't have a clue why they were dying. Then science showed up. One scientist mapped out the places where people were dying and concluded they were dying in specific locations, the ones where there were polluted drinking wells. His solution that saved lives was to boil water before drinking it and clean out the streets from the garbage thrown into the middle of them. That's science, baby. It works. Prayer does not work. Faith does not work.

Christians say God wants us to freely believe so he doesn't reveal his power and presence to us, for if he did, we would be forced to believe.[4] Left completely unresolved is why God would care that we should believe, but we'll leave that aside. For one thing, as I described in chapter 1, Theodore Drange argues that since people want to know the truth about why they exist, then God would not be abrogating our free will by giving us what we want.[5] For another thing, there were people in the Bible to whom God supposedly appeared, like Moses, Gideon, Jacob, Mary, James, and especially the apostle Paul. If God could appear to them without abrogating their free will, then he can do so for the rest of us. If he can't do this without abrogating our free will, then he abrogated *their* free will. Furthermore, and more to the point, if God wanted to remain hidden, then all he had to do was stop the Black Death pandemic with the snap of his omnipotent fingers by neutralizing the infectious disease at the source. If he did this and stopped the disease before anyone was infected, no one would ever know he intervened. He could have remained hidden. It may have required a perpetual miracle, but then why is that a problem for God?

Christian philosophers like William P. Alston argue that "for all we know, God does sometimes intervene" in our world to prevent suffering.[6] But this is a mere possibility without any evidence for it at all. The number of tragic events throughout history and in today's world is strong evidence God doesn't intervene at all. Alston's argument is an ad hoc one meant to explain away the probabilities. It grants that the evidence is against what Christians believe, for if the evidence were otherwise, they wouldn't have to punt to mere possibilities.

Christians are using the "black or white," "either/or" fallacy, also known as "the fallacy of the beard," saying the only alternatives for God are to have a perfect world without suffering as compared to the present one with massive ubiquitous suffering. Then, given such a false set of alternatives, they will conclude I'm asking the impossible of God, since a perfect world would not try the souls of men adequately. But as I said earlier, I can know what a beard is without having to specify which whisker, when plucked, no longer leaves a beard. There are a wide range of alternatives for God, if he exists. If he were to merely eliminate the cases of massive intensive suffering, then this whole problem would be diminished by the same force. Once again, *the probability that God has intervened is inversely proportional to the amount of intense suffering we find in the world, and there is just way too much of it to suppose that he has done so.*

So, why didn't God do anything about the Black Death pandemic? Be reasonable here. This is but one example. I argue that Christianity is a faith that must dismiss the tragedy of death. It does not matter who dies, or how many, or what the circumstances are when people die. It could be the death of a mother whose baby depends upon her for milk. It could be the Spanish influenza pandemic that decimated parts of the world in 1918, or the more than 23,000 children who suffer and die every single day from malnutrition and starvation. These deaths could be by suffocation, drowning, drive-by shooting, or being burned to death. It doesn't matter. God is good. Death doesn't matter. People die all the time. In order to justify God's goodness, Christianity minimizes the value of human life. Far from being pro-life, it is a pro-*death* faith, plain and simple.

But here's the Good News: There is no all-good, all-powerful God. Period. The empirical evidence is overwhelming.

The Force of the Problem of Suffering in the Natural World

Christians just don't have a reasonable answer to this problem except to say they have good evidence to trust in God despite the weight of the suffering in our world. Okay then, how does this so-called evidence of theirs compare to this particular undercutting defeater of suffering?

Christians have philosophical arguments for God's existence. But if you actually read the literature on both sides, they are *at the very best* a wash. That is, given the counterarguments, they do not establish the case at all. As I mentioned in chapter 2, atheist philosopher Dr. Keith Parsons announced he was done teaching philosophy of religion classes because several atheists have "produced works of enormous sophistication that devastate the theistic arguments in their classical and most recent formulations" and, as such, have "presented powerful, and, in my view, unanswerable atheological arguments." So he can no longer "take [theistic] arguments seriously any more, and if you cannot take something seriously, you should not try to devote serious academic attention to it."[7] But he's not alone. Christian apologist Alvin Plantinga has also admitted these theistic arguments don't work, saying, "I don't know of an argument for Christian belief that seems very likely to convince one who doesn't already accept its conclusion."[8] Christian apologist John Feinberg doesn't think they work, for he wrote, "I am not convinced that any of the traditional arguments [for God's existence] succeeds."[9] Christian philosopher and apologist Richard Swinburne specifically rejects the *Moral Argument* to God's existence, saying, "I cannot see any force in an argument to the existence of God from the existence of morality."[10]

These theistic arguments do not lead to any one particular god, even if we were to grant that they worked. Much more effort needs to be done in order to establish that the *Christian* God exists after trying to establish that a creator exists. In order to do this, the evidence for miracles in the distant ancient superstitious past must lead to their particular kind of God. As I've mentioned previously, theists disagree over this supposed evidence even though they all believe in a creator God. Theists are just as skeptical of other distinctive religious miracles as I am of them all.

Take for example the Jews of Jesus' day. They believed in Yahweh, that he performed miracles, and they knew their Old Testament prophecies. Yet the overwhelming majority of them did not believe Jesus was raised from the dead by Yahweh. Since these Jews were there and didn't believe, why should we? No, *really*. Why should we? *Why should anyone?* The usual answer is that these Jews didn't want to believe because Jesus was not their kind of Messiah, a king who would throw off Roman rule. But then, where did they get that idea in the first place? They got it from their own scriptures. And who supposedly penned them? Yahweh. Christians will also claim God needed the Jews to crucify Jesus to atone for our sins, just as he needed Judas to betray him. So God needed to mislead them about the nature of the Messiah too. But look at the result. Because he did this, Christians have also been given a reason to persecute, torture, and kill Jews throughout the centuries for their alleged crime (the Romans are actually the guilty ones). Not only this, but the overwhelming majority of Jews will go to hell (however conceived), where Judas is right now. Does this sound fair for a righteous, omniscient judge? It smells exactly like entrapment, pure and simple.

Beyond this, the supposed resurrection of a virgin-born Son of God took place in an ancient, prescientific, superstitious age where virgin-born sons of God were believed to walk the earth, as biblical scholar Robert Miller shows in his book *Born Divine*.[11] In addition, Richard Carrier looked at the superstitious nature of the people in the Roman Empire in "Kooks and Quacks of the Roman Empire: A Look into the World of the Gospels," and concluded, the age of Jesus was not an age of critical reflection and remarkable religious acumen. It was an era filled with con artists, gullible believers, martyrs without a cause, and reputed miracles of every variety. In light of this picture, the tales of the Gospels do not seem very remarkable. Even if they were false in every detail, there is no evidence that they would have been disbelieved or rejected as absurd by many people, who at the time had little in the way of education or critical thinking skills. They had no newspapers, telephones, photographs, or public documents to consult to check a story. If they were not a witness, all they had was a man's word. And even if they were a witness, the tales above tell us that even then their skills of critical reflection were lacking. Certainly, this age did not lack keen and educated skeptics—it is not that there were no skilled and skeptical observers. There were. Rather, the shouts of the credulous rabble overpowered their voice and seized the world from them, boldly leading them all into the darkness of a thousand years of chaos. Perhaps we should not repeat the same mistake. After all, the wise learn from history. The fool ignores it.[12]

Again, why should we believe what some prescientific, superstitious people said in a lone place on the planet in the past? The past is notoriously difficult to mine for its nuggets of truth. This problem is exponentially compounded by the fact that we are supposed to believe miracles took place in this small place on the planet in that ancient era but not in ours. Gotthold Lessing put a fine point on this problem when he said:

Miracles, which I see with my own eyes, and which I have opportunity to verify for myself, are one thing; miracles, of which I know only from history that others say they have seen them and verified them, are another. . . . But . . . I live in the 18th century, in which miracles no longer happen. The problem is that reports of miracles are not miracles. . . . [they] have to work through a medium which takes away all their force. . . . Or is it invariably the case, that what I read in reputable historians is just as certain for me as what I myself experience?[13]

All that Christian apologists have is second-, third-, and fourth-hand testimony found only in manuscripts dated to the fourth century CE that Christians doctored up, among other texts that they forged, lots of others. The evidence of the gospels would be thrown out as unreliable testimony in any reasonable court proceedings. Even if not, we could not trust these testimonies to the resurrection of Jesus until we could interrogate those so-called witnesses ourselves. Who exactly were they? How did they first learn of the resurrection?

The New Testament tells us that early Christians were visionaries—that is, they learned things directly from the risen Jesus himself through dreams and visions (Acts 2:17, 16:9–10, 18:9, 22:17–18, 23:11), especially Paul (Galatians 2:2; Acts 9:17, 26:19; 1 Corinthians 9:1; 2 Corinthians 12:1–7). Paul even says he learned the gospel message itself from a vision (Galatians 1:11–12), along with the details of the Lord's Supper (1 Corinthians 11:23). In the book of Revelation, Jesus supposedly dictates seven letters to seven churches directly to the author (2–3). These are private subjective experiences. Why should we believe them?

Did these supposed eyewitnesses to the resurrection all tell the same story? Given the canonical gospels, we know they didn't. Did any of them later recant? We don't know. Almost all of our important questions are left unanswered. We do not have anything written directly by Jesus himself or any of his original twelve disciples. Nor do we have anything written by the Jewish leaders or Romans of that time as to what they thought about claims that he had resurrected. We know hardly any of them were converted to Christianity. In the gospels, Jesus always had the last word over his opponents—something I have never seen in any real religious debate. So we really need to know what his opponents said in response to these claims.

There is also a great lack of independent collaborative evidence. We have no independent reports that the veil of the temple was torn in two at Jesus' death (Mark 15:38), nor that darkness came "over the whole land" from noon until three in the afternoon (Mark 15:33), nor that "the sun stopped shining" (Luke 23:45), nor that there was an earthquake at his death (Matthew 27:51, 54), with another "violent" one the day he arose from the grave (Matthew 28:2), nor that the saints were raised to life at his death, then waited until Jesus arose before walking out of their own opened tombs, who subsequently "went into the holy city and appeared to many people" and were never heard from again (Matthew 27:52–53). Could these events really have occurred without subsequent Roman or rabbinic literature or Philo or Josephus mentioning them? These silences are telling.

Christians will argue their faith has unique elements, making the story more credible. Although this is debatable, what does it prove if so? Most religions have unique elements to them, such as Mormonism, Islam, Hinduism, Jehovah's Witnesses, and Seventh-day Adventism, as do smaller religious cults, such as Marshall Applewhite's Heaven's Gate and those led by Jim Jones and David Koresh. In fact, uniqueness is what can propel a new religion forward. But it says nothing about whether it's true at all.

Undeterred, Christians claim that they have religious experiences from their God that confirm their faith. But important questions abound. Why is it that so many people in non-Christian religions claim to have had these same experiences of a different god or goddess? Why is it that so many people on the planet with different conceptions of God all claim to have these same types of experiences? What value is it to have an experience when the content of that experience only confirms what you already believe? We know every believer thinks God agrees with them about everything.[14]

So, does the force of the empirical evidence for the problem of suffering outweigh the force of the evidence for the Christian faith? I think it does, most emphatically. On this rock the Christian faith dies. All Christians can do is argue based on special pleading, skirting the issue, the "you too" fallacy, appeals to ignorance, and begging the question. In other words, they've got nothing, nothing but possibilities, when probabilities are all that matter. Q.E.D.

* * *

If any apologist can honestly and intelligently defend Christianity from these kinds of problems, and do so better than any of the Christian apologists out there whom I have studied, then have at it. It is a losing goal though. It would take someone with the brilliance of the ages to do so, someone who would not duplicate the mistakes of all the Christian apologists I've studied so far. I'd like to say "good luck," but *that* would be insincere. So I merely say be honest life-long seekers of the truth. Doggedly follow the truth. Don't trust your brain. Ask lots of questions. Think like a scientist. Become a generalist. Adhere to the intellectual virtues I spelled out in chapter 3. If you do this you'll have a much greater chance of finding the truth and be better off. Remember most of all, that the best way to defend a conclusion you've reached is to start out being right. If you are a Christian you have started out being wrong.

Notes

Introduction

1. Randal Rauser, "Apologetics and the Problem of the William Lane Craig Clones," *Tentative Apologist*, February 1, 2015, http://randalrauser.com/2015/02/apologetics-and-the-problem-of-the-william-lane-craig-clones/.

Chapter 1

1. See my chapter 6 titled "What We've Got Here is A Failure to Communicate," in *The Christian Delusion*, ed. John W. Loftus (Amherst, NY: Prometheus Books, 2010), pp. 181–206.

2. Richard R. Rubenstein, *When Jesus Became God: The Struggle to Define Christianity during the Last Days of Rome* (Orlando, FL: Harcourt, 1999), and Phillip Jenkins, *The Jesus Wars: How Four Patriarchs, Three Queens, and Two Emperors Decided What Christians Would Believe for the Next 1,500 Years* (New York: HarperOne, 2011).

3. Do some research into the French Wars of Religion and the Thirty Years' War. See especially the important works of Jack David Eller, *Cruel Creeds, Virtuous Violence: Religious Violence across Culture and History* (Amherst, NY: Prometheus Books, 2010), and Hector Avalos, *Fighting Words: The Origins of Religious Violence* (Amherst, NY: Prometheus Books, 2005).

4. Centers for Disease Control and Prevention, "Handwashing: Clean Hands Save Lives," http://www.cdc.gov/handwashing/when-how-handwashing.html.

5. A few paragraphs that follow were originally published by me in chapter eight of *Christianity Is Not Great*, ed. John W. Loftus (Amherst, NY: Prometheus Books, 2014), pp. 176–78, with some editing.

6. The following section comes from the ending to chapter 8 in *Why I Became an Atheist* (Amherst, NY: Prometheus Books, 2008), pp. 164–68.

7. This is an argument I developed in chapter 9 of my book, *The Outsider Test of Faith*, (Amherst, NY: Prometheus Books, 2013), pp. 187–91.

8. This is a truncated version of Drange's argument seen in part 4 of *The Improbability of God*, ed. Michael Martin and Rikki Monnier (Amherst, NY: Prometheus Books, 2006), pp. 337–79.

Chapter 2

1. "Goodbye to All That," posted on *The Secular Outpost,* September 1, 2010, http://secularoutpost.infidels.org/2010/09/goodbye-to-all-that.html. Later Parsons said he wished he had used the word "vacuous" rather than the word "fraud" to describe the arguments. Professor John Beversluis made the same decision when it comes to his writings, saying via email: "Interestingly, Keith and I came to this conclusion more or less simultaneously but independently."

2. I've argued for this in a series of posts tagged as "Ending Philosophy of Religion" on my blog "Debunking Christianity." I answered the following questions: (1) Why do I propose ending philosophy of religion (PoR) as a subdiscipline of philosophy proper in secular universities?; (2) What should we know when it comes to ending PoR?; (3) What exactly is my proposal?; (4) What are the best ways to examine the claims of religion?; (5) What are some practical steps to help facilitate this proposal?; and (6) Why do secular philosophers of religion object to this proposal? See http://debunkingchristianity. blogspot.com/search/label/Ending%20Philosophy%20of%20Religion.

3. Richard Dawkins, *The Greatest Show on Earth: The Evidence for Evolution* (New York: Free Press, 2009), pp. 8–9.

4. Jerry A. Coyne, *Why Evolution Is True* (New York: Viking, 2009), pp. 222–23.

5. Especially in chapters 12 and 16 in *Why I Became an Atheist*, and chapter 9 in *The Christian Delusion.*

6. Jerry A. Coyne, "Adam and Eve: The Ultimate Standoff between Science and Faith," Why Evolution Is True, June 2, 2011, https://whyevolutionistrue.wordpress. com/2011/06/02/adam-and-eve-the-ultimate-standoff-between-science-and-faith-and-a-contest/ See also "Scientists Try to Reconcile Adam and Eve Story, Whiff. Again," *The New Republic*, http://www.newrepublic.com/article/115759/adam-eve-theologians-try-reconcile-science-and-fail. Used with permission.

7. From the book *Incognito: The Secret Lives of the Brain* (New York: Vintage Books, 2012). The essay is available at http://www.theatlantic.com/magazine/archive/2011/07/the-brain-on-trial/308520/.

8. Julian Baggini and Jeremy Stangroom, *Do You Think What You Think?: The Ultimate Philosophical Handbook* (New York: Plume, 2007), pp. 55–92.

9. Richard Dawkins, *The God Delusion* (Boston: Houghton Mifflin Company, 2006), p. 31.

10. This book is scheduled for release in 2016.

11. See especially chapter 5 in *Why I Became an Atheist*, my cowritten book with Randal Rauser, *God or Godless? One Atheist. One Christian. Twenty Controversial*

Questions (Grand Rapids, MI: Baker Books, 2015), and also my anthology *Christianity Is Not Great.*

12. James A. Lindsay, *God Doesn't; We Do: Only Humans Can Solve Human Challenges* (CreateSpace, 2012), p. 89.

13. John Hick expressed this problem in these words: "Neither the intense christological debates of the centuries leading up to the Council of Chalcedon, nor the renewed christological debates of the 19th and 20th Centuries, have succeeded in squaring the circle by making intelligible the claim that one who was genuinely and unambiguously a man was also genuinely and unambiguously God." As quoted in chapter 3 ("The Myth of God Incarnate") of N. F. Gier, *God, Reason, and the Evangelicals* (University Press of America, 1987).

14. Graham Oppy, *Describing Gods: An Investigation of Divine Attributes* (Cambridge: Cambridge University Press, 2014). See also Michael Martin and Ricki Monnier, ed., *The Impossibility of God* (Amherst, NY: Prometheus Books, 2003).

15. George H. Smith, *Atheism: The Case Against God* (Amherst, NY: Prometheus Books, 1989), p. 52.

16. Ibid., pp. 87–88.

17. Theodore Schick Jr. and Lewis Vaughn, *How to Think About Weird Things: Critical Thinking for a New Age,* 7th edition (Boston: McGraw-Hill, 2013).

18. David J. Hand, *The Improbability Principle: Why Coincidences, Miracles, and Rare Events Happen Every Day* (New York: Scientific American / Farrar, Straus and Giroux, 2014).

Chapter 3

1. Daniel C. Dennett, *Breaking the Spell: Religion as a Natural Phenomenon* (New York: Viking Penguin, 2006), p. 31.

2. Just look at the titles of some of these works: Leonanrd Mlodinow, *Subliminal: How Your Unconscious Mind Rules Your Behavior*; David DiSalvo, *What Makes Your Brain Happy and Why You Should Do the Opposite*; Thomas D. Gilovich, *How We Know What Isn't So: The Fallibility of Human Reason in Everyday Life*; Cordelia Fine, *A Mind of Its Own: How Your Brain Distorts and Deceives*; Carol Tavris and Elliot Aronson, *Mistakes Were Made (But Not by Me): Why We Justify Foolish Beliefs, Bad Decisions, and Hurtful Acts*; Michael Shermer, *The Believing Brain: From Ghosts and Gods to Politics and Conspiracies—How We Construct Beliefs and Reinforce Them as Truths*; Robert Burton, *On Being Certain: Believing You Are Right Even When You're Not*; Ori Brafman and Rom Brafman, *Sway: The Irresistible Pull of Irrational Behavior*; Christopher Chabris and Daniel Simons, *The Invisible Gorilla: And Other Ways Our Intuitions Deceive Us*; Dan Ariely, *Predictably Irrational: The Hidden Forces That Shape Our Decisions*; David McRaney, *You Are Not So Smart: Why You Have Too Many Friends on Facebook, Why Your Memory Is Mostly Fiction, and 46 Other Ways You're Deluding Yourself.*

3. Guy Harrison, *Think: Why You Should Question Everything* (Amherst, NY: Prometheus Books 2013), p. 67.

4. Read just one small nontechnical book on this by psychology professor Gary Marcus, *Kluge: The Haphazard Evolution of the Human Mind* (New York: Mariner Books, 2009).

5. Online at www.handwritinguniversity.com.

6. Carl Sagan, *The Demon-Haunted World: Science as a Candle in the Dark* (New York, Random House, 1996), Michael Shermer, *Why People Believe in Weird Things* (New York, Henry Holt and Company, 2002), Joe Nickell, *The Science of Miracles: Investigating the Incredible* (Amherst, NY: Prometheus Books 2013), Guy P. Harrison, *50 Popular Beliefs That People Think Are True* (Amherst, NY: Prometheus Books 2012), David J. Hand, *The Improbability Principle: Why Coincidences, Miracles, and Rare Events Happen Every Day.* (Scientific American / Farrar, Straus and Giroux, 2014), Mike McRae, *Tribal Science: Brains, Beliefs, and Bad Ideas* (Amherst, NY: Prometheus Books 2012), and Theodore Schick Jr., and Lewis Vaughn, *How to Think About Weird Things: Critical Thinking for a New Age.* (Boston: McGraw-Hill, 7th edition, 2013). Don't forget to do an online search for "Think like a scientist"

7. Harrison, *Think*, p. 194.

8. John W. Loftus, *The End of Christianity* (Amherst, NY: Prometheus Books, 2011), pp. 92–98.

9. Stephen Law, *Believing Bullshit: How Not to Get Sucked into an Intellectual Black Hole* (Amherst, NY: Prometheus Books 2013), p. 75.

10. Jaco Gericke, "Fundamentalism on Stilts: A Response to Alvin Plantinga's Reformed Epistemology," *Verbum et Ecclesia* 30, no. 2 (2009), a summary of which can be read online at http://debunkingchristianity.blogspot.com/2009/12/jaco-gericke-fundamentalism-on-stilts.html.

11. Arthur F. Holmes, *All Truth is God's Truth* (Grand Rapids, MI: Eerdmans, 1977).

12. Cordelia Fine, *A Mind of Its Own: How Your Brain Distorts and Deceives* (New York: W. W. Norton & Company, 2008), p. 106.

13. Peter Boghossian, "How Socratic Pedagogy Works," *Informal Logic: Teaching Supplement* 23, No. 2 (2003): pp. 17–25.

14. Peter Boghossian, *A Manual for Creating Atheists* (Durham, NC: Pitchstone Publishing, 2013).

15. Fine, *A Mind of Its Own*, p. 116.

16. Ibid., p. 127.

Chapter 4

1. John W. Loftus, "'Why Christians Should Be Reading John Loftus' Books,' By Christian Professor Dan Lambert," Debunking Christianity, March 2, 2013, http://

debunkingchristianity.blogspot.com/2013/03/why-christians-should-be-reading-john. html. Dan is presently an associate professor of education at Tiffin University in Ohio.

2. John W. Loftus, "If Nothing Else Look at the Trend, From Conservative to Moderate to Liberal to Agnostic to Atheist," Debunking Christianity, March 5, 2011, http://debunkingchristianity.blogspot.com/2010/08/if-nothing-else-look-at-trend-from.html.

3. Robert Price, *Inerrant the Wind: The Evangelical Crisis in Biblical Authority* (Amherst, NY: Prometheus Books, 2009).

4. John Walton, *The Lost World of Genesis One* and *Ancient Near Eastern Thought and the Old Testament;* Peter Enns, *Inspiration and Incarnation: Evangelicals and the Problem of the Old Testament* and *The Evolution of Adam;* Kenton L. Sparks, *God's Word in Human Words: An Evangelical Appropriation of Critical Biblical Scholarship;* and Christian Smith, *The Bible Made Impossible: Why Biblicism Is Not a Truly Evangelical Reading of Scripture.*

5. Matthew Barrett and Ardel Caneday, eds., *Four Views On The Historical Adam* (Grand Rapids: Zondervan, 2013).

6. John W. Loftus, "Honest Evangelical Scholarship Is a Ruse. There Is No Such Thing!" Debunking Christianity, October 12, 2012, http://debunkingchristianity. blogspot.com/2012/10/honest-evangelical-scholarship-is-ruse.html.

7. Thomas Albert Howard and Karl W. Giberson, "An Evangelical Renaissance in Academe?" *Inside Higher Ed*, February 24, 2014, https://www.insidehighered. com/views/2012/02/24/essay-need-evangelical-scholars-reclaim-christian-thought-fundamentalism.

8. "College Accreditation: Frequently Asked Questions," Back to College, http:// www.back2college.com/library/accreditfaq.htm.

9. "The PhilPapers Survey," http://philpapers.org/surveys/.

10. "Theism and Expert Knowledge," Crucial Considerations, January 28, 2015, http://crucialconsiderations.org/rationality/theism-and-expert-knowledge/.

Chapter 5

1. Kenneth Boa and Robert M. Bowman Jr., *Faith Has Its Reasons: Integrative Approaches to Defending the Christian Faith,* 2nd ed. (Downers Grove, IL: IVP Books, 2006), p. 4.

2. Alvin Plantinga, *God and Other Minds: A Study of the Rational Justification of Belief in God* (Ithaca, NY: Cornell University Press, 1967).

3. William Lane Craig, "God Is Not Dead Yet," *Christianity Today*, July 2, 2008, pp. 22–27, available at http://www.reasonablefaith.org/god-is-not-dead-yet#ixzz3IPgVtJPt.

4. Troy Anderson, "A New Day for Apologetics," *Christianity Today*, July 2, 2008. http://www.christianitytoday.com/ct/2008/july/14.29.html.

5. Bernard Ramm, *Types of Apologetic Systems: An Introductory Study to the Christian Philosophy of Religion* (Wheaton, IL: Van Kampen Press, 1953).

6. In 1962 Ramm revised and retitled his book to *Varieties of Christian Apologetics: An Introduction to the Christian Philosophy of Religion* (Grand Rapids, MI: Baker Books, 1962).

7. James K. Beilby, "Varieties of Apologetics," in *Christian Apologetics: An Anthology of Primary Sources*, ed. Khaldoun A. Sweis and Chad V. Meister (Grand Rapids, MI: Zondervan, 2012), p. 30.

8. Gordon R. Lewis, *Testing Christianity's Truth Claims: Approaches to Christian Apologetics* (Chicago: Moody Bible Institute of Chicago, 1976, 1980). Lewis updated the book in 1990 and published it with University Press of America.

9. Norman Geisler, *Christian Apologetics* (Grand Rapids, MI: Baker Books, 1976).

10. Listed in order of date published: Mark M. Hanna, *Crucial Questions in Apologetics* (Grand Rapids, MI: Baker, 1981); John H. Gerstner, Arthur W. Lindsley, and R. C. Sproul, *Classical Apologetics: A Rational Defense of the Christian Faith and a Critique of Presuppositional Apologetics* (Grand Rapids, MI: Zondervan, 1984); Ronald B. Mayers, *Both/And: A Balanced Apologetic* (Chicago: Moody Press, 1984), revised by Mayers as *Balanced Apologetics: Using Evidences and Presuppositions in Defense of the Faith* (Grand Rapids, MI: Kregel Academic & Professional, 1996); Norman L. Geisler, *Baker Encyclopedia of Christian Apologetics* (Grand Rapids, MI: Baker Academic, 1998); Steven B. Cowan, ed., *Five Views of Apologetics* (Grand Rapids, MI: Zondervan, 2000); Boa and Bowman Jr., *Faith Has Its Reasons*; and John S. Feinberg, *Can You Believe It's True?: Christian Apologetics in a Modern and Postmodern Era* (Wheaton, IL: Crossway, 2013).

11. James K. Beilby, *Thinking About Christian Apologetics: What It Is and Why We Do It* (Downers Grove, IL: IVP Academic, 2011), p. 102.

12. Emphasis is mine. Dulles, *A History of Apologetics*, 1st. ed. (New York: Corpus Books, 1971), p. 246. This might be the earliest work detailing the history of Christian apologetics. The second edition of this book (San Francisco: Ignatius Press, 2005) adds just six pages on twentieth-century evangelical apologetics (pp. 353–59). For primary source material, see the two volume set compiled by William Edgar and K. Scott Oliphint, eds., *Christian Apologetics Past and Present (Volume 1, to 1500): A Primary Source Reader* (Wheaton, IL, Crossway, 2009), and *Christian Apologetics Past and Present (Volume 2, From 1500): A Primary Source Reader* (Wheaton, IL, Crossway, 2011). Also consult the books edited by Khaldoun A. Sweis and Chad V. Meister, *Christian Apologetics: An Anthology of Primary Sources* (Grand Rapids, MI: Zondervan, 2012), and W. C. Campbell-Jack, Gavin J. McGrath, and C. Stephen Evans, eds., *New Dictionary of Christian Apologetics* (Downers Grove, IL: IVP Academic, 2006).

13. For a short overview of the various apologetic systems and why they exist, see Beilby, "Varieties of Apologetics," pp. 29–38.

14. John Warwick Montgomery, "A Short History of Apologetics" in *Christian Apologetics: An Anthology of Primary Sources*, ed. Khaldoun A. Sweis and Chad V. Meister (Grand Rapids, MI: Zondervan, 2012), p. 27.

15. Gary Habermas, "Evidential Apologetics," in *Five Views of Apologetics*, ed. Steven B. Cowan (Grand Rapids, MI: Zondervan, 2000), p. 92.

16. Feinberg, *Can You Believe It's True?*, p. 34. He does think, however, that an apologist in today's world must first argue that truth is objective and knowable, given that he deals with this in Part 1 of his book, covering 194 pages.

17. See Kerry Walters, *Revolutionary Deists: Early America's Rational Infidels* (Amherst, NY: Prometheus Book, 2011).

18. J. O'Higgins distinguished between four types of deism in "Hume and the Desists: A Contrast in Religious Approaches," *Journal of Theological Studies* 23, no. 2 (October 1971): pp. 479–80, which is summarized in Norman L. Geisler and William D. Watkins, *World's Apart: A Handbook on Worldviews* (Grand Rapids, MI: Baker Book House, 1989), pp. 148–49.

19. Cowan, ed., *Five Views of Apologetics*, p. 16.

20. Norman Geisler, *Christian Apologetics*, p. 95.

21. Feinberg, *Can You Believe It's True?*, p. 321. This is not to mischaracterize Feinberg as saying these arguments don't have some evidential weight to them. He favors the argument from design, but none of them serves as a deductive proof, so they "don't offer the degree of objective certainty many believers, let alone non-believers would require." He would rather "rely on other evidences 'to carry most of the weight' in an over-all defense of Christian truth."

22. Richard Swinburne, *The Existence of God*, 2nd, ed. (Oxford: Oxford University Press, 2004), p. 215.

23. See my discussion of "Hume's Stopper" in *Why I Became an Atheist*, p. 86.

24. I've briefly argued against these contentions. See chapter 9 and 13 in my cowritten book (with Randal Rauser) *God of Godless?* To assert God is the basis of logic is to fall within the same trap of the Euthyphro dilemma with regard to moral truth. Is something reasonable merely because God proclaims it so, or does God proclaim something reasonable because it is? Reason has shown itself trustworthy by pragmatic effectiveness—it just works. Of course, the brain doesn't reason as well as the presuppositionalist proclaims. Eastern philosophers may reject logic outright as *maya* because it's based on a rationalistic worldview they reject. So how presuppositional apologetics can make a dent in Eastern beliefs is a puzzle to me.

25. Cowan, ed., *Five Views of Apologetics*, p. 217.

26. Ibid., p. 233.

27. Ibid., p. 242.

28. Thomas Morris, *Francis Schaeffer's Apologetics: A Critique* (Grand Rapids, MI: Baker Book House, 1987).

29. The most hard-hitting and persuasive critique of presuppotionialism is still the book by Sproul, Gerstener, and Lindsley, *Classical Apologetics*, section III, pp. 183–338.

30. Alvin Plantinga, *Warranted Christian Belief* (New York: Oxford University Press, 2000), p. 200.

31. Ibid., pp. 245, 262.

32. Richard Swinburne, *Faith and Reason*, 2nd ed. (Oxford: Oxford University Press, 2005), pp. 74–75.

33. Plantinga, *Warranted Christian Belief*, p. 201. Plantinga has defended some arguments for Christian faith, most notably the Ontological Argument.

34. Plantinga, "Reason and Belief in God," in *Faith and Rationality: Reason and Belief in God*, ed. Alvin Plantinga and Nicholas Wolterstorff (Notre Dame: University of Notre Dame Press, 1983), p. 65.

35. David J. Hand explains how unexplainable rare events happen all of the time in his book, *The Improbability Principle*.

36. John W. Loftus, *The Outsider Test for Faith* (Amherst, NY: Prometheus Books, 2013), pp. 70–72, 134–144, and *Why I Became an Atheist*, pp. 43–47.

37. W. K. Clifford, "Ethics of Belief," originally published in *Contemporary Review* (1877), available at http://infidels.org/library/historical/w_k_clifford/ethics_of_belief.html.

38. Alvin Plantinga, *Warranted Christian Belief*, p. 262.

39. Ibid., pp. 245–46.

40. Gericke, "Fundamentalism on Stilts," http://www.up.ac.za/dspace/bitstream/2263/12356/1/Gericke_Fundamentalism%282009%29.pdf. See also his chapter, "Can God Exist If Yahweh Doesn't?" in *The End of Christianity*, ed. John W. Loftus (Amherst, NY: Prometheus Books, 2011), pp. 131–54. For another great response see Graham Oppy's essay "Natural Theology," in *Alvin Plantinga*, ed., Deane-Peter Baker (Cambridge, Cambridge University Press, 2007).

41. Gericke, "Can God Exist If Yahweh Doesn't?" p. 150.

42. Myron B. Penner, *The End of Apologetics: Christian Witness in a Postmodern Context* (Grand Rapids, MI: Baker Academic, 2013), p. 4.

43. Myron B. Penner, ed., *Christianity and the Postmodern Turn: Six Views* (Grand Rapids, MI: Brazos Press, 2005), p. 127. See Myron Bradley Penner and Hunter Barnes, eds., *A New Kind of Conversation: Blogging Toward a Postmodern Faith* (Downers Grove, IL: IVP Books, 2007); and Robert C. Greer, *Mapping Postmodernism: A Survey of Christian Options* (Downers Grove, IL: IVP Academic, 2003). See also John B. Cobb Jr., *Living Options in Protestant Theology* (Philadelphia: Westminster Press, 1962).

44. Beilby, "Varieties of Apologetics," p. 34.

45. Cowan, *Five Views of Apologetics*, p. 317. Cowan can be seen to concur on pages 380–81.

46. Ibid., p. 314.

47. Ibid., p. 316.

48. Ibid., p. 336

49. Ibid., p. 343.

50. Ibid., p. 357.

51. Ibid., p. 343.

52. Ibid., p. 344

53. Ibid., p. 347

54. Feinberg thinks *Reformed Epistemology* "isn't a method for defending the Christians worldview as truth" in *Can You Believe It's True?*, p. 248.

55. Ibid., p. 249.

56. Ibid., p. 320.

57. Ibid., p. 321.

58. I no longer think as I did in *Why I Became an Atheist* (p. 54, see especially p. 474, note 78) that cumulative case–type Christian apologetics can be good ones. Geisler argued against this method in his book, *Christian Apologetics*, pp. 117–32, as I do here. So also does Plantinga in his book, *Warranted Christian Belief*, pp. 268–80. (Plantinga prematurely conceded his argument fails.) Geisler says that "at best" a cumulative case can test for the falsity of a worldview though.

59. Beilby, "Varieties of Apologetics," p. 37.

60. Ibid.

61. H. Wayne House and Dennis W. Jowers, *Reasons for Our Hope: An Introduction to Christian Apologetics* (Nashville, TN: B&H Academic, 2011), p. 47.

Chapter 6

This chapter is adapted in part from the first chapter of *The Outsider Test for Faith*.

1. On this see Michael Shermer, *The Believing Brain: From Ghosts and Gods to Politics and Conspiracies—How We Construct Beliefs and Reinforce Them as Truths* (New York: Times Books, 2011); Pascal Boyer, *Religion Explained* (New York: Basic Books, 2010); and Jesse Bering, *The Belief Instinct: The Psychology of Souls, Destiny, and the Meaning of Life* (New York: W. W. Norton & Company, 2011).

2. Scott Atran, *In Gods We Trust: The Evolutionary Landscape of Religion* (Oxford: Oxford University Press, 2002); Jack David Eller, *Introducing Anthropology of Religion:*

Culture to the Ultimate (London: Routledge, 2007) and *Cultural Anthropology: Global Forces, Local Lives* (London: Routledge, 2009). See also David Eller's chapters on the topic in *The Christian Delusion* and *The End of Christianity*.

3. This kind of science is discussed in Marcus, *Kluge*; Carol Tavris and Elliot Aronson, *Mistakes Were Made (But Not by Me)* (Orlando, FL: Harvest, 2007); Ori Brafman and Rom Brafman, *Sway: The Irresistible Pull of Irrational Behavior* (New York: Broadway Books, 2009); Christopher Chabris and Daniel Simons, *The Invisible Gorilla: And Other Ways Our Intuitions Deceive Us* (New York: Crown, 2010); Michael Shermer, *Why People Believe Weird Things: Pseudoscience Superstition and Other Confusions of Our Time* (New York: Henry Holt, 1997); and Fine, *A Mind of Its Own*. See also Loftus, ed., *The Christian Delusion*, particularly the early chapters by Valerie Tarico, Jason Long, and myself.

4. For this evidence, see Simon G. Southerton, *Losing a Lost Tribe: Native Americans, DNA, and the Mormon Church* (Salt Lake City: Signature Books, 2004).

5. Robert Burton, *On Being Certain: Believing You Are Right Even When You're Not* (New York: St. Martin's, 2008), p. xi.

Chapter 7

1. Some of the material in Part 2 is gleaned from selections of my other books. There are things I said elsewhere that need to have more attention drawn to them, so I share them here.

2. Bo Bennett, "Special Pleading," Logically Fallacious, http://www.logicallyfallacious.com/index.php/logical-fallacies/164-special-pleading.

3. Loftus and Rauser, *God or Godless?*

4. Ibid., pp. 95–96.

5. See my chapter 7, "The Poor Evidence of Historical Evidence," in *Why I Became an Atheist*, pp. 146–69.

6. Bart Ehrman, *Jesus Interrupted* (New York: HarperCollins, 2009), p. 175.

7. Ibid., p. 177.

8. Dale C. Allison, *Resurrecting Jesus: The Earliest Christian Tradition and Its Interpreters* (New York: T & T Clark, 2005), p. 338.

9. James McGrath, "Easter Ehrman," Exploring Our Matrix, April 8, 2009, http://www.patheos.com/blogs/exploringourmatrix/2009/04/easter-ehrman.html.

10. Ernst Troeltsch, "Historiography," in *Encyclopedia of Religion and Ethics*, ed. James Hastings (New York: Scribner's, 1967 [reprint of the 1909 edition]).

11. Pieter F. Craffert, "The Origins of Resurrected Faith: The Challenge of a Social Scientific Approach," *Neotestamentica* 23 (1989): p. 342. Craffert is also the author of the interesting book, *The Life of a Galilean Shaman: Jesus of Nazareth in Anthropological-Historical Perspective* (Eugene: Cascade, 2008).

12. Michael R. Licona, *The Resurrection of Jesus: A New Historigraphial Approach* (Downers Grove, IL: InterVarsity Press, 2010), p.143, also p. 145.

13. Ibid., pp. 139, 143.

14. Ibid., p. 145.

15. Ibid., p. 142. *a priori* judgments are based upon reason alone independent of experience.

16. Bart Ehrman, *The New Testament: A Historical Introduction to the Early Christian Writings*, 3rd ed. (Oxford: Oxford University Press, 2008), p. 229.

17. Ibid., pp. 227–29.

18. Licona, *The Resurrection of Jesus*, p. 143.

19. Ehrman, *The New Testament*, p. 227.

20. Plantinga, *Warranted Christian Belief*, p. 405.

21. Ibid., pp. 409–10.

22. Licona, *The Resurrection of Jesus*, p. 163.

23. Ibid., p. 164.

24. Ibid., pp. 165–66.

25. William Lane Craig, *Reasonable Faith: Christian Truth and Apologetics* (Wheaton, IL: Crossway Books, 2008), p. 11.

26. Craig, *Reasonable Faith*, p. 12

27. Gary R. Habermas and Michael Licona, *The Case for the Resurrection of Jesus* (Grand Rapids, MI: Kregal, 2004), p. 44.

28. Ibid., pp. 44–45.

29. Ibid., p. 32.

30. Ibid., pp. 48–77, and Licona, *The Resurrection of Jesus*, pp. 302–464.

31. Robert Price, "Explaining the Resurrection without Recourse to Miracle," in *The End of Christianity*, ed. Loftus, pp. 219–32.

32. Habermas and Licona, *The Case for the Resurrection of Jesus*, pp. 69–70.

33. Ibid., p. 70. See Gary Habermas, "Experiences of the Risen Jesus: The Foundational Historical Issue in the Early Proclamation of the Resurrection," *Dialog: A Journal of Theology* 45, no. 3 (Fall 2006): pp. 288–97.

34. Richard Carrier, "Innumeracy: A Fault to Fix," Richard Carrier Blogs, November 26, 2013, http://freethoughtblogs.com/carrier/archives/4857.

35. See Hand, *The Improbability Principle*. I know I've recommended this book several times, but it's just that good.

36. James McGrath, "Triablogue-osphere," Exploring Our Matrix, April 6, 2009, http://www.patheos.com/blogs/exploringourmatrix/2009/04/triablogue-osphere.html.

37. John W. Loftus, "What a Delusion Does to an Otherwise Intelligent Mind: Vic Reppert On Methodological Naturalism," Debunking Christianity, June 28, 2014, http://debunkingchristianity.blogspot.com/2014/06/what-delusion-does-to-otherwise.html.

Chapter 8

1. See Coyne, *Why Evolution Is True*, and Dawkins, *The Greatest Show on Earth*.

2. On this, see my chapter, "The Darwinian Problem of Evil," in *The Christian Delusion*, ed. Loftus.

3. John King-Farlow and William Niels Christensen, *Faith and the Life of Reason* (Dordrecht-Holland: D. Reidel, 1972), p. 50.

4. William Lane Craig, "Politically Incorrect Salvation," in *Christian Apologetics in the Post-Modern World*, ed. T. P. Phillips and D. Ockholm (Downers Grove, IL: InterVarsity Press, 1995), pp. 75–97.

5. William Lane Craig, "Diversity, Evil and Hell," in *God and Evil: The Case for God in a World Filled with Pain*, ed. Chad Meister and James K. Dew Jr. (Downers Grove, IL: InterVarsity Press, 2013), p. 238.

6. Ibid., pp. 235–41.

7. Ibid., p. 37. I italicized the relevant sense of the word "possible" five times.

8. Ibid., p. 239.

9. J. P. Moreland and William Lane Craig, *Philosophical Foundations for a Christian Worldview* (Downers Grove, IL: InterVarsity Press, 2003), p. 158.

10. See "What We've Got Here is a Failure to Communicate," in *The Christian Delusion*, ed. Loftus.

11. See Randal Rauser, "What John Loftus Has Is a Failure to Communicate," Tentative Apologist, October 21, 2010, http://randalrauser.com/2010/10/what-john-loftus-has-is-a-failure-to-communicate/.

Chapter 9

1. Walter Kaufmann, *Critique of Religion and Philosophy* (Princeton, NJ: Princeton University Press, 1958), p. 219.

2. Ibid., pp. 219–20.

3. Daniel Howard-Snyder, ed., *The Evidential Argument from Evil* (Indianapolis: Indiana University Press, 2008).

4. See John W. Loftus, "Christian Apologists Must Denigrate Science and Scientists Themselves," Debunking Christianity, December 20, 2010, http://debunkingchristianity.blogspot.com/2010/12/christian-apologists-must-denigrate.html.

5. Loftus, *The Outsider Test for Faith*, pp. 223–26.

6. Loftus and Rauser, *God or Godless?* chapter 13, pp. 109–15.

7. Ibid., chapter 5, pp. 45–52.

8. I highly recommend Russell Blackford and Udo Schuklenk, *50 Great Myths of Atheism* (Malden, MA: Wiley-Blackwell, 2013).

9. See "True Reason: Christian Responses to the Challenges of Atheism—on Kindle," M and M, March 21, 2012, http://www.mandm.org.nz/2012/03/true-reason-christian-responses-to-the-challenges-of-atheism.html.

10. See Tom Talbott, "Other Writings and Reflections," Tom Talbott's Site, www.willamette.edu/~ttalbott/other-writings.html.

11. Edward T. Babinski, "Things Christians Have Been Against," Scrivenings, March 19, 2012, http://edward-t-babinski.blogspot.com/2012/03/list-of-things-christians-have-been.html.

12. Randal Rauser, "Not Even Wrong: The Many Problems with Naturalism," Tentative Apologist, July 18, 2012, http://randalrauser.com/2012/07/not-even-wrong-the-many-problems-with-naturalism/.

13. Law, *Believing Bullshit*, p. 75.

Chapter 10

1. John Dickson, "Atheists Just Go One God Further," Willow Creek Association Blog, March 17, 2015, http://www.wcablog.com/evangelism/atheists-just-go-one-god-further/.

2. See David Eller, "Christianity Evolving: On the Origin of Christian Species," in *The End of Christianity*, ed. Loftus, pp. 23–51.

3. John W. Loftus, "There Is No Such Thing as 'Theism,' 'Christian Theism' or 'Mere Christianity,'" Debunking Christianity, March 5, 2014, http://debunkingchristianity.blogspot.com/2014/03/there-is-no-such-thing-as-theism.html; and "The Argument From Christian Diversity: There is No Such a Thing as 'Mere Christianity,'" Debunking Christianity, October 1, 2011, debunkingchristianity.blogspot.com/2011/10/argument-from-christian-diversity-there.html.

4. Bart Ehrman, *Lost Christianities: The Battles for Scripture and the Faiths We Never Knew* (Oxford: Oxford University Press, 2005).

5. John Dickson, post on his Facebook wall, March 19, 2015, https://www.facebook.com/john.dickson.9406417/posts/10153700820694447.

6. Loftus, *The Outsider Test for Faith*.

7. David Marshall, "John Loftus and the Insider-Outsider Test for Faith," in *True Reason: Confronting the Irrationality of the New Atheism*, ed. Tom Gilson and Carson Weitnauer (Grand Rapids, MI: Kregel Publications, 2014), pp. 75–96.

8. David Marshall, *How Jesus Passes the Outsider Test: The Inside Story* (Fall City, WA: Kuai Mu Press, 2014).

9. Ibid., p. 7.

10. Ibid., p. 10.

11. Ibid., p. 18–19.

12. Ibid., p. 23.

13. Loftus, ed., *The Christian Delusion*, pp. 25–46.

14. Marshall, *How Jesus Passes the Outsider Test*, p. 23.

15. Ibid., p. 26.

16. Ibid., p. 26.

17. Loftus, *The Outsider Test for Faith*, p. 21.

18. Marshall, *How Jesus Passes the Outsider Test*, p. 11.

19. Loftus, ed., *Christianity Is Not Great*.

Chapter 11

1. The prophetic book of Isaiah supposedly predicted the rise of the Persian king Cyrus about 150 years earlier (Isaiah 44:28–45:1).

2. I'm referring to the Deuteronomist history of the JEDP Documentary Hypothesis. See John W. Loftus, "The JEPD Theory in A Nutshell," Debunking Christianity, January 12, 2010, http://debunkingchristianity.blogspot.com/2010/01/jepd-theory-in-nutshell.html.

3. On these questions I recommend reading Richard Elliot Friedman, *Who Wrote the Bible* (New York: Harper & Row, 1987); Israel Finkelstein and Neil Asher Silberman, *The Bible Unearthed* (New York: Simon and Schuster, 2001); William G. Dever, *Who Were the Early Israelites and Where Did They Come From?* (Grand Rapids, MI: Eerdmans, 2003); and Hector Avalos, *The End of Biblical Studies* (Amherst, NY: Prometheus Books, 2007), pp. 109–27.

4. On this question I recommend Israel Finkelstein and Neil Asher Silberman, *David and Solomon: In Search of the Bible's Sacred Kings and the Roots of the Western Tradition* (New York: Free Press, 2006), and William G. Dever, *What Did the Biblical Writers Know and When Did They Know It?: What Archeology Can Tell Us About the Reality of Ancient Israel* (Grand Rapids, MI: Eerdmans, 2001); and Avalos, *The End of Biblical Studies*, pp. 127–64.

5. As argued quite successfully by Thom Stark in chapter 7, "The Shepherd and the Giant: Government Propoganda," of *The Human Faces of God: What Scripture Reveals When It Gets God Wrong (and Why Inerrancy Tries to Hide It)* (Eugene, OR: Wipf & Stock, 2011), pp. 150–59.

6. Gary Greenberg, *101 Myths of the Bible: How Ancient Scribes Invented Biblical History* (Napperville, IN: Sourcebook Inc., 2000).

7. Tim Callahan, *Secret Origins of the Bible* (Altadena, CA: Millenium Press, 2002).

8. James D. G. Dunn, *The Living Word* (Philadelphia: Fortress Press, 1987), pp. 69–70. For a further treatment, Dunn recommends David G. Meade, *Pseudonymity and Canon* (Tübingen, DE: J. C. B. Mohr, 1986).

9. Kenton L. Sparks, *God's Word in Human Words* (Grand Rapids, MI: Baker Academic, 2008), pp. 116–18.

10. Ehrman, *Lost Christianities*, pp. 9–10. See his book, *Forged: Writing in the Name of God—Why the Bible's Authors Are Not Who We Think They Are* (New York: HarperOne, 2001), and especially *Forgery and Counterforgery: The Use of Literary Deceit in Early Christian Polemics* (Oxford: Oxford University Press, 2013).

11. Randel Helms, *Gospel Fictions* (Amherst, NY: Prometheus Books, 1989).

12. See John W. Loftus, "Was Jesus Born in Bethlehem?" Debunking Christianity, December 24, 2010, http://debunkingchristianity.blogspot.com/2006/12/was-jesus-born-in-bethlehem.html. See especially Jonathan M. S. Pearce's book, *The Nativity: A Critical Examination* (Onus Books, 2012).

13. Avalos, *The End of Biblical Studies*, pp. 35–63.

14. See Harry H. McCall, "Why Josephus' So-called *Testimonium Flavianum* Must be Rejected," Debunking Christianity, November 29, 2008, http://debunkingchristianity.blogspot.com/2008/11/why-josephus-so-called-testimonium.html.

15. See the Wikipedia entry "Catholic Church Sexual Abuse Cases" for a summation of these incidents: http://en.wikipedia.org/wiki/Catholic_Church_sexual_abuse_cases.

16. Candida Moss, *The Myth of Persecution: How Early Christians Invented a Story of Martyrdom* (New York: HarperOne, 2013).

17. For a list of the top ten relics, see "Top 10 Relics of Jesus Christ," Listverse, October 17, 2012, http://listverse.com/2012/10/17/top-10-relics-of-jesus-christ/.

18. See Joe Nickell, *Relics of the Christ* (Lexington, KY: University Press of Kentucky, 2007).

19. Austin Cline, "Holy Foreskin! Whatever Happened to Jesus' Foreskin?" About.com, http://atheism.about.com/od/aboutjesus/a/holyforeskin.htm.

20. Robert Todd Carroll, "'Shroud' of Turin," *The Skeptic's Dictionary*, http://skepdic.com/shroud.html; Antonio Lombatti's review of the 2015 CNN documentary about the Shroud of Turin, "The Bible and Interpretation," March 2015, http://www.bibleinterp.com/opeds/2015/03/lom398011.shtml; Charles Freeman's article in *History Today*, "The Origins of the Shroud of Turin," http://www.historytoday.com/charles-freeman/origins-shroud-turin; Jerry Coyne's online essay, "Pope Francis Endorses the Fake Shroud of Turin," Why Evolution Is True, November 29, 2014, https://

whyevolutionistrue.wordpress.com/2014/11/29/pope-francis-endorses-the-fake-shroud-of-turin/; and chapters 7–10 of Nickell's book, *Relics of the Christ*, pp. 111–66.

21. See "Searches for Noah's Ark," Wikipedia, http://en.wikipedia.org/wiki/Searches_for_Noah%27s_Ark. On the story itself, see Robert Todd Carroll, "Noah's Ark," *The Skeptic's Dictionary*, http://skepdic.com/noahsark.html.

22. "Has Noah's Ark Been Found on Turkish Mountaintop?" Fox News, April 27, 2010, http://www.foxnews.com/scitech/2010/04/27/noahs-ark-found-turkey-ararat/.

23. "Noah's Ark PaleoBabble Update," PaleoBabble, April 27, 2010, http://michaelsheiser.com/PaleoBabble/2010/04/noahs-ark-paleobabble-update/.

24. For more on the *60 Minutes* story on it, see "*60 Minutes* on the James Ossuary," BiblePlaces.com, March 24, 2008, http://blog.bibleplaces.com/2008/03/60-minutes-on-james-ossuary.html.

25. Chris Rodda, *Liars For Jesus: The Religious Right's Alternate Version of American History,* vol. 1 (BookSurge Publishing, 2006). See also "Lying for Jesus," Wikipedia, http://rationalwiki.org/wiki/Lying_for_Jesus.

26. Shankar Vedantam, "Walking Santa, Talking Christ: Why Do Americans Claim to Be More Religious Than They Are?" *Slate*, December 22, 2010, http://www.slate.com/articles/health_and_science/the_hidden_brain/2010/12/walking_santa_talking_christ.html.

27. Bill Wiese, *23 Minutes in Hell: One Man's Story About What He Saw, Heard, and Felt in that Place of Torment* (Lake Mary, FL: Charisma House, 2006).

28. Kevin and Alex Malarkey, *The Boy Who Came Back from Heaven: A Remarkable Account of Miracles, Angels, and Life beyond This World* (Carol Sream, IL: Tyndale Momentum, 2011).

29. "'The Boy Who Came Back From Heaven' Recants Story, Rebukes Christian Retailers [UPDATED!!!!!]," Pulpit and Pen, January 13, 2015, http://pulpitandpen.org/2015/01/13/the-boy-who-came-back-from-heaven-recants-story-rebukes-christian-retailers/.

30. Mark Oppenheimer, "The Turning of an Atheist," *New York Times*, November 4, 2007, http://www.nytimes.com/2007/11/04/magazine/04Flew-t.html?pagewanted=print&_r=0; and especially Richard Carrier, "Antony Flew's Bogus Book," Richard Carrier Blogs, November 6, 2007, http://richardcarrier.blogspot.com/2007/11/antony-flew-bogus-book.html.

31. Antony Flew, with Roy Abraham Varghese, *There Is a God: How the World's Most Notorious Atheist Changed His Mind* (New York: HarperCollins, 2009).

32. Valerie Tarico, "Two 'Liars for Jesus' and an Aging Philosopher," Debunking Christianity, November 11, 2007, http://debunkingchristianity.blogspot.com/2007/11/two-liars-for-jesus-and-aging.html. Richard Carrier, while not a medical doctor, claims Flew had a stroke.

33. Timothy Keller, *The Reason for God* (New York: Riverhead Books, 2008).

34. Ibid., p. 23.

35. William P. Alston, "The Inductive Argument from Evil and the Human Cognitive Condition," in *Philosophical Perspectives, 5: Philosophy of Religion*, ed. James Tomberlin (Atascadero, CA: Rideview Publishing Press, 1991), p. 29.

36. Bryan Frances, *Gratuitous Suffering and the Problem of Evil: A Comprehensive Introduction* (New York: Routledge, 2013), pp. 1–5.

37. Ibid., p. 4.

38. Stephen Law, "William Lane Craig: 'Animals Aren't Aware That They're in Pain,'" Debunking Christianity, October 4, 2012, http://debunkingchristianity. blogspot.com/2012/10/stephen-law-on-apologist-claim-that.html.

39. John W. Loftus, "Christians Are Not Credible Witnesses So Christianity Is Not Credible Either," Debunking Christianity, November 28, 2012, http:// debunkingchristianity.blogspot.com/2012/11/christians-are-not-credible-witnesses. html.

Chapter 12

1. This is how I express the problem even though I know of other ways to do so. On the issue of suffering I've written quite a lot in my books, so readers can expect some duplication in Part 3 without my citing references in what follows. My guess is that there will be many new readers to my work with this book, so the duplication of some of my material will be helpful here.

2. There is also a nonmoral category of suffering due to accidents resulting from human neglect and inaction. A very significant portion of human suffering is created by people who didn't know the consequences of their actions. The founding of the city of New Orleans by French explorer Rene-Robert Cavelier, below sea level, is one example of this, as evidenced when Hurricane Katrina ripped through the Big Easy in 2005.

3. James F. Sennett, "This Much I Know: A Postmodern Apologetic," unpublished manuscript. He provided me with a copy of the manuscript.

4. William Lane Craig, "The Problem of Evil," Reasonable Faith, http://www. reasonablefaith.org/the-problem-of-evil.

5. Chad Meister and James K. Dew Jr., eds., *God and Evil: The Case for God in a World Filled with Pain* (Downers Grove, IL: InterVarsity Press, 2013).

6. James K. Dew Jr., "The Logical Problem of Evil," in *God and Evil*, ed. Meister and Dew, pp. 26–37.

7. For a discussion of this issue, see Part 2 in Michael Martin and Riki Monnier, eds., *The Impossibility of God*, (Amherst, NY: Prometheus Books, 2003), pp. 59–124. Note there just isn't one logical problem for Christians to solve, but several of them.

8. J. L. Mackie, "Evil and Omnipotence," *Mind* 64, no. 254 (April 1955).

9. Alvin Plantinga, *God, Freedom, and Evil* (Grand Rapids, MI: Eerdmans, 1974).

10. J. L. Mackie, *The Miracle of Theism: Arguments for and against the Existence of God* (Oxford: Clarendon Press, 1982), p. 154.

11. Dew, "The Logical Problem of Evil," p. 37.

12. Graham Oppy, *Arguing about Gods* (Cambridge: Cambridge University Press, 2006).

13. Oppy, *Arguing about Gods*, p. 288.

14. Ibid., p. 276. I'll spare my readers a discussion of these things. See Oppy's book for more.

15. Ibid., p. 284.

16. Ibid., p. 278.

17. Plantinga, *God, Freedom, and Evil*, p. 58.

18. Swinburne, *The Existence of God*, p. 202.

19. Mackie, *The Miracle of Theism*, p. 162.

20. Gregory Ganssle and Yena Lee, "Evidential Problems of Evil," in *God and Evil*, ed. Meister and Dew, pp. 15–25.

21. See William Rowe, "Evil and Theodicy," *Philosophical Topics* 16, no. 2 (1988): pp. 119–32.

22. William Rowe, "The Problem of Evil and Some Varieties of Atheism," *American Philosophical Quarterly* 16, no. 4 (October 1979).

23. Stephen Wykstra, "Rowe's Noseeum Arguments from Evil," in *The Evidential Argument from Evil*, ed. Daniel Howard-Snyder (Bloomington: Indiana University Press, 1996), pp. 126–50.

24. Ganssle and Lee, "Evidential Problems of Evil," p. 19.

25. Ibid., p. 23.

26. From Loftus, *Why I Became an Atheist*, pp. 230–31.

27. Craig, "The Problem of Evil."

28. Charles Taliaferro, "Evil and Prayer," in *God and Evil*, ed. Meister and Dew, pp. 152–162, and Gary Habermas, "Evil, the Resurrection and the Example of Jesus," in *God and Evil*, ed. Meister and Dew, pp. 163–75.

29. Gary Habermas, "The Truth—and the Comfort—of the Resurrection," http://www.garyhabermas.com/articles/decision_mag/dec_truth_comfort_res_2000-04.htm. An edited version of this article was published in *Decision* 41, no. 4 (April 2000): pp. 8–10.

30. M. Scott Peck, *The Road Less Traveled: A New Psychology of Love, Traditional Values, and Spiritual Growth*, Anniversary Edition (New York: Simon & Schuster, 2002), p. 15.

31. Habermas, "Evil, the Resurrection and the Example of Jesus," p. 166.

32. Ibid., p. 168.

33. Ibid., pp. 170–71.

34. Ibid., p. 174.

Chapter 13

1. R. Douglas Geivett, "Augustine and the Problem of Evil," in *God and Evil*, ed. Meister and Dew, pp. 65–79.

2. John W. Loftus, "What is the Likelihood That a Trickster or Evil God Exists?" Debunking Christianity, January 2, 2010, http://debunkingchristianity.blogspot.com/2010/01/what-is-likelihood-that-trickster-or.html.

3. Andrea M. Weisenberger, *Suffering Belief: Evil and the Anglo-American Defense of Theism* (New York: Peter Lang International Academic Publishers, 1999), p. 74.

4. Ibid., p. 73.

5. Geivett, "Augustine and the Problem of Evil," p. 74.

6. Geivett, "Augustine and the Problem of Evil," pp. 76–79.

7. Jill Graper Hernandez, "Leibniz and the Best of All Possible Worlds," in *God and Evil*, ed. Meister and Dew, p. 97.

8. William L. Rowe, *Can God Be Free?* (Oxford: Oxford University Press, 2006). Rowe answers Robert M. Adams' argument in "Must God Create the Best?" *Philosophical Review* 81 (1972): pp. 317–32.

9. See Nicholas Everitt's discussion in *The Non-existence of God* (London: Routledge, 2004), pp. 243–44.

10. See Richard R. La Croix, "Unjustified Evil and God's Choice," in *The Impossibility of God*, ed. Michael Martin & Ricki Monnier (Amherst, NY: Prometheus Books, 2003), pp. 116–124.

11. Norman Geisler, *Philosophy of Religion* (Grand Rapids, MI: Zondervan, 1978).

12. Hernandez, "Leibniz and the Best of All Possible Worlds," p. 104.

13. Ibid., p. 98.

14. Ibid., p. 105.

15. John Hick, "An Irenaean Theodicy," in *Encountering Evil: Live Options in Theodicy*, ed. Stephen T. Davis (Atlanta: John Knox Press, 1981), p. 43. He calls it a a revamped Irenaean Theodicy after the early church father Irenaeus in the 2nd century CE. His ideas were first developed into a complete theodicy by Hick. It seems as though

to avoid a heresy charge Christians must find someone in the past who argued in a similar fashion.

16. John Hick, *Evil and the God of Love* (New York: Palgrave Macmillan, 1985), p. 287.

17. James Spiegel, "The Irenaean Soul-Making Theodicy," in *God and Evil*, ed. Meister and Dew, pp. 80–93.

18. Ibid., p. 83.

19. Ibid., p. 82.

20. David R. Griffin in *Encountering Evil: Live Options in Theodicy*, ed. Stephen T. Davis (Atlanta: John Knox Press, 1981), pp. 53–55.

21. David Hume, *Dialogues Concerning Natural Religion*, Part 11, 1779.

22. To read a few good critiques of John Hick's theodicy I recommend the responses to his essay in chapter 2 of Stephen T. Davis, ed., *Encountering Evil: Live Options in Theodicy* (Atlanta: John Knox Press, 1981), which Spiegel acknowledges in a footnote. Spiegel shows no awareness however of Michael Martin's devastating critique of Hick's theodicy in chapter 17 of *Atheism: A Philosophical Justification* (Philadelphia: Temple University Press, 1992), nor of chapter 4 in Andrea Weisberger's excellent book *Suffering Belief*.

23. Plantinga, *God, Freedom, and Evil*.

24. Michael Peterson, *Evil and the Christian God* (Grand Rapids, MI: Baker, 1982); Bruce Little, "God and Gratuitous Evil," in *God and Evil*, ed. Meister and Dew, pp. 38–49; and William Hasker, *The Triumph of God over Evil: Theodicy for a World of Suffering* (Downers Grove, IL: IVP Academic, 2008).

25. Law, *Believing Bullshit*, p. 75.

26. Martin, *Atheism: A Philosophical Justification*, 345-46.

Chapter 14

1. Paul Copan, "Evil and Primeval Sin: How Evil Emerged in a Very Good Creation," in *God and Evil*, ed. Meister and Dew, pp. 109–23.

2. R. C. Sproul Jr., *Almighty All Over* (Grand Rapids, MI: Baker, 1999), as quoted by Copan, "Evil and Primeval Sin: How Evil Emerged in a Very Good Creation," p. 114.

3. Ibid.

4. Walter Wink, *Unmasking the Powers* (Minneapolis: Fortress Press, 1986), pp. 11–44.

5. See T. J. Wray and Gregory Mobley, *The Birth of Satan: Tracing the Devil's Biblical Roots* (New York: Palgrave Macmillan, 2005); and Elaine Pagels, *The Origin of Satan* (New York: Random House, 1995).

6. Donald E. Gowan, *From Eden to Babel: A Commentary on the Book of Genesis 1–11* (Minneapolis: Fortress Press, 1988), p. 82.

7. Claus Westermann, *Creation* (Minneapolis: Fortress Press, 1974), pp. 108–9.

8. David Basinger and Randall Basinger, eds., *Predestination and Free Will*, (Downers Grove, IL: IVP, 1986), p. 58.

9. Copan, "Evil and Primeval Sin," pp. 124–37.

10. William Dembski, "Evil, Creation and Intelligent Design," in *God and Evil*, ed. Meister and Dew, p. 262. This chapter is basically taken from chapter 21 of his book *The End of Christianity: Finding a Good God in an Evil World* (Grand Rapids, MI: B&H Academic, 2009), with one additional concluding sentence at the end: "Bottom Line: Evolution, with or without God, does nothing to mitigate the problem of evil" (p. 269).

11. William Dembski, "Karl Giberson Responds to William Dembski," Uncommon Descent, September 29, 2009, http://www.uncommondescent.com/evolution/karl-giberson-responds-to-dr-dembski/.

12. For more on this read, see my chapter titled, "The Darwinian Problem of Evil," in *The Christian Delusion*, pp. 237–70.

13. Kevin Timpe, "Prayers for the Past," *Religious Studies* 41 (2005): pp. 305–22.

14. John W. Loftus, "On God Answering Prayers Retroactively," Debunking Christianity, April 19, 2011, http://debunkingchristianity.blogspot.com/2009/11/on-god-answering-prayers-retroactively.html.

15. Garry DeWeese, "Natural Evil: A 'Free Process' Defense," in *God and Evil*, ed. Meister and Dew, pp. 53–64.

16. Ibid., p. 64.

17. Ibid., p. 55.

18. Ibid., pp. 62–64.

19. David Hume, *Dialogues Concerning Natural Religion*, Part X.

20. From page 446 of my book *Why I Became an Atheist*.

21. Jerry L. Walls and Kyle Blanchette, "God and Hell Reconciled," in *God and Evil*, ed. Meister and Dew, pp. 243–58.

22. Craig, "Diversity, Evil and Hell," pp. 227–42.

23. Walls and Blanchette, "God and Hell Reconciled," p. 249.

24. See John W. Loftus, "The New Evangelical Orthodoxy, Relativism, and the Amnesia of It All," Debunking Christianity, April 19, 2011, http://debunkingchristianity.blogspot.com/2012/12/the-new-evangelical-orthodoxy.html.

25. Walls and Blanchette, "God and Hell Reconciled," p.244.

26. Alan E. Bernstein, *The Formation of Hell: Death and Retribution in the Ancient and Early Christian Worlds* (Ithaca, NY: Cornell University Press, 1996).

27. Law, *Believing Bullshit*, p. 75.

28. See John W. Loftus, "The Nature and Value of Free Will," Debunking Christianity, September 7, 2007, http://debunkingchristianity.blogspot.com/2007/09/nature-and-value-of-free-will.html.

29. Jonathan M. S. Pearce, *Free Will?: An Investigation into Whether We Have Free Will, or Whether I Was Always Going to Write This Book* (Ginger Prince, 2010).

Chapter 15

1. Chad Meister, "Evil and the Hiddenness of God," in *God and Evil*, ed. Meister and Dew, pp. 138–151.

2. Ibid., p. 138.

3. Ibid., p. 139.

4. Ibid., p. 142.

5. Ibid., p. 144.

6. Ibid., p. 146.

7. Ibid.

8. Ibid., p. 149.

9. Ibid., p. 148.

10. Ibid.

11. Little, "God and Gratuitous Evil," pp. 38–49.

12. Ibid, p. 39. Emphasis is his. Little doesn't admit gratuitous suffering exists.

13. Terence Penelhum, "Divine Goodness and the Problem of Evil," *Religious Studies* 2 (1967): p. 107.

14. Norman L. Geisler and Winfried Corduan, *Philosophy of Religion*, 2nd ed. (Grand Rapids, MI: Baker Book House, 1988), p. 371.

15. Little, "God and Gratuitous Evil," p. 42.

16. Ibid., p. 46.

17. Ibid., p. 49.

18. Ibid., p. 42.

19. Bruce A. Little, *God, Why This Evil?* (Lanham, MD: Hamilton Books, 2010).

20. Nick Trakakis, *The God Beyond Belief: In Defense of William Rowe's Evidential Argument from Evil* (Dordrecht: Springer Books, 2006).

21. Karl W. Giberson and Francis S. Collins, *The Language of Science and Faith: Straight Answers to Genuine Questions* (Downers Grove, IL: IVP Books, 2011).

22. Dembski, "Evil, Creation and Intelligent Design," p. 276.

23. Karl W. Giberson and Francis S. Collins, "Evil, Creation and Evolution," in *God and Evil*, ed. Meister and Dew, p. 273.

24. Ibid., p. 278.

25. Ibid., p. 279.

26. Ibid., p. 280.

27. Ibid., p. 282.

28. Ibid., p. 280.

29. John Shook, "God and Evolution Don't Mix," It's Only Natural, July 10, 2011, http://www.centerforinquiry.net/blogs/entry/god_and_evolution_dont_mix/.

30. Dembski, "Evil, Creation and Intelligent Design," pp. 163–64.

31. Giberson and Collins, "Evil, Creation and Evolution," pp. 280–81.

32. Ibid., p. 282.

33. John W. Loftus, "Science Is Predicated on the Non-Magical Natural World-Order," in *13 Reasons To Doubt: Essays from the Writers of Skeptic Ink*, ed. Edward K. Clint, Jonathan M. S. Pearce, and Beth Ann Erickson (Onus Books, 2014).

34. Giberson and Collins, "Evil, Creation and Evolution," p. 281.

Chapter 16

1. See *The Black Death*, translated and edited by Rosemary Horrox (Manchester: Manchester University Press, 1994), p. 63. My information in what follows was gleaned from some online articles and books. See John Kelly, *The Great Mortality: An Intimate History of the Black Death, the Most Devastating Plague of All Time* (New York: Harper Perennial, 2006); and John Aberth, *The Black Death: The Great Mortality of 1348–1350: A Brief History with Documents* (Bedford: St. Martin's Press, 2005).

2. Wykstra, "Rowe's Noseeum Arguments from Evil," pp. 126–50.

3. Steven Johnson, *The Ghost Map: The Story of London's Most Terrifying Epidemic—and How It Changed Science, Cities, and the Modern World* (New York: Riverhead Books, 2006).

4. For the argument to the contrary, see J.L. Schellenberg, *Divine Hiddenness and Human Freedom* (Ithaca, NY: Cornell University Press, 1993).

5. Drange's argument can be seen in Part 4 of Michael Martin and Rikki Monnier, eds., *The Improbability of God* (Amherst, NY: Prometheus Books, 2006), pp. 337–79.

6. William P. Alston, "The Inductive Argument from Evil and the Human Cognitive Condition," in *The Evidential Argument from Evil*, ed. Daniel Howard-Snyder (Bloomington: Indiana University Press, 1996), p. 113. Alston was talking about suffering caused by moral agents, but I presume he would have said the same thing about natural suffering.

7. Keith Parsons, "Goodbye to All That," The Secular Outpost, September 1, 2010, http://www.patheos.com/blogs/secularoutpost/2010/09/01/goodbye-to-all-that/.

8. Plantinga, *Warranted Christian Belief*, p. 201. Elsewhere Plantinga defended some arguments for Christian faith, most notably the Ontological Argument.

9. Feinberg, *Can You Believe It's True?*, p. 321. As noted earlier, this is not to mischaracterize Feinberg as saying these arguments don't have some evidential weight to them. He favors the argument from design, but none of them serves as a deductive proof, so they "don't offer the degree of objective certainty many believers, let alone non-believers would require." He would rather "rely on other evidences 'to carry most of the weight'"in an over-all defense of Christian truth."

10. Swinburne, *The Existence of God*, p. 215.

11. Robert Miller, *Born Divine* (Santa Rosa, CA: Polebridge Press, 2003).

12. Richard Carrier, "Kooks and Quacks of the Roman Empire: A Look into the World of the Gospels," The Secular Web, http://www.infidels.org/library/modern/richard_carrier/kooks.html.

13. "On the Proof of the Spirit and of Power," in *Lessing's Theological Writings*, trans. Henry Chadwick (Palo Alto, CA: Stanford University Press, 1956), pp. 51–55.

14. See Ed Yong, "Creating God in One's Own Image," *Discover*, Not Exactly Rocket Science, November 30, 2009, http://blogs.discovermagazine.com/notrocketscience/2009/11/30/creating-god-in-ones-own-image/#.VdsxjrxViko.

About the Author

John Loftus is a former Christian minister and apologist who received an M.A. and M.Div. from Lincoln Christian Seminary in 1982, and a Th.M. from Trinity Evangelical Divinity School in 1985. While in school he studied philosophy, theology, and the philosophy of religion and majored under Dr. William Lane Craig, today's leading evangelical apologist and debater. He also studied in a Ph.D. program at Marquette University for a year and a half in the area of theology and ethics (1985–87).

Loftus is the author of *Why I Became an Atheist: A Former Preacher Rejects Christianity* (rev. ed. 2012), which he considers his magnum opus, and *The Outsider Test for Faith* (2013), both published by Prometheus Books. He has edited three important anthologies, *The Christian Delusion: Why Faith Fails* (2010), *The End of Christianity* (2011), and *Christianity Is Not Great: How Faith Fails* (2014), also published by Prometheus Books. He cowrote a debate book with Dr. Randal Rauser titled, *God or Godless* (2013), published by Baker Books.

He has traveled the United States and Canada speaking to audiences in Indiana, Ohio, New York, Louisiana, Texas, California, Colorado, Wisconsin, and many places in between, and has participated in seven public debates. He welcomes other such opportunities to speak and debate.

He is a licensed minister with the First Church of Atheism and the Universal Life Church, so he does weddings and funerals (but no baptisms, sorry!). His website is Debunking Christianity (www.debunkingchristianity. blogspot.com), where he tests some of his ideas and arguments. His Twitter handle is @loftusjohnw and his email address is loftusjohnw@gmail.com.